ENTITLEMENT:

CAUSE AND EFFECT

AN

AUTOBIOGRAPHY

BY

MICHAEL B. SCHEFFLER

Entitlement

Cause and Effect

2

In 1948, Nat King Cole recorded "Nature Boy." Later on it was recorded by Sinatra, Dick Haymes, and Sara Vaughn. I do not remember when I adopted "to love and be loved in return" as my mantra, but I did.

"Nature Boy"

There was a boy...

A very strange enchanted boy.

They say he wandered very far, very far

Over land and sea,

A little shy and sad of eye

But very wise was he.

And then one day,

One magic day he passed my way.

And while we spoke of many things,

Fools and kings,

This he said to me,

"The greatest thing you'll ever learn

Is just to love and be loved in return."

Entitlement

Cause and Effect

4

CHAPTER 1: IN THE BEGINNING

The year 1941 would result in the Jewish faith eternally crying tears of blood for the Holocaust and the carnage perpetrated upon them throughout the world. Jewish people were slaughtered by Adolph Hitler and the Nazi regime. American blood was spilled at the hands of the Japanese.

The world, in desperate need of the "Messiah," hardly noticed that on

March 7th, 1941, Michael (Mickey) Barry Scheffler was born.

He was the only male and the youngest of three, born to the Virgin Pearl and the scholar Benjamin. Their eldest child was Marilyn, who was eight, and Karen, who was four.

The Virgin, Pearl, was born on November 3rd, 1910.

The Scholar, Benjamin, was born on May 26th, 1907.

Benjamin, the oldest of four two brothers and one sister, was the black sheep of his family in religion, education, and financial gain. His brothers and sister had much more commitment to religion and education. While he was a common sense, street-smart guy, his calling was to work, while their calling was to educate first and work later.

Pearl was one of seven children—five sisters and a brother, none were educated beyond high school or surrounded by education or religion. They did not have the substance and intelligence Benjamin's family did, probably because of their lack of religious discipline.

As the "Messiah," I referred to them as Mom and Dad, so that I could blend in.

My most cherished memories are of spending Passover Seder nights at my grandparents'. Originally, when my grandfather was alive, he would conduct the services. The prayers were read in Hebrew by my grandfather and at certain points of the prayers he would start to cry and bow as he was sitting and dovening. The excitement of finding the "afekomen" (matzoh), which we each received a gift for, was a highlight of the evening.

When we were ready to leave, my grandmother would go into her tiny kitchen, where she had spent days cooking and baking, and she would give us all fresh baked apple pies to take home. This tradition went on from my earliest memory until my grandmother passed away.

My grandfather passed away when I was five. From that point on, my uncle Morty, my father's brother, ran the Seders, as he read sang and spoke Hebrew articulately. The wonderful memories of those beautifully executed, traditionally respectful, religious moments define in part who I am and defined how I would bring up my children.

My mother was not religious at all. My mom's mother, Leah, was a very English lady, with a sweet, tea-drinking manner that resembled nothing of her children. Grandma had immigrated to the United States from London; she was also a black sheep from a religious, upstanding, well-educated family.

The story goes that Grandma married someone that her family did not approve of. She and her new husband crossed the pond. The husband, (my grandpa) was unknown by his children or anyone else other than Grandma.

It seems he showed up to sire six girls and a boy and then permanently disappeared. The only thing we ever knew about him was that in one photograph my grandmother kept of the two of them, his head was cut off and no other unclothed parts of his body were shown.

My eighteen cousins and I were all very good dancers, leading me to humorously theorize that he was black, and therefore we all were part black.

The seven siblings, my mother included, spent every holiday together along with their respective spouses, their children (my cousins), and eventually the cousins' spouses. Out of all seven, there were two that were not mean-spirited. They all got decent men, though, as they were a good-looking lot, and each of the cousins' life experiences were a direct result of the father's relationship with the mother.

I think my parents, Pearl and Ben, had the brightest and most grounded children. The reason, I theorize, is that Ben was a very bright man and did not let Pearl completely rule the roost. The other reason is probably the leftover remnants of his orthodox religious family.

My sister Marilyn was born in 1932. A Marilyn Monroe look-alike, she eloped with her first husband. He was a very charming, intelligent, good-looking man, who unfortunately became an alcoholic. That marriage dissolved.

Their Son, Saul, born in 1952, fought with drug addiction well into his adult life. Eventually, he found success in Hazelton, where he met his wife, converted to Born Again Christianity, and became a counselor at Hazelton. His sister, Lisa, suffered the same addictions as Saul and successfully defeated her dependencies in the same manner as her brother.

My sister, Karen, was born in 1936 and married to Jack. She was a working mother. Their son, Doug, and daughter, Melissa, are well-grounded, nice people. Karen and Jack have lived in many different parts of the country. Currently, they are living in San Francisco.

My dad's parents: Bessie, my grandmother, was a nice, religious woman with a stern hand and a good heart. My grandfather, Sam, died when I was too young to have any memory other than his deathbed and dovening at the Seder.

The memories of my father's family, who I did not see as often as the others, I have long believed are what family should be and what I wish mine was.

My earliest memory was sitting in a booth in a luncheonette-type restaurant with my mother and my aunt. A radio was playing, everyone was very quiet and listening, and then there were tears. My aunt and others cried. It was the day Franklin Delano Roosevelt died, April 12, 1945. I was four years old.

Other early memories were of a neighbor in our building, Harry, coming home from the war. He was smoking Lucky Strikes, but he had the pack cut in half so he could cut down on his tobacco intake. I was in the arms of my dad, watching this; whatever the reason it was engraved in my memory.

In those earlier years, I remember setting up war games with my toy soldiers, creating all kinds of imaginary scenarios. On one of my cowboy-idolizing days, I straddled the windowsill of our second-floor apartment to serve as a horse to ride off into the night. Fortunately a woman across the street was looking out her window and yelled at me to get off.

Beyond that, there were the times in the Rockaways where we spent summers for two or three years, when I was six or seven. I remember going to the movies by myself and seeing a Western. I was so enamored with it that I was riding my make-believe horse on the boardwalk going home.

I remember having one of many asthma attacks in Rockaway and not being able to breathe. One of my parents gave me an inhaler that relieved the problem. Asthma plagued me from age three to thirteen. I was limited in exerting myself and heavily medicated.

One summer in Rockaway, there was a shower in the back that I guess was unused. For some reason, I was climbing inside it, and I fell on a board with a nail sticking out of it, which went completely through my hand.

1947: Jackie Robinson joins the Brooklyn Dodgers

I was in Times Square with my mother. It was the beginning of the expansion of automation, and we entered a Horn and Hardert Automat. It was the first of a prepared, fast food restaurant. The side walls were columns of twelve-inch square cubicles with glass covers and a money slot similar to a phone booth. You searched the glass-covered shelves for something you wanted to eat and put in a nickel. The glass door opened, you removed your item, the door closed, the shelf automatically spun around, and someone on the other side replaced the item

In those early years, the only real memory of us being a family was Sunday nights. My mother, father and I would go to Parkchester to have "chinx." I could not understand why it was called "chinx" and not Chinese food. I felt it was disrespectful.

On many occasions, during an asthma attack, I would take a bridge chair in front of my apartment house. The chair was under our apartment window so my mother could watch. I was there so as not to exert myself, and my friends would pass by on the way to the schoolyard, games, and fun.

I had to take two hour train rides to Brooklyn every week to visit Dr. Rafkin for medication for my asthma. He was the only doctor that had this special medicine. Supposedly it was not approved by the MDA because it had arsenic in it. It worked for me, and writing about it right now, I can still taste it. The doctor also gave me injections. After a while, my dad learned how and administered them himself.

1951: Julius and Ethel Rosenberg found guilty of relaying US military secrets to the Soviets. The Rosenbergs were the first U.S. civilians to be sentenced to death for espionage.

My father had a gigantic, empty replica of a liquor bottle in his closet where he put all his change. I would raid it continuously and buy my friends candy. One day, a teacher turned me in to my mother as she was wondering where the money came from.

From ten years old on was Bar Mitzvah lessons. My friends and I would walk ten blocks on our way to Bryant Avenue, where the synagogue was. Mr. Dinnerstein, our teacher, would pull you out of your chair by your ear when he felt you weren't paying attention. By the time I was to be bar mitzvah'd, I had to go to his home for lessons, as he was very ill.

During my childhood, we spent our days in school. Afternoons and evenings we were either playing ringalevio, stick ball, or Johnny on the Pony. Weekends we played softball. Not being an athlete, I usually played first base or right field. We played stick ball on the street, and when the ball went down the sewer, we would take a stick with gum on it and lift the ball out.

In the evenings, we would go to the Pines Italian restaurant for pizza on Tremont and Belmont, where Dion and the Belmonts were created. Across the street was Dollinger's toy store, where, many years later, the owner Stanley would become a friend and business partner.

There were two gangs in the area at the time, the Fordham Daggers and the Fordham Baldies. The Daggers were a training camp for the Baldies. One evening, while playing Johnny on the pony in the schoolyard, one of those gangs showed up as they had apparently scheduled a rumble. They yelled at us to get the hell out of there and fast. All my friends ran but me; nobody tells me to run. I walked. After being whacked across the back with a broomstick, I ran.

On Tremont Avenue from Southern Boulevard to West Farms there was the Vogue movie theater, the pool hall, and the Busy Bee. The Busy Bee served paper cones stuffed with waffled French fries, which we ate with mustard and a sour pickle. Across from our schoolyard, PS 67, was Leafy's candy store, where we would buy three cigarettes for two cents.

On 180th Street, three blocks away, there was Witkins Deli, where we went for the best corn beef sandwiches. There was a Jewish bakery further down the block and another movie theatre, the Ritz. We must have been eight or nine when we started going by ourselves to all these places. Which of course wouldn't happen today.

1953: Dr. Jonas Salk announced he had invented a vaccine to prevent polio

Then there was junior high. I don't remember much about Herman Ridder other than the first unrequited love of my life, Sandy Simon. I also remember that Chuck (one of my good friends), got the lead part in the school play, *Sing Out Sweet Land*. I couldn't believe that he got a part and not me, and the lead yet. He did a great job.

I had found some X-rated books in my father's drawer, so I took them to school one day and showed them on the bus. When we got off at the school stop, a big African American guy grabbed me, said he was a detective, and took them away from me.

Through school, we attended a TV broadcast of the Herb Sheldon show; I was wearing a suit, shirt, and tie. I was always dressed more formally than the others, as I was very appearance-cognizant. The particular clothes I was wearing that day were handed down from my cousin Harris.

Herb Sheldon picked me out of the crowd, and on live TV, asked where I bought my clothes. Not wanting to tell the truth, I searched for a name and came up with Robert Hall. When I got home my mother said that I should have mentioned a different name, as that was a cheap outlet. She then made me call them and ask for some kind of acknowledgment for mentioning them on TV.

In the apartment house where I lived, there were many others my age. These were the beginning days of Rock and Roll. We would sing the songs, write our own, and live the dream. When Elvis arrived, we all loved him. I imitated his style and song with a broomstick.

On occasion, we would go over to Yankee stadium and watch a game. One time, I followed Whitey Ford, Billy Martin, and Mickey Mantle into a bar on the concourse and 163rd Street. I walked in right after them and asked for an autograph. The three of them physically threw me out.

1954: Academy Award, Best Picture: *From Here To Eternity*

My bar mitzvah was a very nice affair relative to my friends, considering our financial position at that time. The affair was at the Elsmere Hall on March 21, 1954. My Hoftorah was Saturday morning, and the party was on Sunday evening.

Entitlement

Cause and Effect

Back then, when a boy turned thirteen, we really did become "men." At least in the sense that we were really on our own. We came and went without having to get anyone's approval.

In the spring of 1954, I was on a class trip to Rye, New York. We went to Playland, which was a carnival with rides. Coincidentally, my cousin Harris, who was five years older, was there with his friend, Larry.

When he saw me, his only concern was that they had run out of money and wanted me to give them some. I hardly had enough for myself. It was one of the few times in my life I said no. They were persistent, but I stood my ground. About a month later, Larry was on his way with his family to a bungalow colony in the mountains. He passed me on the street in the back of his parents' car. When he saw me, he stuck his middle finger up and said, "I'll remember you for not lending us the money."

A few weeks later, my mother took a room at the bungalow colony where her sisters were. She had rented a single room for the summer.

The room was formerly the dressing room for the entertainers. It was about ten feet by ten feet and the bathroom was outside the room in the open casino. It had an entrance door and a stage door.

When you left, you had to walk through the auditorium and the coffee shop at the entrance. This was home for eight weeks, and I shared it with my mother and my father the one night he was there. The first day there, as I walked outside, I ran into Larry.

That first year was miserable. He made the eight weeks of that summer a living hell for me. I clearly remember walking from my room in the casino to the concession thinking that I really was not there, and it was all just a bad dream.

No one knew to this day that there was even a problem, not even the perpetrator, Larry. I did not want to show Larry that he got to me. I was afraid to let anyone else know, as they might say something to him and make it worse.

Every summer for the next fourteen years, from the end of June through Labor Day, we went to the bungalow colony in the Catskills. The first few years we would leave on a Sunday morning at 5:00 am, when my father came home from work. My mother and I were there for the summer. My father would come up every week from Sunday morning to Monday afternoon. At that time, my older sister Marilyn was married and an Army wife in Alabama. My sister, Karen, was starting her career in the fashion industry.

On Saturday nights, the adults put on a show in the Casino, no kids allowed. But, of course, we were able to peek through the screened windows and watch as they wore fake penises and performed sexually-themed skits.

My uncle Lou was the star of the show, captain of the softball team. On weekends, when I was outside early in the morning, he took me with him to the store to buy rolls and bagels and fish for his family. It was a rewarding relationship.

He filled in some of the missing male camaraderie for me. We shared a mutual respect for one another all through the years.

Larry hung out with the older crew. Of course, he prevented me from being part of that group, and I was too mature for the younger crew. I wasn't good enough to play on the older guys' softball team, so I started a junior team and a league. I put the team together, called all the other area colonies, and arranged games. I do not remember if we won or lost, but no one could stop me from playing. It was my team.

1955: *On the Waterfront* won Best Picture. James Dean died in a car accident at age 26. Rosa Parks refused to sit at the back of the bus, breaking Montgomery, Alabama's segregated seating law.

Back in the bungalow colony, Silberts, we graduated to two rooms in the attic. I had my own lean-to type of room. We stayed in the attic for a couple of summers. Two miles away was the most prestigious hotel in the Catskills, the Concord Hotel. They had two separate golf courses, The International, an 18-hole championship course across the road from the hotel, and a nine hole course on the hotel side.

I started to work there as a caddy. Every day I walked to the hotel from Silberts while trying to hitch a ride. About 200 feet from the clubhouse was the caddy shack.

The routine was as follows:

When you arrived about 6:00 a.m., you listed your name on a clipboard, following the person who arrived prior to you.

When the caddy master got a call from the pro shop as to how many caddies were needed for the next group to tee off, he looked at the list and decided who to send. His decision was based on a method only he could understand.

At that time, carts were not used, and golfers were not allowed to carry or pull their own bag. A caddy was assigned a single bag for nine holes, or eighteen, or two bags for nine or eighteen.

The amount of money you could make was probably the determining factor in the caddy master's decision of whom to select. The experienced regulars would get the double eighteen; the up and coming newer group would get the double nine. The rest went by size.

In the beginning, I stayed with the plan and managed to get out late in the morning carrying one bag and one round. The real money was doing two bags for two eighteen-hole rounds.

The format needed to be modernized. After signing in, instead of sitting in the caddy shack, I began to sit outside.

The phone would ring in the caddy shack, and two of the regulars would be dispatched to the club house, and I would follow, walking twenty feet behind them. The Hotel and International pro Jimmy Demerit would come out and show the other two caddies the bags to pick up.

He would look at me and say, "I only ordered two."

"Okay, stick around, I'll get you out next."

This became my daily chore: get out early for one double eighteen, have lunch, and carry another double eighteen. The nickname attached to me was "Presser." Between fees and tips, I was earning fifty dollars per day at age fourteen in 1955.

One day, as I finished my day of work at the Concord, someone mentioned that Milton Berle was on the golf course. Figuring out where he could be, I walked through the woods and came up to the sixteenth green. Berle, Phil Silvers, Jan Murray, and Red Buttons were on the green. As I got closer, I stepped on a twig, making a cracking sound just as Berle was about to putt. I never knew Uncle Milty had such a foul mouth.

1956: Grace Kelly married Prince Rainier III of Monaco. Jerry Lewis and Dean Martin ended their partnership after sixteen films

In the Catskills, we had decent-sized bungalows. The social life was fabulous. I had six sets of aunts and uncles and thirteen cousins.

Entitlement

Cause and Effect

The younger crowd was getting older, and the older crowd started to let me in.

Jerry, a windmill softball pitcher, pitched so fast and accurately he probably could have been a pro in addition to being a very funny, bright, guy, He and Albie, a nice quiet guy, became my good friends

There was a bus that went back and forth from Monticello to Loch Sheldrake. Loch Sheldrake was a town with an old fashioned drug store with a long counter in front of the soda fountain.

In the beginning, we would get on the bus, have some fun, and come back. Later on, we set up lawn chairs and all kinds of silly things on the road so that Whitey, the bus driver, would stop the bus. He wouldn't charge us and would turn the lights off on that dark mountain road while going over a big bump. We had great laughs. The bus rides, the golf, the crashing of all the hotel shows, and the best of all worlds.

Dave, Jerry's dad, was a bookmaker and had attached to his side a Damon Runyan character named Folly, a single man who was either his body guard or servant. Dave was also a funny guy. All these guys were down to earth, real people.

Albie eventually worked for his father in the "Trimming Business." When John Gotti was indicted for racketeering, he listed his legitimate employer as "Albie Trimming."

Recently, Albie's son opened a restaurant in Boca. Not knowing this, I ran into Albie there one night and we had a reunion with Albie, his dad, Jack, Jerry, Larry, and a few others.

After the summer, in the city, across from our apartment (915 East 179th Street, Apartment 2B) was a grocery store owned by Hy and his wife Selma. They exemplified the fact that husband and wives should not work together.

After school every day from the age of fourteen on, I worked there. My job was to deliver orders, wait on the people, and take out the garbage. I also would bring the deliveries from the street to the basement and from the basement to the store. I learned that when you stock the shelves, you move the old up front and the new in the back.

When I was through for the day, I went around the corner, from Daly Avenue to 180th Street, took a right turn after about a hundred and fifty feet, and arrived at the Laundromat, where I delivered laundry. Directly across the street there was a fruit store, where I also delivered. Next to the fruit store, there was a shoe repair store, where I shined shoes as well.

Ely, my sister Marilyn's husband, was starting his career at Montgomery Ward, where his older brother was a buyer. He had a friend named Armand. The two of them made a deal with a children's dress manufacturer to take dresses on consignment and sell them at the farmers' markets every weekend. I was one of the salesmen. It was a busy booth and the time went by quickly. It was fun.

When I got a little older, I worked at a camera store for a man named Phil Diamond. He had a mail-order business as well as the retail store. I did everything for him, and although he was twenty years older, we became good friends and kept in contact until he was well into his seventies.

I had all the equipment to take pictures and develop them. I set up a portable darkroom, and would turn our one bathroom into a darkroom whenever possible. I would enlarge photos from 35mm to 8 x 10 prints using a massive enlarger. It was an enjoyable hobby for as long as it lasted.

My mother had few friends; Irene Levy was one. Her husband, Archie, was the treasurer of Radio City Music Hall. I went to see him and asked for a job. They were going to make me an usher, but my height lead them to believe I should be a doorman.

The job consisted of taking tickets, guarding the outer spill doors, keeping the Christmas line in order, and filling in as usher and elevator operator when needed. The uniforms were fancy—tails, a formal shirt, and white gloves.

The theater had its own commissary, so I would eat amongst all the Rockettes, which did not bother me. I even dated a Rockette from Texas. She was about nineteen, and I was a tall fifteen. I took her on a horse and buggy ride around Central Park.

At the opening or first run worldwide debuts, I would be at the door taking tickets as Marilyn Monroe came in for *Gentleman Prefer Blondes*. I saw Jack Kennedy, Sandra Dee, Milton Berle, and many others.

Of all the celebrities, and politicians, the most memorable was Marilyn Monroe, not because of her beauty, but because she had a glow around her head as if there were a spotlight attached to her neck and shining up. I know that this sounds absurd, but time stopped as I stared at her, and while I was in the trance, that glow was as radiant as anything I had ever seen.

There were always the wise guys who wanted to beat the long line outside in the cold. My position was by the outer spill door, which was where celebrities and invited guests would pick up their tickets.

It became a challenge to separate the celebrities from the guys who were trying to con me. Usually I won. One night a guy came to the door and said he was John Rait (a famous opera singer of the time), and that there were tickets at the box office.

I said, "Yeah get to the back of the line." I had never heard of John Rait at the time. Well, sure enough, it was him, and I was red faced.

At times while ushering, I saw some movies fifty times. I can quote the words from every song from some of the most famous musicals of the time.

The next four years, my teen years, were a fun-filled, educationally-rewarding time. I was lucky enough to experience my summers in the Catskills and the rest of the year in the City.

My first year of high school. New friends, bus passes, girls, club rooms, cars, sex, and White Castle hamburgers. The high school was Theodore Roosevelt on Fordham Road in the Bronx, across the street from Fordham University.

It was a five-block walk from my house to the bus, a thirty minute ride on the bus, and then a two block walk from the bus to the school.

The least important thing to me at the time was education. My whole purpose there was to pass my subjects and graduate. My father worked seven days a week from 11:00 a.m. to 4:00 a.m. My mother worked Monday to Friday, nine to five.

No one cared about my marks or was encouraging in any way. To my amazement, mathematics came naturally to me, so naturally that I scored one hundred on the algebra Regent's exam. My primary interests were girls and cars, along with an insatiable desire to be liked.

At the time I also had a crush on a skinny girl with big breasts. All the guys would tease me about it. I would go to her apartment to hang out or take a walk with her. Her father would always be there. His presence was very intimidating.

One weekend, my uncle Al lent me his old jalopy of a convertible, which was great. However, as I was driving without a license on West Farms in front of a police officer directing traffic, suddenly the hood flew up and smashed the windshield. The policeman came over and assisted me in a temporary repair and never asked for my license.

Mel and Lenny were new friends that I met in high school, and we would become a threesome all through school and beyond. None of us had a license to drive yet, as we were too young. But they had access to their father's cars. Lenny's dad came home from work, found a parking spot, and the car stayed there all night.

Mel's dad had a garage, and his father worked late hours. We would go to Lenny's house, take two wooden horses from anywhere on the street, pull Lenny's car out, put the horses in its place, and off we went.

Our music teacher, Jack Cohen, lived in Ardsley, a short ride from Lenny's house in the Bronx. Often we would drive up there and hang out with him. Other times we would just take rides. Our biggest fear then was getting caught by our parents; the driving without a license was a threat, but did not carry any serious repercussions

Entitlement

Cause and Effect

22

CHAPTER 2: ADOLESCENCE

1957: Russia takes the lead by successfully launching Sputnik

Chuck, a school friend, Ralph, and I took a bus ride to Washington, D.C. The three of us had one room at the Mayflower Hotel, we toured every sight imaginable. It was a trip that was most enjoyable, with very rewarding historical sights. If I could I would have a mandatory list; one of the items on it would be extensive tours of D.C. For the education of the workings of the greatest country in the world and the beauty of our National Treasure Memorials.

Ralph had a cousin who lived in D.C., a girl about our age. We had him call her and arrange a date for one of us with his cousin, and two of her friends with the others. We knew the names of the girls that we were each set up with. When we arrived at the house, the girls came down the stairs one at a time. As they reached the bottom, the parents introduced us. The first girl who came down was Ralph's date. They were awkward years, but I lost it.

Never being disrespectful, I just couldn't help myself. She was not pretty. The next down was Chuck's date. Now I really went nuts; she was even worse. Finally, mine arrived. Well payback is a bitch, and mine was even worse than the first two, but we had a good time and had many great laughs from that weekend.

Chuck writes: "I believe we were in the Mayflower in 1957. Just another great experience that I owe to you. I have never stopped traveling since."

Then came dances. I don't know how they were organized. I was doing the bump to "Earth Angel," eyes closed and my body caressing my partner to the song and the beat.

I can replay the sound, the feeling, the picture as if it were yesterday. When the rest of the Doo Ops came out, we wrote our own, we sang them all, and we loved them.

One crush I had was on a girl with long red hair in high school. We went out once or twice, but I think she was just geographically undesirable. From childhood till today, the view of long, flowing hair was an immediate turn on. I am surprised that I haven't fallen in love with a mare with a beautiful mane.

The gym teacher and I had dinner once a week. He was involved with the student body and also coached all the teams. He was an elderly, dapper guy with a big mustache. He wanted to form a golf team. And since I had some experience, I joined.

I became the team captain, the lowest handicapper, the best dressed, and the most charming. Oh, I almost forgot. I was also the only member of the team. He encouraged me to take some interest in the school newspaper, which I did, and became the photographer.

Our school president was another high school crush. I went to her house by bus for a neighborhood walk date. I decided since it was a date that I should shave the nonexistent hairs on my face. I must have had six pieces of tissue on my face for the bleeding when I picked her up. I don't remember if I forgot they were there, or if I thought it was cool, but her family cracked up when they saw me.

In trying my hand at political office, I ran for treasurer in high school and lost. My senior bio listed me as a photographer, a clarinet player for the orchestra, and captain of the Golf Team.

That summer we were back in the Catskills. Each of the hotels had their own specialty; we explored them all.

Thursday nights we would go to Kutchers, they always had a pre-pro basketball team that competed in the hotel league. This particular year they had Wilt Chamberlain and Bob Cousy. Wilt was tall but awkward; Cousy was great.

Saturday night the Concord Shows always had a major headliner, a semi-major opening act, and the hottest bands of the time. Of course these extravaganzas were only available to the hotel guests, therefore each week we had to find a way to get in. Sometimes we would show a key to the guard that we got from caddying. Other times we would sneak onto the grounds through the owner, Wynn Erick's, home. One time a big Doberman Pincher chased us, but we made it.

Once on the property, we had access to everything. Prior to the show, at the lounge named The Cotillion Room, was a gigantic bar with a three or four piece group playing. We danced, drank, and frolicked.

When the show was about to begin, I would walk into the "standing room only" show room. No matter which date I was with, I would give the maître de twenty dollars, and they went into a storage room and returned carrying out a table for two, and set it wherever they could.

We saw performances by the greatest artists of the time, including Johnny Ray, Connie Francis, Allen King, Eddie Fisher, Don Rickles, Shecky Green, Jerry Lewis, Sid Ceasar, Buddy Hackett, Red Buttons, and the list goes on and on.

What a fun time it was.

After the show we danced to Tito Puente, Pachecho, The Cha Cha, Mambo, Merengue, and Lindy. We did them all, and pretty well. Our hopes, our dreams, our visions of the future, friends, and family all came from those wonderful days.

From the Concord at 1:00 a.m. to the The Laurels, in Sacket Lake, on Saturday nights, when the entertainers were finished with their regular hotel performance, they all ended up at Laurels at 2:00 a.m.

Dick Gregory, Jackie Mason, Totie Fields, Felicia Saunders, and many others went there prior to their fame. They ad-libbed on stage and put on a great show.

After the show we would go to Loch Sheldrake for roast pork on garlic bread, get back to Silbert's at 5:00 a.m., and get up at 7:00 a.m. to play golf at Tarry Brae in South Fallsberg.

Whatever money any of this cost me was completely out of my own pocket, all from my work as a caddy. When I write about this now, I cannot believe what a wonderful experience this all was.

1958: Elvis Presley is inducted into the US Army

As school photographer, I was assigned to photograph and interview Nat King Cole. A wonderful man and a great experience. Another assignment was to photograph Queen Elizabeth's visit to New York.

Mel's father owned a deli in Greenwich Village, and I worked there at night. Sometimes with Mel, sometimes alone. I made sandwiches and sold a lot of ice and logs. It was fun. We traveled back and forth by train.

Prior to graduation, I thought I had caught a break. My history Regent's exam was not until two hours after my friends'. So I had the advantage of getting all of the answers from them before I took the test. Common sense should have dictated that the test would be taken by all at the same time. No big deal, I took a makeup test. Other than English, I was about to graduate with an Academic Diploma. My English teacher, out of the goodness of his heart, passed me anyway, and on I went.

My senior prom was a weekend affair. My sister, Marilyn and Ely, had just bought a brand new 1957 Chrysler convertible in red, and they lent it to me for the prom weekend.

As I was driving home with it from their apartment in Queens, I was on Yellowstone Boulevard. A car came down from one of the side streets without looking to his right. He drove right into the back of the car. The car was drivable. So rather than ruin my weekend, I did not let my sister know until I returned the car. That was all they were really upset about, and I felt terrible that I did not let them know as soon as it occurred.

Finally I was turning seventeen, when I could have a junior license. My mother took out a pass book loan of $600.00, which was secured with a pass book from her sister, Rose. I bought a 1954 Oldsmobile 88. My payments were $27.00 per month, and with a junior license, I drove all over. In those days, I kept a twenty in my wallet. If I got stopped, it would fall out when I would show my license. Today any thought of that would put you behind bars.

My mother did not do this for me out of the goodness of her heart. The caveat was that I had to chauffeur her wherever she wanted.

I took a part-time job at Frank's sporting goods on Tremont Avenue and Webster Avenue in the Bronx. Frank taught me how to sell in a retail store. During hunting season, if someone would come in for a pair of warm socks, that was the last thing you would show him. By the time you got to the socks, he had a new rifle, coat, pants, long underwear, and a $500.00 tab.

After cleaning, creating, and using many club houses, we finally had one in the east Bronx we could get to. At that time, I was attracted to a very pretty blonde in school, Lorraine. She was not attracted to me; she liked the tough guys.

When someone asked me what the best memories I had of a former girlfriend were, I said "Lorraine." What was so special about Lorraine? Her friend Martha! (That is stolen from Mel Brooks.)

Martha was Lorraine's best friend. My plan was to get friendly with Martha to get to Lorraine. That turned out to be one of the best educations I ever had. Martha was attracted to me, she pursued me. She wanted me to give her driving lessons, which I did, and we always ended up back at the club house, alone. It was apparent that she was sexually experienced, and although I had a few dalliances prior, nothing compared to this. She taught me everything there was to know about sex, without any inhibitions, and to mutual satisfaction.

Martha lived next door to Mel. Whenever I would drop her off, Mel would call me at home and had to know the details of everything that went on. Being sixteen and naïve, I gave him all the details for the next two years.

During the Summer, I still had my own room in the attic at Silberts, and Martha's friends came to a nearby place for four weeks. She ended up staying with me every night that they were there. The rest of the summer was golf, cards, and hotel nightlife.

As the years went by, Monticello Raceway was built, and that became an early evening attraction. That pattern continued as married couples. It was the best of times.

1959: Liz Taylor's fourth marriage to Eddie Fisher took place

I started going to City College, during their twilight session. During the day, I worked for Lenny's father, who had a candy and cigarette distribution company in the Bronx.

Lenny's dad wanted me to work there full time, which I did not see for myself. I was disappointed though that not only was there no encouragement anywhere in my family for higher education, but my father was encouraging me to take the job.

I dropped out of the twilight session and took a job on Ely's recommendation with Alexander's on Fordham Road. It was for their training program for which I was assigned to the ladies' underwear department for Fred Tessler and the merchandise manager, Francis Simmons.

The next two summers, my mother decided to go to Long Beach and then Lido Beach. Two of her sisters were there, and her mother lived a few miles away in Rockaway. I would drive my car with Peggy Lee blasting "Fever" from the radio. Lido Beach was chosen because my mother wanted my sister to join the Lido Hotel Beach Club so she could meet a guy. I guess they were getting nervous as she was all of twenty three.

My friends and I were going out with some girls from North Woodmere. Mel with Barbara, Lenny with Karen, and I was with Dena.

One of the girls' friends was Trudy. Since we were all hooked up, I introduced Chuck to her. They made an instant connection. They did not hang out with us much, as Chuck did not care for the antics of Mel. That turned out to be one of my most successful ventures, as they married in 1964 and as of this writing are living a very loving, happy life together.

Barbara married a nice guy, who unfortunately died too young. Dena married and divorced. Lenny and Karen married and divorced. Mel and Aura are still married.

Entitlement

Cause and Effect

One night on the strip going to the approach to the Atlantic beach bridge I was in my car and Mel his. We started to race, when from nowhere headlights went on, and a car was following us. When we approached the bridge I went to the tolls and Mel headed for Rockaway; he figured the cop was a Nassau cop and wouldn't follow him over the city line. He was wrong; he got the ticket.

The Army, which at that time was mandatory to serve a two-year stint, came out with a program that if you served six months of active duty and five-and-a-half years of reserve duty, that you would satisfy your draft requirements.

After active duty you would have to attend a meeting once a week and spend two weeks in summer camp for the balance of the contract. Choosing to get the draft behind me and opt for a shorter time away, I joined.

The day I left for the service, Mel went to Martha and repeated everything I had told him in a quest to replace me. What he accomplished instead was a letter she sent to me that made me look up to the curb. Never would I kiss and tell again.

CHAPTER 3: MANDATORY 101

1959: Fidel Castro assumed power

On November 1st, 1959, after staying up all night with Mel, Lenny, and the girls, I took a bus from the Bronx at 2:00 a.m. to Fort Dix, NJ.

Arriving at Fort Dix, the drill sergeants' task was apparently to intimidate all the new recruits. And they were very good at it. They rushed us off the bus with metal rods, obscenities, pushing and kicking us. We were marched through the uniform line, barber shop, showers, and finally, after much more harassment and intimidation, to our quarters. The quarters had two floors that were exactly the same.

About twenty-five double bunk beds were on the left, and twenty-five were on the right. The one bathroom had ten toilet bowls on the left and ten facing them on the right, no dividers. The shower was one open pit that would accommodate twenty or more at a time, with ten sinks and ten urinals in another room. There was no way of being shy. We sat on the toilet facing our roommates, and stood in the shower with all our packages exposed; the others were primarily not circumcised. Talk about intimidation.

Every day we were woken at 4:00 a.m. We had to be showered, dressed, have our bunks made, standing in front of our bunk and foot locker at attention. They checked the bunk, our foot lockers, the uniforms, our hair, and our faces. We were not allowed to move until they were finished with the entire barracks and the drill sergeant yelled, "At ease." We then had to line up outside, exercise, do rifle routines, eat breakfast, and play war games.

Entitlement

Cause and Effect

This was basic training, and it was eight weeks of disciplined training. It's designed to prepare you for survival. And it does. The only time they were civil was shortly after we arrived. They had a one-hour orientation class.

The instructor informed us that the purpose of basic training was for us to understand that we can endure more then we think. That there will be times that you are on a ten-mile march, and when you reach that ten-mile mark, your sergeant will say to march five more miles. You will think there is no way you can make it, but you will.

The experience of basic training, although not enjoyed during the process, should be mandatory for all men and women. It would give everyone the realization that there is no entitlement and would give everyone an experience that would help them get over life's bumps in the road. It would teach people that we are all the same. That we can endure whatever is thrown at us, and that we can learn how to get along with all kinds of people.

After four weeks of basic, half the platoon was given a weekend pass. The other half would get their pass the following week. I was not in the first group, but in my insane mentality of, "I will not be denied," I stuffed my bed with pillows as if I were sleeping and took off on the bus. When I came back, I was of course caught, but somehow, with talk and money, I got away with it, never ever considering the severity of the situation.

Once the training routine was over, my job was in the motor pool, where I ended up driving a five-ton truck pulling a huge Howitzer.

On Friday nights in the barracks, it was our responsibility to scrub the barracks and the toilets, but if you were Jewish, you could get out of it by going to the base Rabbi and participating in Shabbat prayers.

I decided that I should be a representative of the Jewish faith to dispel any of those anti-Jewish feelings that people had that I could not understand. Therefore I did not go to the Rabbi, and instead I stayed to clean the barracks. I have carried that ambassadorship with me all my life.

On one of our ten-mile marches to a bivouac site, where we slept outdoors for two or three nights in the woods, it snowed the whole time. I was eating chicken that the mess sergeant had prepared for us, and while the snow was falling on the chicken, there were ants crawling on it as well. I was so wet and so uncomfortable that I just ate the food and whatever was on it as well. That was one of the lessons. That you can do whatever you have to in order to survive.

One night we were sent to the infiltration course, where we had to crawl on our elbows and knees while our rifles were embedded in the inside folds of our elbows. Directly over our heads they were shooting live tracer bullets. Not an easy task. When we were given the signal to go, I crawled forward and soon was out of breath. I spotted a mound, I crawled over there to lie down and rest for a minute where I would not be seen. While I was there, that mound, which was actually a circle around a deep pit, exploded with a timed mechanism that was installed inside. Not knowing anything other than the explosion, I took off like a bat out of hell, and probably got to the other side before anyone else.

One of the things about being in the Army is that experiencing all this is great for bonding. One of the guys I got very friendly with was Bobby Vanucci. Another was Justin Wernick. One night in the bunk some wise kid started with Jewish slurs. I confronted him, and I ended up with a bicycle chain swept across my face.

Bobby, who was built very well, stepped in, and that was ended quickly. Bobby was also the only guy who got phone calls while there. Every week there was an emergency call for him. All of the calls were from girls telling him that they were pregnant. So in addition to liking him, he became an idol.

Later on, Bobby, also known as Bobby Van, was one of the bachelors along with Joe Namath in Bachelors Three in New York. He became the owner of The Candy Store in Fort Lauderdale, and the benefactor of many good times had after the service. Justin was a podiatrist and had an office in the Garment District.

I used his services for a while and then lost track of him. But each time I went to someone in his field, I would ask if they knew him. Everyone knew him. Justin developed some kind of insole and became a very successful man.

One night we were able to go to a local town, called "Bordertown." Having dinner in a restaurant with tablecloths was a highlight and a delight.

Based on tests that were taken upon entry to the military, you were assigned the tasks you would perform. Based on those tasks, it would be determined where you would go after basic.

My assignment was to be a radio teletype operator, and I was sent to Fort Gordon, Georgia. We left in the middle of the night on a troop carrier airplane. Sitting on the floor in the body of this seatless airplane was my first experience on an airplane.

Upon arriving at Fort Gordon, we were brought to a big open field where we lined up for roll call, and afterward we were assigned to our quarters.

Somehow, I lucked out and ended up with a private room for two. I do not know how, but I did and settled in.

The next morning, at about 6:00 a.m., one of the guys said, "Here take this and follow me." He had handed me a thermometer. After reveille, the first call is sick call. About fifteen percent of the group fell out, including me, as I was following.

The nurse came by the line up and put a thermometer in everyone's mouth. As she passed, they would take out the thermometer and put in the one they had, which was preset to 101 degrees. When she came back, she removed the thermometer and read it: 101. Three days bed rest, which meant we could do anything we wanted for the next three days.

The guys were of the Mormon faith, and they only were interested in fun. We would stay at a motel for two nights, drink beer, and get drunk. This went on continually. I was still able to go to my typing and Morse code classes. The first time that I got drunk on beer was the last, as it was awful, same for wine.

Fort Gordon was a final base for those getting out, so as time went by, I had different friends, as they would be discharged one by one. I was friendly with the Mormon group, but I think they kept looking for my horns. They were a group of guys who had no shortage of money or appetite for fun.

We all signed up at a local airport for flying lessons. Ten one-hour lessons for $75.00. On my first lesson, the pilot said that it was a little windy up there today, and it probably would not be a good day to start.

"Nah, it won't bother me," I responded. Not more than ten minutes in the air, hitting those air pockets and dropping ten feet each time, I threw up all over the plane. I think it took me three or four weeks to get rid of the queasiness. Never went back for the other lessons.

Fort Gordon was a piece of cake. It was very loosely run, with none of the rigid ritual of basic training. One of the guys I became friendly with who was a little older had his car on base. It was a Triumph convertible. Every weekend, we would go to other towns: Savannah, St. Augustine, Jacksonville, Daytona, Augusta, and others. We would sleep in the car and tour.

One Passover, the campus clergy organized Passover dinner in Atlanta. All the Jewish troops were bussed to Atlanta. It appeared at the time there was an abundance of single Jewish girls and a shortage of single Jewish guys.

The bus dropped us off at the synagogue, where they had a meet and greet dance. Afterward we went to a holiday dinner at pre-assigned homes and several parties after dinner. In many cases we danced with some girls, spent the holiday dinner with others, and enjoyed after dinner parties with others. This was not a good holiday; this was a **GREAT** holiday.

To earn some money, I got hold of a cosmetic line designed for the black community. I went from house to house trying to sell it. I am not sure I sold anything, but boy did I have guts.

Joe Rozzo, a Brooklyn guy, befriended me. He said his family owned Rozzo Bros. in New York, a big wholesale fish distributor. I would continually pass their building, so I went in once. They'd never heard of him. That was not unusual; he was a nut.

He went AWOL one weekend and his name was up on guard duty. Being his only friend, I had to cover for him. It was a cold, miserable night.

At the time, my sister, Karen, was a buyer for Carr at their buying office in New York at 1440 Broadway. Karen had a store as part of their group in Augusta. She advised the owners and told me to stop in and say hello. I did, and a very nice friendship evolved. I was invited over to their home on a continual basis.

One of the highlights of being in Augusta was the fact that the Masters was played there. In 1960, a friend and I in the military bought discount tickets and followed Arnold Palmer around the course as he won. It was a very exciting experience.

Once during my time in Augusta, I took the train home, not sure why. It was a twenty-four-hour ride each way, and I stayed home one day.

Finally I was discharged and flew home on a commercial airplane. I have no memory of being met at the airport or how I got home, but no complaints. Again, the Army experience is something that should be mandatory.

It a wonderful precursor to real life.

Entitlement

Cause and Effect

38

CHAPTER 4. NAVIGATED DESTINY

1960: John F. Kennedy defeats Richard Nixon

When I returned from Georgia in May of 1960, I took a job on the sales training program of M. Lowenstein and Sons at 1430 Broadway in New York City.

I purchased a used 1957 Cadillac convertible, silver with red upholstery.

In the training program, I became very friendly with several of the guys, but two in particular, Dave Newman and Jerry Lauren. They were both at least five years older than me. Dave was a character with a sense of humor that was laced with catchy expressions which I picked up and still use.

If you asked him a question, he would look at you with a serious expression and say, "It's a long worm that eats no Indian nuts." On other occasions it would be, "No matter how fast a choo choo train may travel, a giraffe cannot pee up a tree." And last was a one-worder: "Yahootee," after whichever word or expression he'd used. He would then walk away.

Dave, being from an affluent home, was a product of that affluence. He was sure of himself and had some natural talents. He was a three-handicap golfer, and a fabulous handicapper at the flats and trotters.

Jerry was from the background of a very orthodox Jewish family, and he was brought up in religious schools. His older brother, Lenny, had changed the family name from Lipshitz to Lauren.

Jerry's personality was very dry. His talent was, first, that he had the face and physique of an Adonis, a Cary Grant type with all perfect features

In addition to that, he was a very humble and very nice guy. As much as the girls fell all over him, he was not of the nature to ever take advantage.

Dave gave him the nickname of "kiss," because that is as far as he would go. Jerry had a younger brother as well, Ralph. I met Ralph on several occasions while he was selling gloves and ties, and then after he started designing his own ties. He became moderately successful, and you may have heard of him: Ralph Lauren.

On the training program, we would wait in the showroom until a salesman would bring in a customer, and then one of us would assist. While learning the fabrics and the sale techniques, we had a lot of free time. One of the guys was married, and each day in our round-table discussions, he would mention that his wife had such a good job that her boss took her to these expensive lunch places, bought her gifts, gave her bonuses, and for Christmas bought her a fur coat. He was the only one in the room that did not understand that his wife was putting out a day's work instead of putting in a day's work.

Mitchel Aronstein a top executive in the company was manager of the "Fashion Set" Department, which was the design and creation of printed textiles for the ready-to-wear trade. The department consisted of five people: Mitchell, the designer, and detail people. The department was very successful, and whenever Mitchell worked in the showroom with customers, he would only have me assist him.

As the department grew, he requested that I become the assistant manager. I did; I was good at what I did because it was structured, not like sitting around waiting for a customer. Sales people would come in and out all day wanting samples or shipping cuts of particular styles to their customers, and they would make them up in a sample garment. If it sold, so would the piece goods.

One of the sales people who was older and very successful was Burt Rubin. He was a nasty guy who spoke down to everyone. One day I guess I was feeling secure in my job and Burt came in directed a barrage of nasty commands in my direction. I pointed my finger in his face and let him know that he better talk to me with respect. From that point on he was my best friend, and later on I became his assistant. Another lesson learned.

I was assistant to Mitchell for a year. Next to our office was an Executive Vice President, Morty Engle. He was in charge of research and development. He went on an extended trip around the world. He requested that I fill in for him while he was gone. I had no clue of anything going on in his office.

In his capacity, I received a sample of a foam-backed fabric. The grey goods provider wanted to know if the thickness of the foam was good or if it needed to be adjusted. Whatever the decision, he had to make a minimum of 500 yards.

I went to the chief operating officer, Phil Fibusch, and said that I would like to do the fabric in three thicknesses as it would have different uses in different markets. But before I would tell the converter to go ahead, I wanted approval. I did not have the authority to spend the company's money. He stopped me in mid speech and said, "You know, you are a very bright young man. You are going to go far in this company." He gave me the okay to proceed. The next day, as I was coming up the escalator to the 2nd floor, Mr. Fibusch was right behind me. I said, "Good morning, sir."

Whether he recognized me or not, I don't know, but he appeared to have no interest.

Cause and Effect

Years later I was playing golf at Sea Wayne Country Club, a high maintenance private club, as a guest. When we were through playing, we went into the locker room to shower, change, and meet our wives for dinner.

At all of these clubs, the men who enjoy cards play golf early and come back to the card room to play. I walked in to see who I knew and to watch for a little while Phil, the executive from Lowenstein, then retired, was there playing cards. When he was in between hands, I reminded him of the incident. When I got to the part that he did not recognize me, he was not amused.

Morty Engle came back, resigned from the company to pursue his love of sailing. I pursued a waste of time: I became a salesman.

As life experiences taught me later on, unstructured work was not my forte. Starting out, they give you a list of accounts that they have never done business with or only did business with a long time ago. You can't call these accounts and make an appointment. You have to cold call. Most would not see you or they would make you wait hours at the freight entrance to their showroom. It wasn't my kind of thing, and so I fell in to a pattern hanging out with Jerry, Dave, and others, having coffee every day for hours, and then at times going to the track.

There was very little supervision, and no one really cared except for the guys who were smart enough to know that this was their future and worked to get somewhere.

Once or twice a week we would go to the trotters at Yonkers or Roosevelt. Dave would pick at least three winners, and they were never the favorites. He had an uncanny way of reading into their history and matching it to the conditions of that night. Jerry became hooked. To this day, he goes to the races by himself and handicaps. Not for the money; he never bet much. He just loved the challenge.

Dave went on to marry, join his father-in-law's business, and live in Florida, where he owned a floor tile distribution center. Jerry, who was at my wedding, and I at his, met and married the most lovely girl from Deal, NJ. Just the other day, I went online for some research for the book and I saw that Susan had passed away last year.

1961: "Are You Lonesome Tonight?" by Elvis Presley, peaks to number one. Pablo Picasso, age seventy nine, married his model, Jacqueline Rocque, age thirty seven.

In one of our excursions, we were at a country club in New Rochelle called The Eldorado. I came in my car, and Jerry and Ralph came in Jerry's VW convertible. Ralph borrowed Jerry's car to take a girl for a ride and hadn't come back for hours. I took my car with Jerry, and we started looking for Ralph. We found the car smashed into a fire hydrant with Ralph and the girl unconscious in the car. We drove them to the hospital. Ralph had to have a screw put in his leg. Other than that, everyone was okay. I hope Ralph reads this and remembers I saved his life. I sent a snippet of the above to Ralph, and a note of condolence to Jerry; neither one answered.

Through the years, Jerry, Dave, and I kept in touch, and on occasion we met for dinner or lunch. And also on occasion, I ran into all of the other guys somewhere along the way.

A few months ago, I was having dinner at Casa D'Angelo in Boca, and a guy came over and asked if I was Mike Scheffler. I immediately recognized his voice. I knew exactly who he was. It was Larry Sobel from the same group, forty-seven years later. We've had dinner together several times since.

One weekend in the early sixties, Jerry, Dave and I went to Grossinger's in the Catskills for a singles weekend. After chatting up many girls, we left without taking any numbers. On the way back, we stopped for gas. One of the girls we had been talking to was there also getting gas. Not to make the weekend a total loss, I asked her for her number. Sure, she said, and handed it right to Jerry.

The dating period for me consisted of Broadway shows, night clubs, The Blue Angel, Regine's, Jimmy's, The Playboy Club, Copa Cabana, Latin Quarter, The Living Room, and any other place that had dancing and was noted as "in."

One night on the way out of The Blue Angel after watching Peter, Paul, And Mary, a group of people were at the front door exchanging greetings. After inquiring and looking, it was Eddie Fisher, one day back from Rome and his highly publicized dumping by Elizabeth Taylor.

He was escorted by Carlos Romulo, the Ambassador to the UN at the time. I shook hands with both men and would tell the story to all my friends, holding my hand up. Not to be touched, because through Eddie Fisher, my hands have been where his hands have been. Therefore, Liz and I had a thing going on.

In addition to the Lowenstein crew, I had my Army buddies . Bobby Van's father owned a dude ranch in Hunter, New York. During the summer it was a camp for kids, and during the winter it was a camp for us.

Hunter Mountain was nearby. We would ski, snowmobile, party and have a lot of fun. In those days, Hunter Mountain Ski Lodge had a small barn-type house with a huge fire pit in the center and a small bar. The smell of the burning wood, plus the smoke in your eyes, just lent itself to a peaceful, enjoyable, get-away way of life.

One weekend with some other Army buddies, we went skiing at the Concord. On the way up on the chair lift, I wasn't paying attention. I was talking to my friend next to me, and both of us were looking straight ahead.

The chair came close enough to a mountain peak that the tip of my ski caught a twig. I had to jump off the chair or lose my leg. I survived that fall. But my friend kept talking to me. When he realized I wasn't there, the chair was over a deep ravine.

Enjoying the whole skiing experience on a weekend with friends, I followed a better skier than myself down a trail too steep for me. I could not stop. I crashed into a fence and appeared to have sprained my ankle. Rather than cut everyone's day short, I went back to the main hotel in a wheelchair, had drinks and snacks, and then went home.

Two days later, when it was not healing, I had x-rays taken, and it was broken. For the next three months I wore an ankle cast. I drove back and forth from work using my left foot while my broken ankle rested on the car seat.

1962: The US was embroiled in the Cuban Missile Crisis. The USSR wanted to build missile bases in Cuba; Kennedy ordered a blockade. Johnny Carson hosted his first Tonight Show, Peter, Paul, and Mary released their first hit, "If I Had a Hammer"

Back at Lowenstein, Mitchell Aronstein was starting his own converting business and asked me to come work for him, which I did. It was him, the designer, and me. It was still cold calling, but I had the entire garment center as my customers. It was a good opportunity.

At the same time, I started dating Louise, who was working in the secretarial pool of Lowenstein.

After a year or so of dating, Louise and I decided to get engaged. I could not afford an engagement ring, and we agreed that it could wait. Her mother, however, thought it was not right. I agreed and bought a nice ring that I was able pay off monthly.

Louise's mother was a very cold, shallow woman who ruled the roost. Her father came off as a very nice guy, but to this day I am confused about his sincerity. After each encounter of niceties with people, he left most of them with comments to me of what he really thought of them.

Louise's sister, Norma, was nice, married, and subservient to a very "controversial" man. As someone once stated, "When he dies, it would be impossible to compile a minion of ten men to mourn."

Knowing that my family could not contribute to a wedding, Louise and I agreed that we would get married in a low-key, family-only affair. After we were engaged, her mother wanted an engagement party, and she arranged such at Leonard's of Great Neck. A month or so prior to the affair, my paternal grandmother was on her way back from Florida. She was being driven by her daughter, Natalie, and Natalie's husband, Izzy.

They were in a head-on collision, in which my grandmother died. A very orthodox, religious woman, her funeral was conducted in a chapel. The coffin was then taken into the synagogue for an olea (an honor hardly ever bestowed upon a woman).

My father, who was the least religious of his two brothers and one sister, mourned in his own fashion. His brothers would mourn for one year as tradition dictates, which meant not attending any festive occasions. Needless to say, they did not attend the engagement party.

My father, after having a few drinks, and facing his family not being there and his mother's passing away, spent the rest of the evening crying. We called his brother, Morty, who lived nearby. He came over and somewhat controlled the remorse.

The arrangement with my in-laws-to-be was that we would have the engagement party. The wedding would be in a rabbi's study. But Louise's mother wanted a wedding, so she booked Leonard's for the wedding and allowed me to invite six couples. I objected, stating either that we should stay with the original plan, or else that the friends and family who watched me grow up would need to be there. That was agreed to, and invitations went out.

Natalie, my father's sister, had a five-year-old daughter, Amy, and she refused to come unless her daughter was invited. Fearing a repercussion from the engagement party for my father, I spoke to my future father-in-law, Harry.

Meaning well, he told me to tell her to come, but not to tell his wife. Of course, I did not think of letting the caterer know, so after little Amy disrupted the wedding ceremony with her loud and undisciplined behavior, and after they went to the dining room and found no place setting for Amy, the three of them left.

Other than that, the wedding was a beautiful affair without any problems. We spent the night at the International Hotel and left for Miami the next day on a plane with Allen King.

We were at the Deauville Hotel on our honeymoon. The weather sucked, and Florida was boring. We were bored. Rather than have a memory of a boring honeymoon, I went to a travel agency, and made arrangements for Nassau, Bahamas, only air. I wanted to physically see the hotel before I booked it.

On November 22, 1963, after taking a cab from the airport in Nassau, we stopped at a hotel to see if we wanted to stay there. Louise stayed in the cab and I walked into a hotel lobby. The clerk was listening to the radio and said, "The president and governor of Texas were just shot." For a few moments I wondered who the president of Texas was and then, of course, I realized what he meant. As the day went by, my fears were confirmed with the news of Kennedy's death.

Nassau was in mourning with all the flags at half-mast. The night clubs closed in respect, and a somber mood intoxicated the entire island.

When we were returning from our honeymoon, I started to get anxiety about getting on a plane. Somehow the fact that I was married now, or for reasons unknown, I developed a tremendous fear of flying, which plagued me for many years to come. Fear or not, there was no choice, so we flew home.

We settled in at our apartment, and went back to our respective jobs. Louise was still working for M. Lowenstein and Sons. And I was at the end of the line at Mitchell Aronstein's, as he was not going to make it. Like most startups, there was not enough capital to sustain the learning experiences, and he went out of business.

Louise was having a lot of problems with birth control. While prescribing birth control pills for Louise, the gynecologist told her that she might have a reaction of nausea, and that if it was bad enough to come back, and he would give her a shot to take care of it. The reaction came, and we went to the doctor, who injected her with Thorazine.

From the doctor's office, we took the subway and went to work. While crossing 40th Street off of 6th Avenue, in Manhattan, Louise fainted, and we were transported by ambulance to the hospital. The prognosis was that she should have been advised to go home to bed after taking the drug, and that the drug should not have been administered in the first place.

In search for a new doctor, my sister recommended Virginia Werden. She had the magic touch to finally get the pill to be tolerated and was a very impressionable doctor. A few months later, Louise was staining; we called Werden and left a message. Around midnight, the doctor called back and asked Louise a few questions. Werden told Louise to come right to the hospital.

Thinking they were both nuts, I begrudgingly drove to Doctor's Hospital in Manhattan at one o'clock in the morning. When we walked in, they put her in a wheelchair. To me it seemed like a dramatization of one of the popular doctor sitcoms on TV.

In the waiting room, after some time, Dr. Werden came out and stated that what Louise had was an ovarian cyst and it had to be operated on. I was in shock and awe of how she suspected this over the phone and embarrassed that I did not calculate the possibility of a real medical problem.

The next day she was operated on. Dr. Werden came out and said that everything was fine, and the cyst was gone. And by the way, Dr. Werden said, "She is pregnant."

I was relieved at the medical resolve but now in total fear as I was not prepared for parenthood.

I voiced my fears to my in-laws, who were at the hospital. They assured me not to worry. I learned that day when someone tells you not to worry that you had better worry.

When I was able to go back and see Louise, in a private room in the very pampering hospital, she was fine and elated with all the news. I asked why she was in a private room, fearing the expense; Louise had no idea. I asked Werden why Louise was in a private room, and her response was, "If you go first class, the ability to stay there will follow." I followed her advice for as long as I could.

Within the next few days, Louise wanted to know when she should stop working. I told her that when she felt it was necessary, or when she was able to collect unemployment, she should stop. One week later, she was laid off and collected unemployment.

In my quest for a job, Milton Cohen, my "controversial" brother-in-law, and his partners were just coming off a financial embezzlement in their cutlery company. It seemed that Harry, Louise's father, had a brother, Teddy, who owned Elite Electrical Supply in Brooklyn. He financed Milty, Sam, and Chet to go into business.

They were on the road selling, and Teddy handled the books. One day they realized there might be something wrong. They checked the books and discovered that Teddy was ripping them off. They left Teddy, opened their own place in Brooklyn, and assembled and sold cutlery to the premium trade, as well as gas station giveaways.

Milty suggested that I come work for them. I did, learned the product, the way to assemble it, and their techniques in selling. I was twenty-two, ready to go out on the road to sell to retail stores. I asked something about what to do if the people pay in cash, and nothing was said in response. A week later while working on Saturday for my father-in-law, he said, "You were asking personal questions to Milty. Don't do it anymore."

It was hard for me to comprehend that instead of saying something directly to me, Milty had Harry tell me. Not happy with that kind of environment, I returned the samples and said goodbye. The brothers Sam and Chet were real nice guys; when Sam's son, Jeff, came into the business, it spiraled upwards from there. Years later, through Jeff's effort, the company became very successful.

Now, floundering. I worked for Concord Fabrics, Charter Fabrics, and finally Loomskill Fabrics. I was making a bare living, hanging out with Dave Newman, Shelly Rich, and Jerry Lauren.

1964: Best Picture: *Tom Jones*

Louise and I lived in an L-shaped living room in a one bedroom apartment in Kew Gardens Road, in Queens. On Saturdays, Harry's lead electrician, Carmine, and I installed landscape lighting for all the people I knew who were moving into their new houses. Carmine deducted the material and we split the rest of the money. Working by myself, I built a wall closing off the dining room with sheet rock and wallpaper, and a nursery was prepared.

On September 11th, 1964, Wendy Lynn Scheffler was born.

What a pleasure to have a little girl. She was definitely Daddy's little girl. When she would wake up in the middle of the night, I walked her in her carriage up and down the hallway of our apartment house. I put the New York Times on the bed, a pair of glasses on her face, and photographed her at nine months reading the Times. I posed her and photographed her. When she was very cranky, the carriage bed went on the back seat of the car and we drove around until she fell asleep. I changed her diaper and did everything else a loving father would do. There was no greater feeling I had ever had prior to the sensation of holding my own child in my arms

As she got older, in the morning as I was leaving for work, I found her sitting right in front of the color TV. That was a no-no in those days, so I made her move back. I went out the door, waited a few minutes, and came back in. She was back in front of the TV.

On two occasions Wendy had to be hospitalized. The first time was for a virus that caused exceptionally high temperatures. The second was a hernia, which was operated on by a doctor recommended as the best in that field. He weighed over four hundred pounds, with hands to match. How he could operate on those tiny kids is beyond me, but he did.

During the viral scare, I did get a sincere "Don't worry." My brother-in-law, Ely, said to me not to worry about the money because he would pay for the best possible medical care I could get. It wasn't necessary, but it was sincere.

As she grew, the summers were spent in the Catskills at the same bungalow colony with all my cousins and friends, and their wives and children. It was like sleep-away camp for the kids, but with their parents there. Wendy had kids her age, relatives and friends, swimming pool, swings, and all the activities to keep her occupied all day.

CHAPTER 5: NICHE

I was working for Loomskill Fabrics, an upscale printed-fabric textile firm. As usual, the cold calling and the old accounts were not my thing. If I could get in front of the customer, though, no problem. One month they offered a $500.00 bonus for the largest sales volume of closeout by a salesman. I won. The people who buy distressed goods are easier to get to, as they do not rely on reorders. They make a decision and close the deal.

The company was heavily invested in a new fabric—printed knits with a backing—that served as a lining. The fabric was ready to be cut and sewn. Al Bressler of Breli Originals was an acquaintance through my sister and Mitchell Aronstein, and he was easy for me to get to. He ended up making sample dresses, which were successful in the stores. He placed the largest dollar-value order the firm ever took.

In order to cultivate other accounts, it was necessary to hang around the back door entrances of the manufacturer's offices for hours upon hours and days upon days. Eventually, as proven by some of my constituents, you develop a relationship and get them to test your goods.

For whatever reason, I could not do that. I could not sit there and wait or call and leave messages and never to get a call back. Only these past few years of my life have given me the ability to accept patience as a necessary part of life.

1965: Best Picture was *My Fair Lady*

Carmine and I were each making more money working Saturday and installing landscape lighting as I did for the entire week at Loomskill. I left the textile industry and started working as an electrician for my father-in-law.

He had three employees. Ronnie was a long-time employee and a big-time pain in the ass. Steve was also a long-time employee who was more cooperative then Ronnie, but also difficult. Izzy was an elderly helper. Steve was mostly constructive, but Ronnie did whatever he could to work against me.

After working full time for about three months, I was enjoying the work. I was not enjoying wearing work clothes instead of suits and having un-manicured fingernails as opposed to my previous weekly manicure.

My father-in-law, Harry, had a major heart attack. While in intensive care, the doctors were not optimistic that he would recover. Milton Cohen, Louise's sister's husband, at the height of the realism that recovery might not occur, took my mother-in-law Pearl's hand and turned her engagement ring around so that the doctors would not see it. It was a typical ring of the times. There was nothing about the ring that would have had any impact on the doctor's bill. Fortunately, the doctors were wrong. Harry recovered to within eighty-five percent of prior capacity. He was hospitalized, bed-ridden, and incapacitated for several months. While he was recuperating, the only one who took any initiative to handle the everyday activity of the business was me.

I dispatched the men to the jobs we had, figured out which ones to go to and how anyone would get paid, etc. No one else was offering to do it, so I took over. I dispatched Ronnie and Steve and myself. I answered the messages on the machine at the end of each day and applied responsible business practices to an industry that at that time in history had none.

1966: the Best Picture was *The Sound of Music*

At the end of the day, the answering service had calls from people who had no electricity or no heat. In the past, when the men were busy, the calls where never returned. I took every service call that came in and went out at night alone. By common sense and trial and error, I made the necessary repairs and sold new jobs. We were so busy that I took it upon myself to do the wiring of a brand-new house all alone.

It was a good fit; I found my niche from which to build!

When I took over, the business's checking account balance was negative $30,000. Ninety percent of our business came from home builders. It was a very competitive industry, and it was very slow to get paid.

The builder, in order to operate with the lowest capital possible, provides promissory notes, spread out every thirty days over a year, which work the same as a postdated check. The electrical supply houses, in order to fill your orders, take a slew of postdated checks. Then the builder renegotiates the notes and the supply house cannot deposit the checks. This results in a negative balance and a continuing negative cash flow.

Time went on and our customer base grew. The base reversed by design to more home renovation then home builders. The business was booming. I loved the action. I had found my way.

Laurelton Electric was growing so big that we moved from Harry's garage to a storefront on Merrick Boulevard.

There were two major problems. First, Harry did not have an electrical license. The license we were using was his brother Teddy's, for which Teddy received a monthly check.

As the business grew. I was in fear that any day he would either raise the cost prohibitively or take away the license.

The second problem was that there was no money. None of Harry's, none of mine, none in the business. That problem was never solved, but my relationships with bank managers all through my business career gave me a lot of leeway. In those days, that could be done. They let me overdraw my account and cashed my payroll when there were no funds. I always came through when I told them I would. The first bank I used was Bankers Trust in Queens. Peggy Dwyer was the manager. When she retired, she sent me a note in appreciation of the fact that I never let her down, and that she enjoyed doing business with me.

1967: Israeli and Arab forces battle. The Six-Day War ends with Israel occupying the Sinai Peninsula.

The test at the time for an electrical license consisted of questions and answers pertaining to antiquated methods of installation and connection. There was no one who could pass that test without special tutoring. An electrical inspector, Sal Mugavera, started a class that had a waiting list. At the time, the class cost $300.00. He had previous tests and answers, and twice a week we would go there and review them. It was a one-year ordeal; school at night, work by day.

The weekend prior to the test, a few other students and myself rented a motel room and tested each other all weekend. I passed the written and practical tests with a total score of 98.5. That school today under different ownership charges somewhere around $7,500.00 per class. George Riley, the head of the license board, and myself became friends. Whenever there was a minor problem, I called him, and it was taken care of. These personal relationships, which were typical in the business world back then, are not tolerated today. That takes away a lot of the fun of being in business.

1968: Arthur Ashe became the first black person to be ranked number one in tennis. NBC cut away from a football game to show *Heidi* and missed the Raiders' rally to beat the Jets, 43-32. Nixon was elected president. Senator Robert F. Kennedy died.

One of the builders we were working for, Nathan Apteker and Arthur Feder, built thirteen two-family homes in Far Rockaway. We did the electrical work. When they were finished, they were all rented and then mortgaged to the maximum. They offered them to me with a slight down payment. I took over the existing mortgage and carried a second mortgage. I was a land owner. The income and expenses left enough room to make a profit. I formed a corporation called Wendy Lynn Management, and I became a landlord.

It was a learning experience, to say the least. After selling me the two-family homes, Nathan and Arthur also had a sixty-family apartment house that they had just refinanced. I bought that too.

In real estate especially, if you mix different types of businesses together and one business fails, the others are brought down with it. To be safe, it is always prudent to operate each entity as its own corporation. I formed a new corporation, Welm Management (Wendy, Elyssa, Louise, and Mike) for this new addition to my real estate holdings.

The apartment house came with a couple that managed the building, Penny and Dale. Dale was a sheet metal welder with a regular job. Penny was a housewife who seemed to run everything. In a conversation with Penny, she said she was looking for other employment. I offered her a job. To my great fortune she accepted. I had no idea at the time that I was getting a woman with an IQ probably twice as high as mine and married to a man as nice and as smart as they come.

They were not only responsible for a great deal of my success, but also, from then through this very day, they provided a lifetime of devoted loyal friendship, and love. Penny writes:

> That first day in 1968, when I began work as "Girl Friday" for a twenty-seven-year old electrical contractor in Queens, New York, I never dreamed that I was beginning a friendship that would endure over forty years, only eight of which were spent in his employ. We were a most unlikely pair. Mike was tall, handsome, and charismatic, with a flair for the latest male fashions. That, together with his perfectly groomed hair and nails, suggested a career in the jewelry, fur, or garment industry rather than electrical contracting. But Mike was working and cramming hard to become a master electrician.
>
> He was about to assume ownership of his father-in-law's small electrical business once Harry retired. I was ten years older than my new boss, and born of southern Christian Protestant parents with American roots reaching back to the Revolution and the Indian Wars in the Carolinas, Georgia, and Alabama. In Arkansas, my father had been a Bible-pounding minister of the Baptist faith whom I adored and revered and whose religion I accepted and followed. I was pampered by my father, and I was taught by my mother, a strong southern belle, to be a lady. As a quiet, stay-at-home mother for fourteen years, I was a bookkeeper returning to the job market in an effort to find an identity of my own more than to earn a living.
>
> I could not have foreseen the pressure cooker in which I would spend the next eight years, nor the total devotion, the thrill of accomplishment, and satisfaction I would experience as I worked for Mike Scheffler as he clawed his way, against all odds, to the top of his field. Those people he encountered later

may have believed that Mike came easily to success. To them, I would say, 'It was by sheer guts and determination to succeed that he went from a tiny office in Laurelton, Queens, New York to a suite in the Empire State Building.' I was there in those years of struggle, and I know the truth.

He kicked and clawed his way to be a force in the electrical industry in New York after starting with nothing more than two electricians, his father-in-law, a $75.00-a-week secretary, an accounts receivable consisting of five manila folders, a dirty office on a Laurelton street corner, and a steely determination to succeed...

1969: New York Jets behind, Joe Namath surprises the world with a Super Bowl victory over the Baltimore Colts, 16-7

We had found a connection to New York Jets seasons tickets. Because of Joe Namath's presence, I bought six seats at $350 each from the connection. Then whatever the price was for the tickets. Our seats were on the fifty-yard line in the mezzanine directly behind the Jet's bench.

Doing work for builders was very tough. The only way to make money on private houses was to sell the homeowner extras. The builders were taking bids from everyone in the industry, so if you got the job, you knew that your price was too low to make a profit. The reason you wanted the work was that skilled workmen were in such demand that you did not want to let any of yours go. I would take whatever job I had to keep the men working.

In order to make some profitable sense out of it, I offered the builders a deal. Each time they were to sell a house, they gave me the buyer's contact information. Whatever extra things I sold to the buyers, I would give the builders twenty-five percent.

The builders loved it. I would make appointments to meet the owners at the site. I had a catalogue of all of the might-as-well items, the luxury items, and the security items. Sales averaged $2,000 per house, and everybody was happy.

The Rockaways were within twenty minutes of our offices and had a burst of activity. We were working for a home builder, Sidney Pullman. There were a lot of new homes being built and sold, in addition to many existing homes being renovated.

An older electrician, Richard, owned G&E Electrical Contractors, which was located in the Rockaways. I bought his business, his truck, his two offices, his customers, his good will, and his neighborhood advantage. I stayed with his name in Rockaway for ten years and gradually merged his business and mine into one.

1970: Four students at Kent State University slain by National Guardsman at demonstration protesting incursion into Cambodia

My accountant had a client, Biltrite Fixture Company, owned by Max Fuchs and run by his son, Richard. Their base business was that they were the New York supplier of Hussmann refrigerated cases. That was actually only a small part of their business. Richard, having a capital base provided by his father, took it a step further.

While he was working with all of the supermarket owners, it was always their desire to open more stores. Richard made that possible. If they found a location that made sense, Richard would do the entire renovation, including the cases. The only thing they had to do was to stock the shelves.

For this he was secured by the lease and all the contents of the store. He charged for the cases, the construction, the trades, and the interest. Once the store was open, they paid him weekly, in cash, for ever and ever and ever.

That in itself was a cash cow. Armed with money and building three or four locations at a time, he would collect all the estimates from all the trades. A contractor, such as myself, would estimate all three or four locations.

Richard would negotiate the price for each location. After the price was agreed to, he wanted to know what discount he would get for paying for all the jobs in full, right then. In a horrendously terrible cash-flow business, you started to salivate at the thought. Whatever it took, you walked out with a large check. Richard added a cash cow onto a cash cow. Cash is king.

We became good friends; like me, he was more of a man's man. However, he liked to consider himself more of an intellectual. While I enjoyed dining and drinking, he enjoyed reading, primarily about the Mafia.

Through Richard, I met all the owners of these supermarkets. They all became friends. We serviced their stores, homes, and telephones for many years.

As the business was growing, my in laws, Harry and Pearl, moved to Florida. I sent them a check every week for the next sixteen years until 1982, four years after Harry died.

One of the new bells and whistles was a product called Instant Hot. You would turn the knob and boiling hot water would come out for instant coffee, tea, or whatever. It required drilling a hole in the counter top, connecting the water with an easy connector, and an electric circuit.

The unit cost $75.00 plus labor. We sold it for $375.00. Harry saw it and started to sell them in the condo where he lived in Florida. I would send him ten at a time. We both did very well with it.

As I was learning construction, I decided that central air conditioning systems were easy enough to design and install. I added A/C onto my existing electric company, and proceeded. Everything went well on paper. I sized the units, which I bought from Carrier.

The only thing I could not control was the duct work and refrigerant. I contracted to a sheet metal subcontractor for both. I learned you cannot be in the contracting business without controlling your own forces.

The builders would call and ask me where the duct work was. I had to call the sub, and he either did not answer or would lie, ruining my own reputation. I quickly got out of the air conditioning business.

1971: Best Picture: *Patton*

As we were growing, we had to walk away from some jobs because of the union, Local 3. In order to get around that, I made a deal with a sweetheart union, Local 199. I enrolled two of my men and paid their dues and benefits. If Local 3 came on the job, as long as we showed the union card, there was nothing legal they could do. A sweetheart union lets you pay them for the ability to say that you're union, but they don't bind you to any exorbitant rates or benefits.

That did not seem to work because Local 3 was so powerful. They intimidated and harassed my men, the deliveries, and the property owners. The men refused to work on those jobs. I finished the one year contract with Local 199. I sent a certified letter stating that I do not wish to renew my membership. Never heard from them again.

Louise and I were leaving the house for a much-needed extended weekend in the mountains at the Hotel Nevele when a woman approached me and served me with papers. I had never had any court or legal experiences before that date. The papers were against me, personally, from a woman I had never heard of. It was a criminal complaint without any other specifics. I spent a fearful weekend wondering what this was and what I did that I could be held criminally liable for.

On Monday morning, I found out it was that union, Local 199. Even though I had not renewed my contract with them, they were suing me for nonpayment of those union benefits, which they could pursue criminally.

Chuck, my friend, was then a lawyer with Cravath, Swaine, and Moore, one of the top law firms of the time. He agreed to accompany me to court. We were in a Manhattan criminal court room with hookers, gangsters, and derelicts. When the case was called, Chuck said, "Your Honor, this is a business contract and does not belong in this court." The judge was very impressed.

The judge said, "I'll tell you what belongs in my court. You will not tell me." I pleaded not guilty and the case was set for another day. Scared, distraught, and anxious, I called Uncle Morty, an attorney. I sent him the papers, and within a few days he called me and said to bring $5,000 in cash to his office. I did, and the case was dropped.

"It's all about money."

Joe Senzone, a spot builder we were doing work for, had a piece of land in Rockaway that could accommodate thirty new homes. He was looking to get it capitalized. I was anxious to be a builder, and asked if we could be partners. He agreed, and we shook hands at a 50/50 partnership.

Aside from seed money, I would provide the electrical work. He would provide his expertise. I formed a corporation called Sandalwood Estates. I hired an architect, had plans drawn and filed with the city, and we were ready to go.

Joe then decided that his expertise was worth more than my electrical work, so 50/50 wasn't fair. We settled at 60/40. Two weeks later, he wasn't happy with that either, and tried to negotiate for a bigger percentage.

Feeling that I was being duped, I took my loss and abandoned the project.

1972: Best Picture: *The French Connection*

From the time I started and was building the business, I was drawing a menial salary. In those six years, nothing changed. We did more business. We had higher receivables and higher payables but were still cash poor. I made a decision. I worked hard, long hours, and from then on I was going to draw a more realistic salary.

The acquisition of G&E Electric was very profitable. I sent out postcards to all other electric companies in the yellow pages, asking if they were interested in selling their business.

Eventually, we acquired a company in Merrick, Long Island. Their clients included two of the largest air conditioning contractors in Nassau County. We had at least two central air conditioning jobs to wire on a daily basis for several years.

There is nothing that comes without paying a price. At 3:30 one morning, I received a call from the NYC Fire Marshall. He advised me that one of the two-family homes I owned in Rockaway had burned to the ground, and that a woman had died.

He started asking all kinds of questions, some of which I did not have the answer for. I said I would go to my office and call him back. Extremely concerned over the tragedy and fearful that I might be culpable in some way, I dressed and got to the office at about 4:00 a.m.

As I arrived, three of my incoming lines were ringing. All of the calls were from different NYC Fire Marshalls. I took all of their numbers, which were all the same. When I called back, of course, the Fire Department Main Office was closed.

I assumed that these were fire insurance adjusters or ambulance chasers for adjusters. They had woken me in the middle of the night and scared the hell out of me all so one of them could get my signature on a piece of paper so that they could represent me.

The fire was discovered later to have been caused by a woman falling asleep with a lit cigarette in her hand. I rebuilt that house and continued on.

The Bell System was forced to allow private phone systems to be connected to their telephone lines. Multiple phone users were able to purchase equipment from vendors other than The Bell System.

A salesperson contacted me representing a public company called Dictograph to try to sell me one of these systems. It was a phone system that you paid for monthly, just the same as Bell, but it cost a lot less and came with many more bells and whistles. It seemed to be natural for me to be in that business.

We started negotiations to partner myself and Dictograph. As it turned out, it was a public shell without any financial backing. They could not produce the product they were selling.

We formed our own company called Custom Communications and established a relationship with a new phone manufacturer, Tie Communications. Dictograph was falling apart. I hired the sales and installation people. I started selling to everyone I knew. It was an easy sale. The phones were sleek and loaded with features never offered by Bell.

If the sale was $10,000, I presented it as a monthly payment in comparison to their current monthly payment for equipment to Bell. I showed a spreadsheet showing the cost over five years, and the savings were enormous.

We sold the product on a monthly payment. The leasing company took the monthly commitment and paid us a lump sum which was a profit center as well. This was prior to computers, fax machines, cell phones, and email.

We had an electric typewriter with memory and taught it to produce a professional proposal with mathematical formulas with very limited input.

It printed out the spreadsheet showing Bell's charges and increases, our charge, the monthly difference, the annual difference, and a five-year cumulative difference. All the customer had to do was sign the lease and give us two months of lease payments in advance.

It was very hard to walk out of anyone's office without making the sale. I sold to every member of the Golf Club, friends, acquaintances, electrical customers, etc.

After solving some of the installation bugs, we had a good thing going. We had offices at 101 Park Avenue, Queen's Boulevard, and Laurelton.

From hooking up with leasing companies during this peak, I decided that the leasing companies and banks were making a good profit on their money. I formed another corporation with a partner, Morty Acker. We took the monthly payments from the customer in our own corporation.

I was paid for the phone system. The difference and the interest was our own profit, which Morty and I shared. In the end I sold the accounts to Bob Barrish of Long Island Sound for a decent profit.

1973: Spiro Agnew resigned as Vice President. Secretariat won the Triple Crown. The best movie was The Godfather. The best song was "The First Time Ever I Saw Your Face," by Roberta Flack.

Sydney Graber was an acquaintance and insurance broker of Harry's. He had an insurance office on Merrick Road in a building he owned near the parkway.

He also owned the building I was in. He wanted to sell it, and I wanted to buy it. I purchased it for $50,000. I put up a down payment, and he carried the balance, which I paid off monthly. The new corporation I created for that building was Merrick Properties, Inc.

The building provided a positive cash flow from the beginning until, many years later, it was sold for a substantial profit.

These acquisitions were more fun in the negotiation and purchase than they were for the financial gain. The thrill was the "action" in creating the art in which to close the deal.

In addition to all of the new customers we were acquiring, I had full-page ads in all of the Yellow Page books in all five boroughs of New York. They were renewed every year, and at some point they were costing me $8,000 per month. That was the information highway of the times, and a very lucrative one.

Our offices consisted of ten phone lines and six office staff, expediters, and salespeople. The phones rang so often it could have been a slot machine casino. Every request for work to be done or for an estimate to be made was promised to be done the next day before noon.

Each work request or estimate was written on a three-copy work order. One was filed numerically, one was filed alphabetically, and one was placed in a metal file hung on the wall with seven compartments one for each day of the week. At the end of each day, I would schedule the work orders and estimates. I had pads made up which listed the mechanic's name on the top and the date and day of the week on the side. Each mechanic either returned to an unfinished job or went to the start of a new one.

There were two estimators, Bernie and Neil. Both were knowledgeable, neat, and well-spoken. They were electricians who I had made my estimators. I would schedule their estimates mostly geographically. Each estimate and work order was numbered in the order I wanted them done. Ninety percent were scheduled, as promised, before 12:00.

At the end of each day, the work orders would be returned to my desk with either a check, cash, or a description of what was left to be done. The estimates came with a deposit and a new work order written. We converted seventy-five percent of our estimates into work orders.

At 7:30 a.m., the men would come in the back door and take their work order out of another metal box on the back wall with a compartment with each mechanic's name.

Calvin, a long-time (35 years) employee and friend was in charge of the material. He laid it out the day before. The mechanic pulled his work order, went to the counter, got his material, and off he went.

Every day I waited in the back parking lot making sure the guys would move out quickly because I could not get back to my desk until they left.

This system was cultivated through the years as the business grew. In the beginning, I handled all of the estimates. Then I had Bernie take half of them, while Neil and I did the inside estimates and the organizational duties. As we grew I hired an inside estimator, and Neil shared the outside with Bernie.

Bernie and I would go out for a drink a few nights a week. He would drink without showing any wear, and the next thing you knew, he would pass out on the floor. I liked Bernie, but his compensation was growing beyond what I could afford. When I decided not to increase it one year, he left and went into his own business. As the main estimator, he had relationships with some good accounts, which he convinced to go with him, thus souring our friendship.

At the end of 1973, we employed twenty-two electricians and helpers, owned eleven trucks, and installed 5200 individual jobs over the course of that year. In all, from 1966 through 1973, we installed over 25,000 jobs, of which fifty percent were repeating customers and fifty percent were new.

We entered 1974 with an established individual customer base in excess of 12,500. Seventy-five percent were homeowners and twenty-five percent were commercial.

Entitlement

Cause and Effect

70

Our customer list included religious institutions of every denomination, hospitals in every borough, builders, celebrities, decorators, auto dealerships, McDonalds, Duane Reed, Dykes Lumber, Peter Pan Bakeries, Cohen Optical, Lucille Roberts, Gap, Bed, Bath and Beyond, Burger King, Food Emporium, Key Food, Met Food, Pioneer Supermarkets, Smilers, chains of all kinds, Loews Movie Theaters, general contractors, day care centers, and the list goes on and on.

That was the foundation that I orchestrated, created, enhanced, finessed and worked my ass off for. I did build that myself.

With all due respect, Mr. President, I did Build this Business, Myself.

CHAPTER 6: SMELLING THE ROSES

1968: President Lyndon Johnson announces he will not seek reelection. Martin Luther King, Jr. is slain in Memphis, Tennessee.

While building my business, I was also building my family.

On July 21, 1968, Elyssa Lara Scheffler was born, which pluralized Daddy's little girl.

The same twenty-second disappointment that she was a girl, not a boy. But twenty seconds later, I was over it. I was also disappointed that when I called my mother to tell her, she said she was going to go up to the mountains for the weekend, as she had planned, and that she would see her new granddaughter the next week. I got over that too.

Elyssa was planned, so there was no fear of finances. We had bought a house in North Woodmere in 1967 for $27,500. The bassinet was set up in the bedroom, with a nurse to assist Louise for the first three weeks.

Elyssa went to nursery school and day camp. She was in the same dance class as Wendy and had all of the same things that Wendy did. In the Catskills, we had a bungalow large enough for my parents and us to share. When Elyssa was just starting to walk, there was a big tree outside our place. We gave her about thirty feet of rope and tied it to the tree, so she had a good time exploring.

We spent the next three or four years doing that summer routine. They had a day camp for the kids. My dad would play gin all weekend; I would play golf and cards. We would go out all night long with our friends to the hotels and just have fun.

The married couple bungalow colony routine is that the wife goes to the colony as soon as school ends and returns on Labor Day. The men come up on Friday and go back Sunday night. Like all of the other men, I came up on weekends and was home alone during the week.

One night during the week, I met my sister, Marilyn, and her boyfriend at the time, Wally, for dinner at the Doriental Restaurant on 57th between Park and Lexington. It was directly across from the Lombardy Hotel where Richard Burton lived.

All the people in the restaurant knew Wally and called him by his first name. The food was served based on what you were in the mood for. There was no menu. Instead, they asked what main food you wanted and the rest of the meal was created by the kitchen staff. I was very impressed. As I left, I told Ivan, one of the restaurant partners, that I would be back the following week. I told him that my name is Mike, and that I wanted the same treatment.

The following week, I walked in with some people and got the first-class treatment. That spurred a twenty-year relationship with Ivan, his brother, and his partner, Jimmy, and all of the waiters and bartenders. They did business with me as well, at their homes and in the restaurant.

1969: Richard Nixon inaugurated as the 37th President of the United States. Senator Edward Kennedy pleads guilty to leaving the scene of a fatal accident at Chappaquidick, Massachusetts in which Mary Joe Kopechne was drowned.

BACHELORS 111

Joe Namath had the nightspot, Bachelors 111. One of his three partners was my friend Bobby Vanucci, a.k.a. Bobby Van. The NFL wanted Namath out of the club because one of the other partners was a connected gangster, my friend Bobby.

One night Louise and I went to the club. Bobby was there and he sat down with us. After a while, I said, "What is this bologna about you being a gangster?"

He excused himself and did not come back to our table for the rest of the night. Years later I visited him several times in Florida. Bobby went on to own a very popular disco in Fort Lauderdale called Mr. Pips. The disco attracted the most beautiful women, had the top entertainers, and was an afterhours place for all the major celebrities in and around Miami.

That event occurred during the years I was building my family and business. I was not in touch with Bobby then and did not know about the disco until its time had passed. Later on he owned a very popular club in Fort Lauderdale called The Candy Store. I did visit him there.

1970: Best Picture: *Midnight Cowboy*

POT

Back in the Catskills for the summer. My cousins were all into pot. I was afraid of anything that might make me not be in control of myself, so from the very beginning it was not my thing. At first, I was disappointed in the others for using it, but then I realized I was just isolating myself. I accepted their use of it, but it was not for me.

One day, the whole group took a walk down a dead-end street so that they could get high smoking pot. My car was equipped with a police siren as an alarm which I could activate manually. I drove up to the top of the hill on the side they could not see, turned on the siren, made the wheels squeal, and drove full speed down the hill. They all ditched their cigarettes and were pretty pissed at me. It sure was funny.

FLORIDA

For many years we continued to go to Florida for Christmas vacation, which I loved. We always drove. We fished, we boated, we played on the beach, stopped off at Pedro's, the Mexican place, both ways. It was a fun time. When the Auto Train was in operation, we were on its maiden voyage.

MEXICO 1971

I had been working seven days a week, fourteen hours a day since 1966. Penny, who was my ally, my friend, and my shining light, did everything and anything to assist, including payroll, which was over twenty employees at the time. In those days it was on a one-write system, for those of you who might remember.

An overtime expense was inadvertently left out for one of the men. When he told me, I asked Penny to correct it, which meant the withholding, the unemployment, and all the reports had to change. Anyway, she told me, "No, let him wait until next weekend." She was upset that I even asked her.

Without her knowing, I paid the guy in cash out of my pocket, as I knew he needed it. However, I felt hurt and betrayed. It was the first time she ever said no. In fact, she was right. I should have suggested just paying him like I did. And then correcting it in the following week.

It was time for a vacation, and I told Louise to find a place. We decided on Mexico City and Las Brisas in Acapulco, in September.

We fell in love with the Mexican people as soon as we arrived in Mexico City. We did all the tourist things, the churches, the ruins, the bull fight, the Sunday floating fiesta along the canals of Xochimilco.

We visited the site of the prior Olympics, and then went on to Acapulco, which at that time was the playground of the rich and famous. There was a night club in the center of a very sparsely-occupied town called Armando's Le Club, where I had read all the celebrities hung out.

We danced there every night. I was looking for Sinatra. No celebrities. In the room overlooking Acapulco bay, just the bedroom and bathroom were indoors. The pool, the bar, and the swing were all outdoors, and were very private, and very romantic.

Each morning by 6:00 a.m., there was a pot of coffee and a plate of rolls and pastries left in a two-sided sliding opening. We had an open Jeep and access to their bay-front pool, a natural seawater inlet. We were surrounded by luxury and beauty.

During the day we would go down there, and in the afternoon, we would swim at our private pool. There was something about the Mexican people and the sun that resonated with total relaxation.

Having read that Acapulco had live sex shows, on that first trip, we met a couple at the pool. They agreed to join us to go see one. We took a cab into the woods in a desolate area, up and down mountainous terrain, and finally arrived at this big veranda with a dance floor and a stage and no other patrons there. We sat down, and ordered a drink.

The manager approached and asked if we would like to see a show.

I said sure.

He asked, "The stage, or a private room?"

We opted for the private room.

What would you like to see?

The consensus was two women and a man.

He then brought over eight girls and had us pick the two we wanted. He requested that our wives pick out the man, but they passed.

We then went into this private room, and he bolted the door closed. At that point I was getting a little frightened, and I said, "Our friends are picking us up here in an hour. So be sure to let them know we are in here."

The show began, and since it was the off season, I guess to cut down on the overhead, the guy in the show was played by no other then our host. They proceeded to perform a ménage à trois in our presence. An experience, a lot of giggles, no need for a curtain call.

We explored all of Acapulco. I loved it then, and love it to this day. I made approximately forty more trips to Acapulco. I'm a little afraid to go now, but it has an immediate presence of relaxation. Once the trip was ending, I was relaxed and thinking about flying home. My fears surfaced to the point of trying to figure out how to drive, cruise, or swim home. I had no choice. I flew in fear and got home.

The vacation made me make a decision that separated me from most. I enjoyed my work, but decided to not count my money. Instead, I decided that the fruits of my labor would be spent on roads, left to travel. I adopted the following quotation:

"Don't let making a living prevent you from making a life."

SLEEP AWAY

After that vacation, I was so relaxed that I was able to be more creative, with renewed vigor. I had a built-in pool installed in the backyard. I wanted to spend the time with my girls in the pool.

The first summer we had it was amazing. I invited everyone, friends, kids, and family. I had no idea that Wendy would soon be going to sleep-away camp. I felt that she was being pushed at six, going on seven, but her friend, a neighbor's daughter, Julie, who was the same age, went as well.

I gave in. We took Wendy and her bags to the camp bus. When it was time to leave, she ran off the bus and grabbed onto my leg and would not let go. Louise put her back on the bus. We went home, I locked myself in the bathroom, and cried.

On visiting day, four weeks later, the same thing happened. Everything was fine until we were leaving and she wrapped her hands around my ankle. I was ready to take her home. Louise said, "Just keep walking." That evolved into ten years of sleep-away camp.

In my opinion, it is a tremendously successful education for children to live with other kids and be independent from their parents, and like college, it is a bonding of friendships that last a lifetime. Another of the things I would put on my mandatory list.

After a while, the pool was just good for a few weeks a year when everyone was home. We would have food fights, hose fights, pool games, etc.

1971: *All in the Family* debuts on CBS

While I Debut on Broadway

One of the original customers, the most demanding, and one we finally got rid of, was Stanley Seaman. Somehow in the period we were doing business, he got me to invest in a Broadway musical called *The Ballad of Johnny Pot*, starring David Carradine, produced by Gretchen Wyler and Peggy Cass.

As an investor, you go to the opening productions on the same night as the critics. The story was about Johnny Appleseed, but instead of planting apple seeds, he was planting pot. It was a very formal opening, tuxedos, suits, and ties.

The show had ten musical scenes. There was a five minute standing ovation for each song. In addition, the production received a fifteen minute standing ovation at the conclusion. These, of course, were all the investors.

Afterward we went to Sardi's with the investors and producers, Gretchen Wyler and Peggy Cass, and waited for the reviews. I believe at the time the review was on channel five by Joel Klein. We were all upstairs in the restaurant, as soon as Joel Klein came on, total silence.

His words were: "Ladies and Gentleman, I have to correct my review of the play I saw last night. I told you that I had seen the worst play I have ever seen in my life. I need to correct that to the second worst play. Tonight I saw the worst."

Gretchen Wyler said, "Bastard." Peggy Cass said, "Son of a Bitch." The show was panned in all the papers the next day; the producers vowed to keep it open anyway. The show closed nine days later, with my investment.

"We make a living by what we get.
 We make a life by what we give." Winston S. Churchill

My parents were celebrating their 40th wedding anniversary. I wanted to make them a surprise party. Karen and I agreed to split the expense. Marilyn was in a bad phase of divorcing Ely, so she was not expected to contribute.

Entitlement

Cause and Effect

Milton Cohen, Louise's brother-in-law, called me the day before the affair and said that he would not be coming to the anniversary party and was very insulted. "Why? What happened?" I asked.

"You did not invite my parents, and I am insulted."

"Oh my God! It was a terrible oversight. Please give me your mother's number. I will call immediately."

I called and begged, telling her that I would have her and her husband picked up and brought home. His mother said that I should live and be well and drop dead. Later on, when discussing it with Louise, she said, "Don't you remember that you asked my sister and brother-in-law to give you a list of who they would like to be invited, and he specifically said not to invite his parents?"

He attended the party, but would not look at me or talk to me.

We arranged the party at Leonard's in Great Neck. I took my parents that night across the street from Leonard's to a popular restaurant and hangout on Lakeville Road and Northern Boulevard, Andre's.

Fearing that with my father's heart condition, a sudden shock might be detrimental to his health, I planned on letting him know at Andre's while we were having a drink what was happening. They took it in stride. We walked across the street to Leonard's. The room was full of all of their friends, acquaintances, and relatives, and everyone had a great time.

That was the first catering hall party that I made, and did not realize that the band played for fifteen minutes and then took a break for fifteen minutes. It was a mood breaker. I told them I wanted continuous music, and they conformed.

At the toast that my sisters and I gave our parents, champagne was served, and everyone lifted their glasses. At the end of the toast, people were looking for more champagne, but that was all we had arranged for. Regardless, I told the caterer to keep pouring. It was a great success.

At the end of the evening, when we received the invoices, Karen said that she did not agree to continuous music or unlimited champagne, and she paid for half of everything else. I did not realize that I was obligating her for something that she deserved to make a choice in, so I paid the difference and that was that.

FEAR OF FLYING

Because I was still afraid of flying, Louise and I took a cruise from New York to the Caribbean islands on the Leonardo Da Vinci. We took the Italian Lines, which at that time was the line to go on because the food and the service were the best.

It was just as presented; the food was too good. It was very enjoyable. We met people, danced, and enjoyed the sightseeing. It was a very relaxing way to vacation. All you had to do was drive to the boat, unpack your bags, and you were on vacation. In those days people could come aboard and have a bon voyage party, which we did. The following year we sailed on the Michael Angelo. We did many other cruises, but after a while, unless the ports were interesting, going on cruises was not for me.

CHAPTER 7: LOST AND FOUND

1972: Eleven Israeli athletes at the Olympic Games in Munich are murdered. George C. Wallace of Alabama was shot.

My childhood dreams consisted of a house with a white picket fence, a job earning ten thousand a year, and a son. The first two were easy to exceed, but the latter took me three tries. On the third try, I even used Dr. Werden's method of determining the woman's temperature during ovulation for when the eggs would be fertile enough to produce a boy. Whether that worked or not we will never know, but the result was that after two beautiful, much-loved daughters, I finally had my son.

On June 5th, 1972, Adam Craig Scheffler was born.

He was ordained from the very beginning. His bris, attended by hundreds of friends, took place at our North Woodmere home while the second floor construction was taking place.

Socially and financially, I appeared and basically was on top of my game; everyone was attracted to me. Not because I was attractive, because I exhumed financial success. My father, who I held in such great esteem for no special reason other than he was my father, was there with his two brothers, Morty, an attorney, and Leo, a sweater manufacturer, both of whom I loved and respected, and I admired their intelligence and traditional way of life.

The day was the most proud day of my life; I fulfilled my dream and was able to share my exuberance with all those I truly cared about. The Moyle preformed the circumcision, and the religious aspect was carried out to perfection.

My father held the baby, and I almost passed out. But life prevailed, and the custom, the joy, the respect and tribute to the family religion and myself was done.

Through the years my love for all my children was equal, yet my son was some kind of chance to improve upon my own evolution.

My dad was special to me from the earliest I can remember. Not because he was my dad or a male presence in my life, but because of the way he handled things, and especially because of the way he dealt with me. He never said, "You can't do that because I said so." Actually, I never heard, "You can't do that." Instead there was always a calm, common sense approach. I would say I am going to do whatever. He would reply, "Okay, but if you do that, this is what will happen." He would explain the dangers or pitfalls of what I had in mind. In the beginning, I would do it anyway. However, he was always right.

From a long as I can remember, on Valentine's Day, my sisters and I woke up to a valentine-shaped box of chocolates that my father had left. I saw it as a loving, out-of-the-way gesture. I was so appreciative of it that I continued and embellished upon it with my children for long into their adulthood.

I do not know if my father had any job prior to being an elevator starter in the lobby of 200 Madison Avenue. However, that was not his real job. He was actually a bookmaker, taking bets, collecting, and paying. Apparently, he did well.

New York was not active in prosecuting bookmakers. In 1933, Fiorello Laguadia became mayor of NYC and was determined to crack down on all forms of illegal profiteering. Dad figured it was time to move on and looked for a business to buy. The liquor business in those days was more financially successful than most. The only business he found to buy was a bar and grill called McCabe's, on Fordham Road in the Bronx.

My uncle Morty, Dad's brother, although a practicing attorney, felt he could enhance his income as a partner.

The business never yielded more than a living, and Morty did not see the benefit from the long, late hours he had to work. So Morty left, and Dad continued.

From that point on, Dad worked from 11:00 am until 4:00 a.m. I never spent much time with him, as he was hardly home.

Whenever my dad got upset, and that was usually with my mom, it was over money. He could not get past his anger without tearing up, which was a trait I inherited to a degree.

One summer at the bungalow colony, my friends and I were in the in the casino, and I went to play a song in the jukebox (Sha boom, Sha boom, yaydadada). The jukebox door opened, exposing the coin collector, and we took the coins and used them to keep playing songs.

That must have been a Saturday, because my dad came up late on Saturdays. On Sunday morning, while having the standard family breakfast with my parents of strawberries with sour cream and onion rolls with butter, my dad started talking about the jukebox robbery.

Slowly, deliberately, he carefully mentioned that someone broke in to the jukebox and took the money. The police were called. They took fingerprints and they expected to have an arrest any minute. He was good. I was scared to death, and I blurted out it was me. It was me. Of course he already knew that.

When I was working as a caddy, each week I gave my earnings to my father to put into a savings account for me. When the day came that I wanted the money to use in the purchase of some coveted item, my father informed me that my money, "was used up on me a long time ago." I wasn't happy about it, but I knew the money I earned as a caddy couldn't begin to pay for all the years of love, housing, food, and support my father had invested in me.

My dad was tall and thin as a kid, and basketball was his favorite sport to play. I, too, was tall and thin, and basketball was the one game I did excel at. I let him know that I was pretty good and on a winning team. We played at the public school in the gym, on the sixth floor of a walk-up only entrance. To my shock and awe, one night my dad walked those six flights and came to watch me. There was never a parent around when we played our games. It was a wonderfully rare moment, that I could share myself with him.

My friends, Mel and Lenny, were going to celebrate graduation with their parents at a restaurant in Manhasset called Lorraine Murphy. I never even thought to ask my parents to dinner, as I do not ever remember them sharing any occasion of mine with me. However my mother must have found out about it through Mel, which is how she found out everything about me, and my mother and father joined us. It was an experience I never had before. And a great feeling to be in a social atmosphere with your family.

After high school, I took a job on the training program of Alexander's Department Stores on Fordham Road and the Grand Concourse. It was ten blocks from my father's bar on Fordham Road and Jerome Avenue. Once in a while, I would go over and have lunch.

On one occasion, I walked in and my father was not at the bar. I walked to the kitchen, and he and his waitress Marion were locked in a kissing embrace. They had not seen me. I went back to the bar and sat down. When they came out, my father went behind the bar, and Marion sat down next to me. At which point I told her to get her things and get out. She was fired.

As I walked across the street, my father came barreling out, calling me. I did not answer, but he caught up with me and was very upset about what I said to Marion and so he smacked me in the face. That was never mentioned or discussed again with anyone until the point where it made no difference.

One weekend that year, we were at a country club in New Rochelle as guests of my sister Marilyn and brother-in-law, Ely. My dad, who was an excellent gin rummy player, was playing cards and had an angina attack. Not knowing it was angina, we went to many doctors and the prognosis was angina and the only cure was relief by way of nitroglycerin.

While in the Army, in Fort Gordon, Georgia, I learned that my dad had sold the bar and took a job as a bartender at Yankee stadium and Yonkers raceway. I do not know the cause, but that information made me cry.

Dad related a story to me about his first time working at Yankee stadium. He was given a jug of premixed Bloody Marys. He poured it for each order. Everyone at the bar was high and having a good time. He found out afterward that the mix did not have alcohol in it.

After the Army, I was involved with the guys at work with gambling on sports, horses, cards and stocks. Somehow I got the idea I could make fifty dollars per day by betting on baseball, and if I lost, increasing my bets until I won. Before I knew it, I owed the bookmaker five hundred dollars. I was so upset as to how I would come up with the money that I could not sleep. When my dad came home he saw I was awake and I had to tell him why. He gave me the money to straighten it out.

Some time later, my sister Karen was getting married. During the planning of the events, my dad did not have enough money, and his brother Leo was going to lend it to him. When he came back from Leo's place, he seemed unhappy, and I asked him what was wrong, He was hurt because he could not believe that he had to sign a note, which Leo then put in his safe. My dad was hurt, and till recently, I probably would have been also. I now understand when it comes to money everyone has their own way of dealing with it and there is no right or wrong.

Ever since I bought my house, my parents were invited over every Sunday, along with some friends. I would barbecue or do a lobster bake. I kept a bottle of Seagram's VO for my father at all times, which he drank straight in a shot glass.

On occasion when there was a reason for him to come over to my offices, he would sit at the opposite side of my desk and watch me. He was in awe of my being able to transfer from one call to the next and one business to another. He was very proud, and I was very pleased to make him so.

In the early '70s, at my suggestion, Dad bought a new car. He was a little short, and I gave him whatever he needed. He returned it within a few months.

Every weekend during football season, I would make my picks, my dad would make his, and then we would go over them and decide who we were going to bet on. After we agreed, I phoned in the bets, and whatever the outcome we split it.

During the summers, we had shared a huge bungalow with two full bedrooms and bathrooms that the owner built for us. My dad loved steak, and on very special occasions he used to take us to Dominick's in the Bronx. Monticello had a very serious steak and seafood house called The Old Homestead. Every few weeks during the summer, I would take all of us there.

Ever since the first episode he had with angina, it had become more frequent and more painful. There was a lot of publicity, about a doctor at New York Hospital named Dr. Spencer, who was working on techniques such as coronary artery bypass grafting, which was the beginning for what is now modern cardiac surgery. I made an appointment with Dr. Spencer in the New York Hospital, something that was hard to do. When we arrived at the hospital, there was no place available to park. I dropped my father off and waited.

When he came out, he related that the doctor had said that as long as he is still able to walk and go to work the surgery can wait until it becomes necessary. It made sense to me, but later on I wondered if he told me the truth. I never forgave myself for not going in with him or at least following up with the doctor. I do not know if I would have been in favor of the surgery at the time, as it was scary, but at least I would have known the true prognosis.

Christmas, 1972. I was taking my mom and dad with us to Florida. They had never been more than one hundred miles from the Bronx. They had rented a room at a hotel on the beach. We were staying at a hotel near my in-laws and my parents.

A few days before we left, Uncle Morty had a stroke, which left him paralyzed on one side and speech-impaired. After he was hospitalized and stable, I decided to continue with our plans. Each time we would stop to eat or for gas, I would call to see how he was. We were arriving in Jacksonville, Florida, and I called to see how he was doing. Morty had had another heart attack and passed away.

My father and I flew back. We attended the funeral, sat shiver, and returned to Florida. I took my parents on an overnight cruise to Freeport from Miami. It was the only time my father was at a gambling casino and an elegant one at that. I was proud to have given them that pleasure.

Three months later, my uncle Leo, my father's other brother, died of complications from a minor operation.

I don't believe my dad had an enemy in the world; Uncle Lou was a painting contractor, and back in the day, when my dad had some money, Lou had told me that he was in a bind with his company and could not meet his payroll. He said he went to my dad, who handed the money right over to him.

My father wasn't around much when I was growing up, but he did the best he knew how to do. He gave me life, love, and many of the things an adolescent boy craved. I realized that any money I ever earned would be because I stood on his shoulders as I grew to manhood and learned to make my own way.

Louise and I came home from having dinner with Ray and Lois, friends we had met on our honeymoon. They had come back to our house for dessert after dinner, when I received a phone call from my Uncle Lou. He said, "He's gone." I had no idea what he was talking about. I said, "What's gone?"

"Dad," he said.

On October 27th, 1973, Dad died.

I fell down in hysteria. I had spoken to my father only a few hours ago, when we were selecting our picks for football to place bets on. He said that he had a cold, but was fine. When I got over to his house on Yellowstone Boulevard, the ambulance drivers were rolling him out with the blankets over his head. I went in; no one seemed very upset.

Two of my mother's sisters were there with their husbands for a previously-arranged card game. He had just keeled over and died. My father, as most others in those days, was a member of a lodge, The Knights of Pythias. They had plots and arranged the funerals and interment. The funeral was at the Forest Hills chapel on Queens Boulevard. The chapel was filled with people, and it was a standing-room-only crowd. At that time, I was still the rock star, a status that the illusion of money gave me.

Ninety-five percent of the mourners were friends of mine who'd come out of respect for me. Karen lived in New Jersey at the time. Marilyn had an apartment in Riverdale.

Because the people who would come to the shiva were primarily from Queens and Long Island, I suggested to Karen that the shiva be at my house. She agreed, but I do not think with a full heart. After the procession to Wellwood Cemetery in Farmingdale, we went back to my house, where the traditional boxes were placed, the mirrors were covered, the water outside to wash your hands, and food for everyone to eat.

Early in the evening Karen and Jack were leaving, and Karen said, "I will not be back the next night."

"Why?" I asked.

Her answer was, "I do not like this kind of food."

I said, "What food would you like?"

"Chinese," was the answer.

I said, "Fine, tomorrow night there will be Chinese food."

Never before did I understand the Shiva or the wake. As people came, they ate, they drank, and they told jokes, and to me it seemed disrespectful. I learned differently from this experience. While everyone was there, you were able to take your mind off of your sorrows; the event served its purpose.

The Rabbi came and assembled the men in the house and conducted a minion prayer to mourn your loss that requires ten men to be present.

Karen is not a big food person. Her request for Chinese food was just a way that she was able to get out of whatever was bothering her, and it was probably me. I liked people; she did not. I liked spending money; she did not. The Rabbi was patronizing to me; she was not into religion.

That night I went to bed and grieved for the loss of my father all day and until the next, when more people came over for the Shiva. I totally forgot about the Chinese food, as people had sent over food every day as a token of their compassion.

When Karen got there, she looked for the Chinese food. I realized I forgot and told her, "I will order it right now." She turned and left. We did not speak for a while after that.

It took maybe twenty years before I could recall my father's death without my eyes tearing. I still have the bottle of VO, and I still drink a toast to the most unconditional adult love I have ever experienced.

He was at my house almost every weekend, and he came to my office and watched with pride as I jumped from one call to another. I don't think he took pride in his life, but he was a very street smart guy, and I loved him.

I adored my father; the memory of him inspires me still. My father's death was a devastating blow. I trusted my father; I believed in him. I loved him; I needed his love, admiration, pride, advice, and friendship. Most of all, I wish that he had stayed around a little longer, as I would have had the pleasure of making his life a little more comfortable, and I could have enjoyed the pride he would have in me.

I am proud to have had that foundation, from which to build.

"The experiences of our fathers are the foundation for our sons."

Entitlement

Cause and Effect

92

CHAPTER 8: LAS VEGAS

My friend and customer Richard Fuchs had a ritual of all the guys going to Vegas for five days every three months. I was continually asked to join them, but I never wanted to take away from my work, so I never went. Now, after my father died, it was different. I needed to get out of the funk that the death of my father left, so I decided to go.

The only casino gambling I had done prior was about four times at island casinos, playing for whatever cash I had in my pocket. At the most, four to five hundred dollars. Richard asked how much credit I wanted at the casino. I had no idea, so I said two thousand dollars.

From the first time I entered the first-class lounge of TWA in New York in 1974, to the time I arrived back at Kennedy, I was in an adult toy store. By the time you would get to Vegas, and the treatment you would receive, you thought that 747 you came down on was yours.

The money, the women, the sex, the food, the service, the respect, the suites. The showrooms, the shows, the restaurants. You had the feeling that everything was yours. This was your own kingdom; your pockets only had hundred dollar bills, and lots of them. I did not feel like James Bond. There, I was more like Howard Hughes.

Everyone knew my name (Mr. S); everyone said hello. You imagined you were finally being recognized for this handsome, debonair, world-renowned figure that you were.

Every woman, waitress, croupier, and stranger fluttered their eyes and stared into yours with a slight smile and major flirtation. You knew it was all make-believe, but somehow you convinced yourself that they were making believe for everyone else, but you, no, you are special.

The whole psychologically charged atmosphere puts you in a euphoric state that lasted as long as you can stand it; for me five days and nights every three months was enough.

I can never remember having such wonderful friendships and camaraderie at any time in my life before or after. All you had to do is think about something you wanted to eat, something you wanted to see, somewhere you wanted to go. It was there before you could get the words out of your mouth. I know for a fact that Paul Anka was watching me there, and that is how he was inspired to write "My Way." He let people think it was for Sinatra, for financial and safety reasons. But it was based on me.

The whole experience of Vegas, at that time, is that you are in a make-believe world. Nothing is real, but they make you think that you are a very important person, and you get lost in it.

If you take time to think rationally, you know that none of it is real. The beautiful young woman flirting ,the casino managers and employees know your name and call you Mr. S, the shows are free, the food is free, the liquor is free. The money is chips. Whatever you end up owing the casino, after you are back home, is real, though. A week or two after you return, a local hotel representative calls and asks how you would like to pay...no pressure. It was a fabulous experience for a few days, for a hard-working person to clear their head, as long as you understood that none of it was real.

We left for Vegas on a TWA 747 first class, from the TWA club at the airport. We sat in the upper deck and our seats turned so that we could face a table and play cards. Whatever the reason, flying first class cured me of my fears.

A friend of Richard's, Tony Grasso, was part of the group. I had met him a couple of months earlier at a party at Richard's house.

He was crude, uncontrollable, and a wise guy; I did not like him. At the TWA first class lounge, Virginia Graham, a TV talk show host, and Tony, with his quick, smart, and vulgar ways, were engrossed in humorous conversation. The four-letter-word vernacular made me cringe, and I was embarrassed; however, she did not seem to mind. In fact, she was enjoying the interaction, and it continued on the flight to Vegas.

Once we were in Vegas, we went to the Sands Hotel. We were each given a corner suite one above the other. Richard had us all come into his room, where he ordered five or six rolling carts of food, all VIP—no charge.

Later on, we went to the casino, where I found out that my credit line was not two thousand but ten thousand. We played for a couple of hours. I lost some and went up to my rooms. The adrenalin was flowing in me, so I decided to go back to the casino.

I pressed the button for the down elevator and when it stopped Tony was inside; we went down together to the lobby.

The Sands was one of the few hotels that had a lobby; the others were all casino. The elevator doors opened to an elegant lounge of couches and chairs. A beautiful young woman sitting there looked straight in my eyes, and I back at hers. Without turning away, I nudged Tony.

"Tony, is she a hooker?"

"Nah," he said, in his Bronx Italian accent. "The elevator doors opened, and she fell in love wit you."

As we walked into the casino, Tony said, "Would you like to see a show?"

"Sure," I said.

There was an entrance on our right with the curtains closed. Tony opened the curtain said, "Look, there's Danny Thomas," closed the curtain, and walked away. We went our separate ways, and I continued to play craps until I was just about broke.

I was leaning on the table with my elbows and holding up my head. There were four of us playing; it was 4:00 a.m. One shooter each time; he threw the dice. He threw them up in the air and a lot of times they came up the hard way: twos, threes, fours, and fives, which paid from fifteen to twenty to one.

Having little money left each time he would shoot, I would throw twenty-five dollars each the hard way. He worked it for me, and eventually I was just about even, so I went back to the room at about 5:00 a.m.

I guess from stories, movies, and assumptions my subconscious had the ability and knowledge to do the following: I thought of hiring a prostitute, which I had never done before.

The thought led to a conversation with myself which went like this: "What for? It will be over in fifteen minutes. Who needs it?" Then I thought, "Okay, oral. Same thing: who needs it?"

Then I said, "What if I get someone to stay the night, have intercourse, sleep, oral, sleep, and on and on?" Having no idea how I would even go about this, I convinced myself that it was okay.

There was never any conversation with the guys on this subject. Whatever method I would use to go about this came from somewhere deeply hidden in my brain. I called the bell captain and said, "Please send up a nice, warm package."

I took a shower, went into the living room, and then came a knock on the door.

This was 1974. I was thirty three. I opened the door, and there stood this twenty- or twenty-one-year-old beauty with a body to match in short shorts and a bikini top. She came in, we sat on the couch, and she said, "Okay, you want to party." I said, "Well, I was thinking more of you spending the night. What is the cost?"

She said, "A quick party is one hundred, the night is six hours, five hundred." I was totally intimidated by the whole experience, so I said that I heard that the whole night is less than that. She said, "Well, if you want, you can go downtown by the jail house and wait for a girl to come out. That would be much less." So after more small talk she said, "Do you want to party or not?"

I was scared to death. I said, "Thanks anyway, but no thanks," gave her two hundred dollars, and sent her on her way; that was my first experience with a hooker. Other experiences were just coincidental and never culminated. That was the first of many trips to Vegas over four years.

This make-believe part of the world fed my irresistible desire to be irresistibly desired.

On my trips, mostly with the guys, but sometimes with Louise and friends, each time we were given suites previously used by and named for Frank Sinatra, Dean Martin, Sammy Davis, etc. It felt like living in the lap of luxury, and we all had a great time.

The first-class airfare, the suite, the food, the entertainment; it was all on the house. The following are some of my experiences with the guys.

On true love:

A love-struck friend fell in love with a hooker; he flew her back and forth from Vegas to New York and was really crazy about her. When we were there, she was always around.

She became a friend of all of us. She was cute and personable. He truly believed that they had a love connection.

On naivety:

One friend of mine was an older gentleman. For the five days we were there, he had this very young, very attractive woman with him. Still being naïve, I could not understand it. I asked him if she was a pro. Indignantly, he said, "Absolutely not." I could not figure it out. Of course, as time went by, I realized that she was a pro, and I felt pretty stupid. He became a business partner of mine in later years.

My deli-owner friend:

Remember that this was in the early '70s and that I was in my early thirties. All the other guys were fifty or older. We all ate dinner and breakfast together, then we all went our separate ways. Some played poker, some craps, some blackjack, some baccarat.

On this particular morning, this one friend came down for breakfast in shock! He was very serious in telling us that he had an eye-opening experience that was such a sexual turn on that he was still salivating about it.

While he was sexually involved with a woman, he felt a warm sensation. Apparently, she had urinated, and he found this to be the thrill of a lifetime. I was sitting there wondering if these guys were from outer space. What the hell could be so stimulating about that? But as I say, we are all products of our experience.

My overweight friend:

He was a big guy, a lot heavier than Tony Soprano; he had an Italian deli in the Bronx.

Supposedly he was the son of a made Mafia guy and therefore he was a made man as well and connected one way or the other. I say supposedly because if I don't actually see something I leave room for doubt.

At breakfast, he put on a white priest collar and sat with us. He called over every girl he saw and offered to take their confession. It provided some unforgettably hysterical moments.

My nutty friend:

Tony, my new crass friend, had been in a very serious automobile accident where the young lady he was with was killed and he was crippled. Supposedly it was a hit. After months of recuperating, we had a party for him in Vegas, and the guys got three hookers. We all went into one suite where they were supposed to take care of Tony. He wasn't interested; he was in a wheelchair. So my nutty friend dared the three of them to make him climax. Now I would have a difficult time just being with one of them alone. Never mind three hookers and five guys watching. He had no problem.

On Don Adams & Mort Sahl:

The Sands had a very elegant dining room called The Regency Room, with booths and tables for whatever made you comfortable. I was sitting in a booth with my back next to the booth behind where Don Adams (*Get Smart*) and Mort Sahl (the comedian) were having dinner. They were older celebrities at the time. I eavesdropped on their conversation, which was about women and the fact that they cannot understand them. I left there thinking, "What the hell is wrong with all these people?" I understood women, and I was not nearly as experienced as them. Little did I know how wrong I was.

On Chip Hookers:

As I was playing craps, I was in my second or third week of trying to give up smoking, so I asked the croupier for a cigarette, which I just let dangle, unlit, from my mouth. I was betting with twenty-five dollar chips and probably covering the board with about five hundred at any given time. The young lady next to me was betting as well, one five dollar chip at a time. I paid no attention to her, as craps is a very fast game that requires your total attention.

When there was a break in the game, as someone crapped out, she turned to me and lit my cigarette. I did not stop her because I found her attention flattering. I was so happy to find a female that was not motivated by money. As I continued to gamble, and as I was playing one hundreds, she was playing fives; whenever she was on a losing streak, I threw her a twenty-five dollar chip.

We spent some time together, and I told her I would be there for five days; she offered to stay with me. Eventually it was time for dinner with the guys. When I walked in with her, all the guys were seated, and I was the only one with a woman.

I felt uncomfortable, so I took her outside, gave her some money, and said I would call her next time. I soon realized, after being reminded, "She saw you at the crap table and fell in luv wit you," that she was a hooker, but more commonly known as a chip hooker. They pretend to be attracted to you, and play alongside you, and as all gamblers do, they get tossed chips all along the way. They probably make out better than the others.

On Wayne Newton:

On another first-class trip on TWA, I was sitting next to a very attractive, young woman.

We talked and she explained that she had met Wayne Newton somewhere, that she was a dancer, and that he was going to put her in his show. He had a suite waiting for her at the Sands, and she was to call when she got there. I tried to say that maybe his interest was in something other than dance, but she was very adamant that this was a legitimate, above-board arrangement. While checking in to the Sands, she was there in the lobby with no suite, no reservation, no Wayne Newton.

I offered to let her have the other half of my suite, but she was confident he would show.

On the legal eye:

In later years, I missed a flight with my friends and took the next one out. Sitting in first class, there was only one seat empty, and it was the one next to me. The doors closed, and we started to taxi when the plane stopped and went back to the gate. They opened the door and in walked a body that was the most magnificent I had ever seen. She had the seat next to me. She was an attorney, and she had an employment agency for attorneys. We had a fun flight.

On Reno:

I went to a business convention in San Francisco, and afterward I drove to Reno, watching the beautiful, and dangerous, scenery. When I arrived, they checked my credit with Vegas, and they treated me like a king. They gave me front row tickets to Sammy Davis Junior's show, a suite, and they comped everything.

On one of the trips, I was mistaken for Donald Southerland. On several others Barry Manilow. Today, it's between Brad Pitt and George Clooney. (Just kidding!)

Some few years after all these trips, Tony, who I had learned to love, was found dead in his office with six gunshot wounds to the body. The case was never solved.

We all had a very easy way with money. If I needed money, I would call Richard, and he would give it to me, and I would give it back. It was the same with others. They took from me, I took from them, never a document, never interest, just a way of doing business. It was a product of my experiences.

When I read about the Magic of Vegas that existed the 60s, with the rat pack and all the famous entertainers performing in lounge type atmospheres, gambling next to you at the tables, I realize that my experience in Vegas in the 70s was probably as much as a turn off to them as Vegas is to me now.

I have only been back twice in the past thirty-five years, as to me it is not the same place. Las Vegas had a somber elegance in the way you dressed, dined, and gambled. It all made you feel special; that was the attraction. Today everyone just blends in.

CHAPTER 9: NEW HORIZONS

Prior to my thirty-fifth birthday, I joined the prestigious Lido golf club, as they had made an attractive offer for membership if you were under thirty five. It was a great place in addition to the golf course. The main house was on the beach side, and the food and events were a wonderful experience.

Every Friday night they had a shore dinner and music. They had a great big oval bar area and some really nice people, all of whom were very successful businessmen. I became friendly with many of them, and did electrical and telephone work with them through the years. It was always a rewarding experience.

Tournaments or matches were taken very seriously by golfers, whether it was the club championship or a match for one dollar. I actually saw a member in a one dollar match kick the ball out of trouble when he thought no one was looking.

One tournament that they had every year was "pick your own partner." Everyone picked whomever they thought could help them win. I picked Abe. He owned an office furniture business in New York. He had Parkinson's, which made it difficult for him to play, but he enjoyed the camaraderie and exercise.

The fact that I asked him to be my partner in a tournament made him ecstatic to have the opportunity to play. He and all his friends instantly became my friends.

Years later, when Wendy was thirteen, we made her Bat Mitzvah at Lido. An affair for a girl was just coming into vogue. It was a magnificent affair. Everything was perfect, the atmosphere, the food, the music, and the guests. It was a very proud moment.

In those years, although ten years older, Louise and I socialized a great deal with her sister and brother-in-law. When we joined Lido, they joined, as well as their friends and ours, Seymore and Claire.

The women never got involved, other than the Friday night shore dinners. The three of us were there every weekend. Seymore made a few friends there. Milton Cohen was quite the opposite.

The only time Louise became involved is when they had a special day at the beach. One season the lady members created a color war day for all sports, with cards and fun things for all to participate in. It was extremely enjoyable.

These people were from a special generation. They were a minimum of twenty years older than me and were self-made. Some of them owned businesses that were well-known throughout the nation, but they were not impressed with themselves. Nor were they trying to impress anyone else, and much to my surprise, their wives were of the same accord. The two generations above mine seem to have had the basics of life in a much more orderly fashion.

1976 MONTE CARLO

The Loews was the first American hotel to open in Monte Carlo. My travel agent cousin, Harris, got us and two couples of our friends on a chartered flight with him to Nice. Our travel party consisted of four couples. The charter had mechanical problems and never took off on the night we were scheduled; we all went back to my house to sleep as the flight was rescheduled for the next day. Somewhere in the middle of the night, we lost two couples, since we were all nervous about flying with that plane and airline. Harris and Orysia wanted to go, though, and they kept pushing me.

I finally agreed as long as they would travel with me to another location. Since I had never been to Europe before, they agreed, and we left and arrived at Nice. When we arrived at the Loews Hotel they were overbooked, therefore they set the charter flight up at the Hotel de Paris. It was complete chaos in checking in as everyone was upset that they were bumped.

The ugly American emerged as people were yelling, "You know who I am? I can buy this hotel." Had they taken a moment to smell the roses they would have realized that The Hotel de Paris was a class act with an old formal setting with high down mattresses and a charming bar and restaurant. It was pure elegance in comparison to the Loews.

By the time we got to our rooms, it was late, and everyone was exhausted from the traveling. We went to sleep; I woke about 11:00 p.m., having read back home of a disco in Monte Carlo that Princess Caroline frequented. I got dressed and went there. I saw no one famous, and it was no different than American discos. But I needed to see it.

The next day, we took a car and toured all of Monte Carlo. That evening, we went to the Monte Carlo Casino, all dressed very formally; I played *chemin de fer*, feeling very special. If anyone had asked my name at that time I would have said, "Bond, James Bond." I bought tickets for the next afternoon train to Trieste, Italy and then Venice and Rome.

Trieste was because Orysia said it was a duty-free port attached to communist countries and things were very cheap. I agreed to Trieste with Venice afterward; I arranged for sleeping cars for the overnight trip. When we boarded the train, the sleeping cars were not yet attached. You traveled in the bench seats facing each other like a restaurant booth without the table.

I thought there would be a dining car, but there wasn't. We were starving when the train pulled into Ventimiglia, where the sleeping cars were attached. On the platform was a vendor selling bags with food in it. I had no idea what was in it, but I bought four of them. The contents were one apple, one loaf of Italian bread, half bottle of red wine. It was superb, perfect, and delicious.

We started out for the sleeping car with our one huge suitcase. The European train system is beyond belief. Prior to computers, how they were able to organize the whole thing was amazing. However, you needed to have some prior knowledge, and with no one speaking English, we were lost.

As we walked in the direction we were pointed, we found out that although I had paid for two first class cabins, they only had one. Not accepting anything at face value, I walked to other sleeping cars and found that they in fact had rooms available. What I did not realize was that in the middle of the night the cars are switched and routed to different places. If I had taken the other cars' cabin, we would have ended up in Munich, they would have been in Trieste.

After some time of trying to piece the broken English and broken Italian, we only had one first class sleeping car and the option of a second class sleeping car. We gave the girls the first class, and we went to the second.

Not knowing what makes the class difference, we headed in the direction we were told. To our dismay, we were sleeping in a cabin with two other men. For reasons unknown, the whole thing made me giggle uncontrollably, leading Harris to do the same. The other two guys just slept and snored.

The next day, we were back in our booth and on our way to Trieste. We passed the train station for Venice and went about an hour more to Trieste. Historically, when I travel, I get constipation for the first few days because of the change in diet.

When we arrived at Trieste, it was time to let nature take its course, and I walked swiftly ahead looking for a bathroom, asking and following. I found a door, walked in, there were urinals and closed doors with a woman standing there. I walked out, immediately turned around and went back, as the decision was no longer mine.

She handed me two sheets of sandpaper and opened one of the closed doors. I walked in and there was a tiled floor with a hole in the center. I walked out again, but I had to go right back. When in Trieste, do as the Triestians. I did, and it was very uncomfortable, but we then walked around Trieste.

We got back on the train heading for Venice. I calculated the time we would arrive and allowed myself fifteen minutes before to sponge bath in the spacious train bathroom. As I was sponge bathing naked, the train stopped and my three world-traveling companions banged on the door and said that we were there.

I dressed, ran, grabbed that big suitcase, and followed them off the train. Remembering the Venice station when we passed it, I recognized that this was not it: this was Venezia Mestre. We got back on the train, and the next stop was Venice.

We arrived in Venice and spent the day shopping and sightseeing. In the evening, Harris and Orysia went back to Monte Carlo. Louise and I took the train to Rome. It was an overnight trip, and again, we had no clue as to how to find the sleeping car. One of the trainman brought us to the compartment of a person they knew who spoke English. The man was extremely gracious, and told us to come back at the next stop and he would lead us to the sleeping car.

At the next station he walked us across the tracks to a train that was not even attached to our train. The conductor told us his name was Vittorio Gassman. (He was a famous and accomplished actor and director. Shelly Winters was married to him in earlier years. Vittorio and she were a regular feature of Hollywood gossip columns.)

We arrived in Rome about 6:00 a.m. on May 1st (May Day in socialist politics). I looked for and found an English-speaking tour guide with a limo.

We saw all of Rome, although Louise slept through half. We had lunch at the originating restaurant of fettuccine Alfredo (called Alfredo), walked to the top of the Vatican, walked through the Cupola, walked through the catacombs, saw the Fountain of Trevi, Spanish Steps, Mussolini Terrace, Parliament, the street where Sophia Loren lived, the view of St. Peter's through the Cavalieri di Malta Keyhole, the Appian Way, Colosseum, and the Roman Forum.

After our tour, it was back to the Spanish Steps, the Hassler Hotel, and the stores, which were closed for May Day, as well as the Sistine Chapel.

We boarded the train, found the sleeping cars and returned to Monte Carlo.

RIO

My cousins Harris and Orysia had a deal from their travel agency to go to Rio De Janiero. We went and saw all the sights of Rio. Orysia was pregnant at the time and suffered a miscarriage, which prompted them to fly back to the US. In my quest to see as much of the world as possible, we took a cab to Sao Paulo, which was about a twelve-hour trip. We drove through and came back.

The only special memory I took back was of the Girls from Ipanema. On the plane (a 747) coming back, I left my gold lighter on the food tray, which they had collected. When I asked the stewardess what I could do, she led me to an elevator, where I went down into the bowels of the aircraft and went through all the trays. I found it. Imagine that happening today.

1978: Pope Paul VI died at eighty, and the new pope, John Paul I, who was sixty five, died unexpectedly after thirty-four days in office. He was succeeded by Karol Cardinal Wojtyla of Poland, who took the name John Paul II. Jim Jones's followers commit mass suicide in Jonestown, Guyana.

LAS HADAS

Always wanting to see the hot spots of the World, the playgrounds of the rich and famous, whenever I read or was informed, I planned my next vacation.

Herma and Don, our neighbors and friends at the time, noted an article about this brand new resort, very exclusive, just opened to the public. The resort was Las Hadas in Manzinillo, Mexico, which gained fame in the movie *10*, which was filmed there.

We planned a trip to Las Vegas, and from Las Vegas to Las Hadas. We arrived at the sands in Vegas, were reimbursed for our first class tickets and were escorted to two magnificent suites. We headed to the casino.

We were playing baccarat, all afternoon and evening. It was 2:00 a.m. We were catching a morning flight to Mexico City. I was up ten thousand dollars. The shoe ended, and it takes about ten to fifteen minutes for them to set up the next shoe. I said, "Okay, let's go to bed. We have to get up early."

They convinced me to stay for one more shoe, and as you can guess, I lost the ten thousand. I had the ten thousand dollar credit line. I was so mad at myself that now I had to stay to win back where I was. It was 5:00 a.m. and my credit line was used up. I went to the manager of the Baccarat Room and told him I wanted to cash a check.

Being a smart guy, watching me chase the money, the manager said, "Mr. S. It's 5:00 a.m. Go to sleep, and I would be happy to cash a check for you tomorrow." My response was the stupid Ugly American. "Who the f--- do you think you're talking to?"

He cashed the check, and I lost all that as well. Never did I overly impress myself again. The next day we flew to Mexico City, and on to Monzanillo, where a three-hour Jeep ride took us to the hotel; it was as magnificent as advertised. Fortunately we met some New Yorkers who were condo owners on the property. They guided us to restaurants in the area that we would have never gone to without help. On our giant veranda, we had a cocktail party for all the people we had met with music, champagne, and hors d'oeuvres.

During the day, we were at the pool, learning and playing backgammon. It was a fabulous experience. Esquire Magazine rated the hotel among the eight most luxurious hideaways on the planet. Vogue went even further, calling it "a delicious dream, the world's ultimate playland." Playboy topped that with its supreme accolade, "A better version of heaven."

Patino—who was one of the world's richest men (if not the richest man, at the time)—is said to have built Las Hadas pretty much on a whim. Some say he did it to upstage playboy Aga Khan's opulent Costa Smeralda resort in Sardinia.

The room where we stayed was showcased in the hit movie *10*. One famous scene showed Dudley Moore, playing a soused songwriter, cavorting with Bo Derek's character, in a fabulous Las Hadas bedroom while music from the record *Bolero* set the romantic mood.

HEMLOCK FARMS

Another memorable experience was our time at Hemlock Farms. I was planning a trip to St Thomas with the family for Christmas, when someone told me they were renting a ski house in Hemlock Farms, Pennsylvania for the entire winter.

When I found out that the cost was the same for the whole winter as for the ten days in St. Thomas, that is what we did. For about four years, we rented in Hemlock Farms. Friends joined in renting their own places, and we had a crew for the adults and the kids.

Friday night, upon arrival, we would go to Mt. Haven Lodge, where we would all meet for dinner and have lots of laughs. In the morning, we would go to one of the various ski areas. As our skills improved, so did the mountains we skied.

The younger kids went to ski school. Everyone had fun during the day, and it was back out to dinner Saturday night. We had the fireplace going, and there was always a jigsaw puzzle in progress. In between skiing and dining, it was a very family-oriented, wonderful time.

The first few years we went there, the snow was almost unbearable. Driving up, it looked like I was driving through Star Wars in outer space. On weekends outside of ski season we always went to the toy store or to a carnival or on a play date, or rarely, a museum. I enjoyed exploring and being with the kids.

We spent four years' worth of winters skiing at this resort. As time went by, everyone in the family became decent skiers, and we eventually outgrew the mountains in Pennsylvania.

SUN VALLEY

During another Christmas, we went to Sun Valley, Idaho. We rented a condo on the grounds of the Sun Valley Resort. There are two separate slopes, Baldy Mountain, which has trails for beginners and intermediates, and Sun Valley Mountain, which has trails for intermediate and expert skiers. I made my family ski Baldy first, to get their ski legs, and then we went to the big mountain. When we took the chair lift to the top, it became so cold that when we got off, Adam just lay down in the snow and cried.

Now that we were at the top and sitting in the chalet, we could tell that this was a mountain much larger than any we had ever skied before. I tried everything I could think of to find a way to get down without skiing, but there was no way. We traversed the mountain and the moguls, and we all survived safely.

While we were in Idaho, we took horse and buggy rides, bought cowboy hats, walked through the charming village of Sun Valley and Ketchum, met people, and formed future friendships.

George Hamilton and I discussed the fact that we both had new boots and they were killing us. Adam had a conversation with Melissa Gilbert. We took videos of everything, even Wendy falling down and claiming there was something wrong with her boots.

At the beginning and end of each day, I had one of the kids act as a news anchor and they interviewed us. When we got home, I edited and spliced and made a fun memory of the trip.

TAM O'SHANTER

The economy brought anyone marginal to reassess their expenses, and as it should be, luxuries were eliminated. Golf Clubs were the first to be eliminated from monthly expenditures, and even Lido was not spared.

It was too difficult to maintain the facilities in comparison to the money coming in from membership and dues. Little by little, the amenities started to decrease. At first, we were looking to increase the membership. I was on the Membership Committee. In the final analysis, however, they sold the property to the county; it became a golf club within a golf course. There were no longer any amenities, and unless it was only golf you wanted, it was not enjoyable.

Over the past years, I had been a guest many times at Tam O'Shanter. It was a golf course and club house that was very similar to Lido. I joined. Tam O'Shanter was no exception in losing membership. I wrote a letter to the board suggesting they offer financial packages and rule changes to entice new and younger members to join.

From that letter, I became Chairman of the Membership Committee, developed packages, met with every potential member, and filled the place to capacity. From that success, I was made a board member, and then the chairman of the House Committee, and then the Vice President.

All day long during those years, you would hear on the PA system, "Mr. Scheffler, call the operator." I was involved in so many things that I was kept busy all day from golf to cards to board and committee duties.

Because my efforts were fruitful, I liked it. During that period, I went from a twenty five handicap to an eighteen. I won a lot of tournaments in my class, including a UJA ten thousand dollar prize tournament.

When I was an eighteen handicap golfer and winning tournaments, I decided I could really be a good golfer. I took daily lessons and accomplished the reverse, which eventually made me give up the game.

My name still appears on about five plaques at Tam. I was friendly with a great group of people not much different than the people I had met through Lido. And they were lots of fun. They had a rule that you had to be twelve to be in the locker room, and Adam was only eight. I convinced the Board to lower it to eight.

One of the friends I had made at Tam O'Shanter, Sol, was president and a really nice guy. Sol owned an Army Navy store in Queens. One day it burned to the ground, and he was vacillating between rebuilding or doing something else. He was such a natural salesman with his niceness and easy mannerisms. I offered him a job. He took it and was with me for about ten years, helping me with anything and everything. Sol passed away a few years ago, and I truly miss him.

EUROPE: MY WAY

Hal and Lucille were recent friends at the new golf club, and they planned a trip with Louise and me to Europe. I was empowered to make all the arrangements. I bought maps and books and chartered the course from the beginning point to the end via car and train without any reservations.

We flew into Germany, toured Berlin, and visited Dachau, where I could not stop the tears from rolling down my face. The camp was left or restored with the frames of each building in place, and movies were shown of exactly what happened to those poor people.

We rented a car, toured Germany, Austria, Switzerland, Italy, France, and Spain, and ended up in Marbella for a week of rest amongst all the oil barons, sheiks, and their entourages of non-virgins.

Hal exemplified the "Ugly American." He complained about everything from the service to the language barrier. He was a total embarrassment, and I was never socially friendly with him again.

Going through Germany and the Black Forest, we came into a ski town, Garmisch. We went into a local tavern, made friends, and were invited to someone's home that night. It was interesting, but scary.

In Baden-Baden, Germany they had spas and natural hot springs. I walked into a casino and played *chemin de fer*, (real baccarat). There was one fellow there who spoke English, and when I got the shoe, he went partners with me, and we made a few dollars, but the idea of sitting there in these elegant surroundings amongst German aristocrats after coming from Dachau...hmm.

These were the days prior to cell phones. As we got to each place, I called home to make sure the kids were okay because no one could have reached us if they needed to. Louise never even gave the children a thought. If she were there without me, she would have never called home the entire time we were away.

I am not saying she did not care, she just wore rose-colored glasses, never thinking of negative possibilities. Louise had a different feeling with the kids; she believed that they should never go on vacation with us she would say. Let their husbands take them, when they get married.

I had a beard and mustache at the time, and one morning in Paris, I shaved it off. No one noticed until I brought it up a few days later.

Then, and maybe now as well, when you traveled by train from France to Spain, the train rails in Spain were a different size than the ones in France. While you were sleeping, the train was lifted by a crane, the carriage holding the wheels was removed, and a new set to accommodate the new tracks was put on.

In Austria, I saw a sign on an optometrist store with the same last name as mine. I went in and introduced myself. The guy mumbled under his breath and walked to the back room.

In Switzerland, the lush mountain terrain was breathtaking. We took the Gondola in St. Moritz and Gstaad, and went around Zurich and Geneva. Every place we went was very formal; shirt and tie were required for dinner at all times.

In Italy, we toured a fabulous town called Assisi. Where I never got to go was Capri and Positano. Don't think I ever will get there, either.

It was a very exciting and rewarding trip, the pre-planning routes without reservations made it easy, relaxing, and memorable.

CHAPTER 10: COLLECTIVE BARGAINING

1977: Elvis Presley died at Graceland, his Memphis, Tennessee home. He was forty-two years old.

For many years, Laurelton Electric was a sore spot for competitors and the Union. Our full-page ads in the yellow pages, combined with a fleet of lettered trucks, made us recognizable to all. At times, we would find one of our trucks turned over. Other times, the conduit we ran in the ground as a raceway for wires were filled with concrete.

In 1976, before I realized what was going on, I received a letter from the Department of Labor that there was going to be a vote for all my employees to join or not join the union Local 3.

The way this kind of situation comes about is that they stalk the employees. They tell them how much better they would be in the union, and have them sign a card of intent to join. When they have thirty five percent of a company's labor force signed, they submit the company to the Department of Labor. With those signatures they can petition the Labor Board to call for a vote.

The only decent lawyers I was ever able to obtain were through Chuck, my childhood friend. He gave me the name Bill Krupman of Jackson, Lewis, who was a first class, smart guy. He briefed me on how to "legally" approach each of the employees and explain the benefits I was giving them as opposed to the union. He outlined my speech to each, and it all worked. We defeated Local 3, the most powerful union in the United States, and the law states that they must wait two years to try again.

I had no idea that this kind of thing could be done; I thought that if someone wanted to have a union company they joined. I did not know you can be forced.

At the same time, a family business in Little Rock, Arkansas, where Penny and Dale came from, needed to be operated by competent people. Penny and Dale were going home. There in Little Rock they were both able to use their talent and skills to succeed in everything they endeavored to undertake. When she left, I broke up her duties, and at some point, I distributed them to four different people.

It made no difference. No one person or group of people could replace Penny. I could only be thankful for the time she gave me, and I am ever indebted to the rare love and sincere friendship they bestowed upon me.

Sidney Graber, who sold me the building, had a son-in-law who was a plumbing contractor, called Krupnikoff and Sons. Two brothers, Lenny and Herbie. They had a storefront next to mine. They had made money with other investments and were getting tired of the business. I kept telling them that if they ever wanted to get out, I would take it over.

 In 1977, they sold it to me for ten thousand dollars. They did not have a license and were paying another plumber two hundred a month for use of his. I continued the payments, and I took their one employee, Bob. Their largest account was one commercial apartment complex run by Hillard Sax, an extremely overweight man with an ego ten times his own size. Their other accounts were all the local residents that called whenever they needed a plumber.

The plumbing business was a much easier business to run. Estimating consisted of units, one sink, one toilet, one bath, one shower. The estimate at that time was one thousand dollars per unit.

The electrical business, to be competitive, required measuring the wire, pipe, connectors, parts, and estimating the labor. Labor was really an educated guess.

Sometimes you were right and sometimes you were wrong. It all depended on the mood of the mechanics on any given day.

In the late '70s, the biggest electrical supply house in New York and possibly the country was Central Queens Electric. The originator, Harry Berken, changed the entire complexion of the construction business. The process at the time was this: you bought the merchandise you needed on your account and when the supplier felt the balance was getting to be high, he would call and you would give him a series of notes or checks for a nominal amount in comparison to what you owed.

The builders also received the benefit of paying the subcontractor the same way. As many of us grew beyond our means, Harry did as well. He was the first to file bankruptcy in the electrical business. The manufacturers all took a bath and changed their way of dealing with the suppliers. Everything had to be net thirty days, meaning our balance had to be paid within thirty days from receiving the goods or the suppliers would be cut off. They passed that way of doing business on to us, and we tried, with very little success, to pass it on to our customers.

Years later, Harry Berken's son, Mitchell, who was a little older than me, opened another supply house called Kennedy Electric. We did business together and had a decent relationship. His dad, Harry, hung out at his shop and did whatever business he was still into.

Harry came to me one day and said he could rent out fifty percent of the space of the building I owned to the City of New York on a lucrative ten-year lease. I made the deal, paid Harry his commission over several years, built the space that the City paid for, and had a Class A tenant.

As we were building the space for the City, I needed a space for my offices. After searching everywhere, I ended up with a broken-down building on South Conduit Avenue. I bought the building, remodeled the inside and out, and made it into a beautiful space with three stores to be rented out and a paved parking area in the back.

Two electric signs adorned the top of this brick-and-metal office front with narrow slits for windows. Between my office and all the others were half-glass walls, as I had the need to see what was going on all around me.

The property was along the Belt Parkway, and the two electrified signs, in bold red letters, read, "Laurelton Electric" and "Krupnikoff Plumbing." I was quite proud.

One year later, there was an empty lot that was for sale on the next corner. It was owned by the same people. I bought it and immediately rented it to a used car dealer who bought it from me some fifteen years later.

Jerry, a builder and general contractor with whom I did electrical and telephone work, was a friend as well. He was having a problem with a city job he was doing. The job was bonded, and the bond was in limbo until resolved. The bond was canceled, and he was unable to get new bonding.

He was forced to file personal bankruptcy. He had contracts to build four new post offices, but without bonding, he could not do them, so he turned them all over to me and put me in touch with the bonding company.

My accountant prepared a personal financial statement showing a net worth of over two million dollars. This of course was ninety percent real estate.

In his words, "This statement is factual if there were buyers here right now with checks in their hands for all the values listed." Because of this, in 1977, I obtained a two million dollar line for bonding, became a General Contractor, and built four post offices. While building the post offices, I was the electrical contractor, the plumbing contractor, and the general contractor.

Those responsibilities required hiring of electricians, plumbers, and laborers for miscellaneous jobs and cleanup. I hired loads of laborers at minimum wage. And just at the opportune time, when a huge payment was scheduled, I was introduced to what is called the "Davis Bacon Act." It is not a vaudeville performance or a sandwich.

The Davis Bacon Act is the reason that unions make large political contributions. The unions convinced the federal government to require a minimum wage in each state to work on any federal contract coincidentally it is the exact wage the union gets. That way the feds, who legally cannot demand that you use union labor, can legally demand that you use union labor.

The two years were up, and I was too involved in the day-to-day operations to think about it. They were not; they interviewed the guys working and asked them about their duties, their hourly rate, and their home address, and they submitted it all to the government, claiming laborers were electrical apprentices, plumbers were steamfitters. They bumped everyone up to the most expensive trade rate they could for their presentation to the government. There I was, finishing all these jobs; the Post Office was preparing a huge payment for me. With the union's guidance, they held up the payment. I had to submit what I paid each employee, their trade, and their social security number.

Again with the union's guidance, they reclassified the trade of each employee. Everyone I hired at a minimum hourly rate or above were given six times what I paid them; a laborer, who swept up at the end of each day, was paid $1200.00 a week.

From the money that was due me from the project, they paid each employee the difference. I was out of the general contracting business, and both Louise and I were on the hook personally for the remainder of the work, which was $250,000 of bonded debt.

Like any other businessman, I did not offer my wife as a personal signature, but in order to be bonded, and having no thoughts of not producing, that was a requirement.

The union had accumulated the necessary signatures, and another vote was held in my offices. I was locked in my private office and not allowed out until everyone was gone. The vote was won by the union by one vote.

There was an appointed person to watch the vote for each side. We objected to two people they called in that were let go several months prior. The union objected to two of our votes as they considered them executives.

We were deadlocked with the union with two objections on each side. The process was to argue each case in front of the Department of Labor, and this went on for over a year. At the trial, the union was very intent on bringing up my excursions to Las Vegas.

The deciding Judge was a young, attractive blonde, just out of law school. The entire trial seemed more like a circus act than anything else. In the final analysis, all four votes were disqualified, and therefore the union won. My lawyer said this only means that I have to negotiate with the union, not that I had to automatically join.

I played with that for six more months, until finally I realized that I could win many skirmishes, but in the long run I couldn't win the war.

The process you just read about is called "Collective Bargaining." It is what is currently bankrupting the country, and things will probably get ugly before it changes.

In 1980, Laurelton Electric became an employer of Local 3 electricians. The union had made it very clear to me that I was simply considered a salesman. The electricians were paid by me, but they worked for them.

The fact that the men I had were unionized and not from the ranks gave me a chance, at least for a while, to still make money with my customer base. But as my workers became indoctrinated into the group of brotherly love, the production went down considerably, the cost to operate now was excessive, and the learning curve of being a union contractor compared to a nonunion contractor was enormous.

A nonunion electrician could put a wall outlet in within one hour for thirty dollars plus material. A union electrician installing the same outlet would take four hours at a cost of eighty dollars per hour plus material. The question is, "Who gets screwed?" If the contractor survives, it's ultimately the consumer.

It took over five years to restructure my customer base and to learn how to deal with these conditions, especially at that time, when the industry was on a turnaround of one hundred and twenty days on receivables.

Entitlement

Cause and Effect

124

CHAPTER 11: FORTUNE TELLER

1980: Richard M. Nixon resigned; he was the first President to do so. Patricia Hearst, the nineteen-year-old daughter of Randolph Hearst, was kidnapped. Vice President Gerald R. Ford, of Michigan, was sworn in as the 38th President of the United States.

One Friday night, Stan and his wife, friends from Tam O'Shanter, joined Louise and I for dinner at Marco's in Lawrence.Stanley said, "Max and I just bought ten standard-bred horses." (They're called Trotters.)

I asked him to explain.

"The ten horses were two hundred and fifty thousand dollars, and I bought ten percent."

"Let me understand. Max put up two-hundred-and-twenty-five thousand, and you put up twenty-five thousand. Correct?"

"Yes."

I thought about it for a minute and realized that it would be fun to go to the track and watch a horse race that you owned, and I thought the kids would get a big kick out of it too. I told Stanley, "I want ten percent of your ten percent." I gave him $2500.00, I was the proud owner of one percent of ten horses.

Max, another friend from Tam, was a very successful man, a furrier; he had owned horses for many years. I loved him. He was a man's man, a happy guy with a great personality, and a fabulous friend. One of our friends at the club was a money manager for celebrities. Max convinced him to have a client invest in one of our horses named Apache Circle. Connie Sellecca and Gil Gerard were our partners, and to seal the deal, Max and I had dinner with Gil and Connie.

They had a three-month-old baby, and they were showing us pictures of a new way to teach kids to stay afloat in the water by throwing them into the pool at three months old.

Thirty days later, Stanley called and said, "You owe me three hundred and thirty dollars."

"For what?"

"Your share of the feeding and staking of the horses."

Never having thought about that aspect of horse ownership, I gave him the money. The following month, he asked for six hundred and forty dollars, and the following month, five hundred and twenty five.

Now, after the fact, I found out that these horses lived an average of twenty years. The next morning, I was shaving and having a very serious conversation with myself, a habit I acquired from my father. I said, "You are a f---n moron. There is no way out of this thing. You can't go and say, 'Here are your horses back.' For twenty years, I am going to be feeding ten one-thousand-pound animals."

The next day, Stanley called. One of our horses was running that evening in a race at Yonkers Raceway. He said, "Let's go up and watch." I said, "Sure."

We went and bet on our horse, Fortune Teller. He won the fifty thousand dollar purse easily, which means, as owners, we get the lion's share of twenty five thousand. We won our bets and posed for photos in the winner's circle. For a couple of hours, I forgave myself.

The next few weeks, as Fortune Teller was running, we watched and bet. He won every time.

We were going into the winner's circle after every race.

As the race stakes got higher, you went to the winner's cocktail party, newspaper interviews, etc. I was pretty proud of myself, thinking about what a smart investor I am.

On August 2nd, 1982, Fortune Teller was running in a race at the Meadowlands for a two million dollar purse against all the two-year-old, best-winning, record horses in the business. It was the largest purse ever offered to that date.

We bet, we watched, and boy, what an exciting thing to win easily in that kind of field. Big time winner's circle and parties. Good profit on the betting, and a really fun experience.

After that race, fifty percent of Fortune Teller was sold to Lana Lobel Farms for four million dollars, payable over two years. My weakness or asset in life has always been to act on impulse without doing my due diligence. This was one time it worked in my favor.

Fortune Teller was then booked all over the country as a three-year-old; we flew around to the various race tracks to watch him race. As a three-year-old, while competing, he developed a rare horse impediment, which caused him to put his head down and pull over to the side.

We were in Montreal to watch him race. Adam was with me. We watched the race, visited with the horses, toured the area, and flew home. In those days, you wore a jacket and nice clothes when you were flying. Max had a box of cigars, so rather than carry the box, he put some in his jacket pocket and some in my jacket pocket.

We checked in and went to immigration. I was asked if I was bringing any illegal substances into the country, and of course said no. Then they asked me about cigars. I felt my pockets and said, "Oh, yes, these are cigars that I am carrying for my friend."

Not being a cigar smoker, it did not dawn on me that Cuban cigars were illegal to be brought back to the United States. They confiscated the cigars and listed me as a known smuggler.

I love Max, but unfortunately, as happens to all nice guys, he was shafted by all and died broke.

Fortune Teller finished his three-year-old tenure and was put out to stud. He was at Lana Lobel Farms in Bedminster, New Jersey. Through the years, the family and I visited him. The breeding of horses is quite an interesting process. In fear of the female hurting the male, the stallion is led into a stall where a mare in heat has her rear half exposed to his view and smell. Separating the mare and the colt is a gym-type horse—a pommel horse, the kind that gymnasts use to perform their routines. As the stallion gets excited, he mounts the gym horse. They then take this huge hollow canister with its sides filled with hot water and slide it over his penis and move it up and down.

When the horse ejaculates, they take that sperm and freeze it. It can be used for impregnating hundreds of mares. At that time, the stud fee for Fortune Teller was four thousand dollars, bringing in close to a million dollars for one (one-sided) sexual experience.

If any of those horses impregnated with his sperm became winners, the stud fee would become significantly higher.

Max took his profits and bought a whole slew of new horses. Stanley took his and bought a new house. I took mine, and other than visiting Fortune Teller, retired from the horse business.

I did take one of my dates to visit him, and one of his friends, "Oil Burner," stuck his head out to say hello. She petted his nose, and he preceded to make me extremely insecure. Sometimes, being a person who doesn't do their "due diligence" works out for the best.

CHAPTER 12: IS THAT ALL THERE IS?

Somewhere along the way, I started to feel that my life was not fulfilled. I wanted more. I wanted a social life that was more than my own efforts. I wanted social relationships that were based on more substance than I have known. This was not for purposes of financial gain or association; I wanted to grow intellectually.

My opinion of myself intellectually was about average. My school grades were just passing. My family never encouraged me to procure any higher education. After I entered the business world, I was continuously being told that I was a very intelligent guy. Of course that was based on their perception of what they assumed was my financial success.

To put it in perspective, Steve, who I inherited from my father-in-law, and was now my key employee said, "If you are so f—n smart, how come you ain't so f---n rich?" My consideration of my intellect was thereby humbled. The lesson learned is, "You can't let praise or criticism get to you. It is a weakness to get caught up in either one."

Louise was a pleasant, trivia-knowledgeable person, but was not as emotional or demonstrative as I would have preferred. The relationship I had with Louise was not fulfilling, primarily because I was the dominant figure and she was the subservient woman. It was that way from the beginning, as that is how I thought relationships were supposed to be. Now I wanted more. I wanted a partner, a friend, and a lover. Up until then, all I had was a slave in all of those areas.

I did not feel loved. I felt obeyed, and cooperated with to a point, but not loved. I do not know what part I played in this being what it was. I could have been totally responsible. I could have been partially responsible. I could have had needs that were too much for anyone to satisfy. I truly do not know.

My discontent grew; I never discussed it with anyone, and I was not sending out any signals. However, I was finding several woman were aggressively flirting with me. As a young man growing up, there was never an outwardly-aggressive female pursuing me. The aggressiveness was from me. I scored on an average basis, with a lot of hard work. Whatever I wanted, I had to go after. Women did not call men in those days; at least not the women I knew. Now, all of a sudden there was a lot of attention thrust in my direction. The first thing that happened was with a couple we were getting friendly with: a very pretty girl, and a very jealous husband.

We invited them to Friday night at Lido for the shore dinner. It was a tremendous display of food and great music. It was probably the last remnants of the Great Gatsby days. During the course of the evening, her husband pulled a muscle in his leg and sat at the table with one leg up on a chair. Louise pushed me to dance with his wife. As we were dancing, she rested her head on my shoulder and started rubbing my back in a very provocative way. Being naïve, I said, "I do not know what you are doing, and I certainly do not know how to react to it."

As the evening went on, she became a little tipsy, and said she needed air. Louise said, "Take her out to the ocean air. She will feel better." Lido's clubhouse was located on the ocean side, and the golf course was located on the bay side.When we got to the beach it was completely dark. All you could see was the white of the waves breaking on the beach. I did not solicit it (out of fear), nor did I prevent it. We ended up very passionately kissing. Anything further than that was under my control, and I prevented it (again out of fear).

By the time we walked back to the clubhouse, about an hour later, the party was over and the only two people left and waiting in the parking lot were Louise and her husband. It was an awkward moment, but we got in our respective cars and headed home.

Louise was fine with the whole thing, and we got home went to bed. At about 4:00 a.m. the phone rang. I picked it up while Louise remained asleep. It was the woman, she asked to speak to Louise.

"What? Why?" I asked.

"My husband is very upset, and I want to apologize to her."

"Not to worry. Nothing to apologize for. She is not angry. It's not a problem. I will speak to your husband in the morning."

The following day I did call and explained that we just lost track of the time, and I certainly was sorry. During the next few weeks, she called the office many times and wanted to go further with the relationship, and although very tempted, I could not do it. She would call me and play a recording of the Carpenters' hit, "I'm on Top of the World."

One day I got a call from her husband. He wanted to know what was going on with his wife and me. It seems she wrote a note about me as to how much she loved me and left it where he could find it. I did not know what to do. I told him I was in the middle of something and I would have to call him back.

The first thing I did after a good deal of deliberation, because I could not tell him that his wife was pursuing me, was to call him back and say, "There is nothing going on with your wife and me." As he questioned me further, my response was that I acted only in his best interests.

My interest was not sexual, therefore I was not interested in someone else's wife. What I wanted was to love and be loved in return like in *Love Story*. I was smart enough to understand that all of a sudden I did not become a chick magnet. Whatever was going on was the void that we were all feeling in our lives.

The smartest thing to do is to understand and correct that void within yourself to maintain a solid, continual family base, which, to me, is the essence of life.

I said to myself, "Okay, all of a sudden women are coming after me. That never happened to me when I was single; why now? And if I do want a relationship with this person, who happened to be in the right place at the right time, what about the rest of the women in the world? Then it is not me that became this Don Juan, but the fact that there is something lacking in my marriage, which apparently causes me to transmit signals without realizing it."

As usual, on Sunday I would have my parents over, and whoever else would be available. One Sunday I started to think of whom to invite, and as I went through the list I realized that I had exhausted the depth of my friendships.

When my dad came over that day, I told him that there was something missing in my life. I needed to continually surround myself with others. I do not know what, but something is tugging at me whenever I am not working. My dad cited all of the material acquisitions and lifestyle that I had, and told me I was crazy.

I consulted my doctor and friend; he advised that I see a psychologist, which I did. I spent about four years with him. I brought Louise in as well, after a while Louise basically said that she was happy with her life and did not see the need to change. I went on with the psychologist, Ted, and we became more like friends instead of patient-doctor. We mutually decided to move on.

Later that year, the summer of 1979, all three kids went to sleep away camp. I told Louise that when they left I wanted to separate and before they come home, we could decide what to do.

My mother was in a bungalow colony for the summer, so I lived in her apartment in Queens. For that period, July 4th weekend, I went to Lake George; while there two things happened. One was I decided I did not like the woman I was with because we were buying supplies for the cottage, and she became impatient with the young lady assisting us and considered her a hick, as we were these big city people.

The second was, not having cell phones, by the time I checked my service for messages, there had been a slew of people looking for me, as Harry, my father-in-law had passed away. I came right back, picked up the kids from camp, and after all settled down, brought them back and continued my sabbatical.

Louise had volunteered at the hospital as a candy striper; I felt that was a beginning to have a more meaningful life. I returned before the kids got home, and we continued for another two years. As soon as I moved back in, the candy striping stopped, and the severity of the situation, for her, disappeared.

Although the next few years were filled with good times, they did not remove the need I had.

During Christmas of 1982, we went as a family to Mt. Snow, where there was no snow, and it was a horribly boring experience. I do remember that at dinner one night, I made Adam try escargot, which he vehemently did not want to do. But I was firm and told him that he must try something first and then if he didn't like it, fine.

After that vacation, I knew I had to go. I did not find any emotional or intellectual need being satisfied in my life. I went back to my prior therapist and he suggested that he and I had pretty much exhausted our ability to make any further progress. He recommended another therapist for me to see.

I met with Bob. After a brief catch up of my life, he said, "I can help you stay in your marriage or get out. The choice is yours."

I chose to leave. He was very helpful. It was not an easy thing to do. Without the support of a professional, I would never have had the guts to go through all the guilt, fears, and loss of family time.

This is not a choice anyone should make without first exploring every possibility of avoiding it. Just prior to moving out, before anyone else was aware of the situation, I was returning from dinner one evening, and I received a phone call from a friend of my mother's, who said that she did not show up at the card game and there was no answer at her apartment. Since I had a set of her keys, I drove over and opened the door, and she was lying on the floor talking calmly in words that did not connect at all.

It appeared to me that she had a stroke. I called 911. I followed the ambulance to the hospital; the primary damage was to the left side of her brain, and no other damage was apparent as there was no paralysis.

When we visited in the hospital, there was no way to make any sense of what she was saying. However, Marilyn and Karen seemed to carry on a conversation with her, each taking away something different, but each sure they knew what she was saying.

After pulling a lot of strings, I got her into Sloan Kettering in Manhattan. The difficulty was that the insurance covered you if there was paralysis, but that just a brain injury was not enough. That was a tough battle to overcome, but somehow we did it.

She was there a couple of months with no improvement to her speech. We arranged for full-time nurses, and she came home. One week later, she died. I was separated from Louise at the time.

The shining star I had been when my father died no longer sparkled, and the funeral was attended by no more than twelve people, which is probably a good deal more than mine will be.

After the mourning period was over, I took an apartment at North Shore Towers, which is a three-building complex with an underground arcade. At that time it had a beauty parlor, coffee shop, movie theater, restaurant, and cocktail lounge. It was perfect for me, as every night I would come home and go to the lounge. I lived in each building over the period I was there, each in a different apartment, each very spacious, with huge balconies and beautiful views.

The night I moved in, the place was filthy. A single young guy had sublet it to me. I just put my clothes down, drove to the Doriental, sat at the bar, drank, and cried.

Entitlement

Cause and Effect

136

CHAPTER 13: ABOUT ME

Who are we?

From what I have gathered, the most applicable theory is that we are a product of our experiences. Research says that who we are is also the experiences of our ancestral genes. But, if so, why then are siblings born of the same parents, in most cases, completely different? What of the things we are that emerge prior to our own experiences?

From the time I was in the womb until I was three years old, my surroundings were the same. My two sisters have few things in common with each other, and neither have anything in common with me.

Right or wrong, nice or not, smart or not, who is to judge? All I believe in is what I have experienced. There are some obvious explanations for how I became me, and then there are some inexplicable reasons that I am me.

I attribute a major part of who I am to religion. Not to being religious, but to being exposed to the discipline of religion. My exposure was not that long, but it was powerful enough to do its job.

What gave me the idea that I would behave in a manner different from what people have said about the Jewish people? What was the experience of pride, of being in a synagogue and listening, watching, with little understanding of what was being said? What made me believe as follows?

It is my opinion that religion is a moral code. However one chooses to believe, practice, preach, display, and pray, they have the right to do so and be respected for it. I am as proud to be of the Jewish faith as I would be having been born into any other faith. I have no objection to any article or celebration of any religion.

What I never could understand is disdain for any religion. In my case, being that I am Jewish, I continually search for what causes anti-Semitism.

From the time I first became aware, I was trying to understand why. There can be no other explanation other than those diseases most common to humanity, greed and envy. The following quotations are a small sample of conclusions by some non-Jewish people.

"Some people like the Jewish people, and some do not. But no thoughtful man can deny the fact that they are, beyond any question, the most formidable and the most remarkable race which has appeared in the world. " Winston Churchill

The following is paraphrased from an article by Olive Schreiner, a South African novelist "

It appears it is difficult for many nations of the world to live in the presence of the Jewish people. They embarrass the world as they have done things which are beyond the imagination. They brought the world the Ten Commandments. They violated the rules of history by staying alive. They outlived all their former enemies. They angered the world with their return to their homeland after 2000 years of exile and after the murder of six million of their brothers and sisters."

"They aggravated mankind by building, in the wink of an eye, a democratic State which others were not able to create in even hundreds of years.

"Whether in Science, Medicine, Psychology or any other discipline, Jewish people taught the world not to accept the world as it is, but to transform it. Some nations continue to go out of their way to find a stick with which to hit the Jewish people.

Their goal is to prove that Jewish people are as immoral and guilty of massacre and genocide as they themselves.

"All of this in order to hide and justify their own failure to even protest when six million Jewish people were brought to the slaughterhouses of Auschwitz and Dachau.

"They enjoy that the Jewish people remain in a struggle with another people who are completely terrorized by their own leaders. They close their eyes to the fact that nations which received, and in any way dealt fairly and mercifully with the Jewish people, have prospered."

The following is from Dennis Miller Live on HBO. Although he is not Jewish, he recently had the following to say about the situation in the Middle East:

"The Palestinians want their own country. There's just one thing about that: there are no Palestinians. It's a made up word. Israel was called Palestine for two thousand years. As soon as the Jewish people took over and started growing oranges as big as basketballs, what do you know, say hello to the 'Palestinians,' weeping for their deep bond with their lost 'land' and 'nation.' They could've had their own country anytime in the last thirty years, especially several years ago at Camp David.

"But if you have your own country, you have to have traffic lights and garbage trucks and Chambers of Commerce, and, worse, you actually have to figure out some way to make a living. They only want to destroy Israel. Chew this around and spit it out: five hundred million Arabs, five million Jewish people. Just reverse the numbers. Imagine five hundred million Jewish people and five million Arabs. I was stunned at the simple brilliance of it. Can anyone picture the Jewish people strapping belts of razor blades and dynamite to themselves? Of course not.

Or marshaling every fiber and force at their disposal for generations to drive a tiny Arab state into the sea? Nonsense. Or dancing for joy at the murder of innocents? Impossible. Or spreading and believing horrible lies about the Arabs baking their bread with the blood of children? Disgusting. Now, as you know, left to themselves in a world of peace, the worst Jewish people would ever do to people is debate them to death."

Beyond the core of religion, I continue to try to understand how I became me. The second most influential force was being in the military. I was not there for long, but long enough to learn that by being forced to do what you think you cannot do you discover that your boundaries are limitless. A necessary requirement to succeed in life.

My mother had been on a stepstool cleaning in our apartment 2B at 915 East 179th street in the Bronx. She fell and fractured her leg, and a neighbor called the police. I was walking home from playing in the school yard. The closer I got the more I realized that the ambulances and people lined up in the street was my building. When I walked into the lobby, the commotion continued up the stairs toward my apartment on the second floor. Until I came to grips with what had happened I was very frightened.

Two weeks later, I was riding my bike and saw my cousin Joan with some of her friends. I had passed them in the street and made a U-turn to go back and fell. I went to get up and as a I stood on my leg, one part went left and the other right, so my mother and I were in casts for the next three months.

Not too long after, I was riding my bike and I went to jump the curb, which was a common occurrence, and somehow the bike stopped short and I went over the handlebars; in stopping my fall, I broke my arm.

My mother said that the asthma medication I was taking had arsenic in it, which weakened the calcium in your bones. Having asthma from age three to thirteen must have had an influence on my persona; I would imagine a good one, as being appreciative of not being ill, when a lot of time was lost being ill.

The first summer at the Bungalow colony, I was lost because of a bully. That was a very lonely year for me. I would take long walks in the woods enjoying nature, wondering how and when the various man-made stone partitions were put there. Enjoying being alone at a little frog pond in the woods with an imaginary girlfriend.

At fourteen, there was a deep sense of romance within me, with an appreciation of the beauty of nature and people. There was a natural water spring on a road leading from our place to the town of Monticello. Opposite the spring was a hill that led up to a field with blueberry bushes. Beyond the field of blueberries was a huge drop into the Catskill valley with a panoramic view that extended miles. I sat there and had a feeling of solace as I enjoyed the scenery and the peacefulness.

That same feeling was apparent on the golf course right at dawn when the grass was soaked with dew and the view and the serenity were breathtaking. On those occasions, as well, I imagined a female partner was with me and I was showing her the beauty.

At that time, The Loretta Young Show debuted on television. Watching her walking down a winding staircase in her long gown and flowing long hair determined what would continually attract me.

Somehow still fourteen, while at the bungalow colony, I arranged to have a date with a girl named June. We went to the movies in Monticello a mile away. By taxi. I paid for both of us and we went home. A week or so later, my mother found out about this whole thing from the girl's mother. When she confronted me with the facts, she was only concerned with who paid.

When she found out that I paid for both of us, she became very angry. She was so mad that she lunged at me, her fingernails scratching my chest, leaving scabs for weeks. I wonder, if and how that may have had an influence on who I am.

The people that resided in our Monticello community for the summer were mostly middle class Jewish families, not showy in any way; no one bragged or claimed poverty. It was all just social, and no one knew what you had or what you didn't.

Bob and his wife were in their late forties, a generation younger than most. Very pleasant, nice-looking people. Bob was a salesman making a living and enjoying the social atmosphere of the summer surroundings. Somehow he became a partner in the business of selling TVs and other appliances on credit to people who could not afford them. They would pay weekly, and when they didn't pay, the appliance was removed, refurbished, and resold. Apparently he was doing well and collecting a lot of cash.

He was enjoying his new successes. He bought a fancy car and made reservations for the Concord show every Saturday night. Invited all his colony friends and paid for the tables, dinner, champagne, the show, everything. Everybody loved him.

That lasted about two seasons. His business started to fall apart, as those things usually do. It all dried up, and he was broke. During that period, when I was about sixteen, he gave me a lift back to the city. He said, "You know when I was making and spending money, people would listen to every word I said as if pearls of wisdom were coming out of my mouth. Now they wouldn't even spend the time to have a cup of coffee with me."

That had a big effect on me. I had watched as the freeloaders kissed his ass, and now they said, "Sayonara, baby." To me, it sucked.

This was one of the major things, along with my mother's envy and people's anti-Semitic remarks about money, that gave me a loose regard for money.

Whenever I could, I helped people who ran into bad luck, including Bob. I lent him money years later, never expecting to get it back.

"You can't live a perfect day without doing something for someone who will never be able to repay you."

When my friends and I would get on the subway to go somewhere and they would behave too loudly, I would walk to another car out of embarrassment. Why?

When my sister called upon me to babysit, I did so, but I was giving up time with my friends and started to resent it tremendously. This was one of the first times I realized that I could not say "no."

As a doorman in Radio City at the time, you were given a uniform. Tuxedo jacket as an usher, tails as a doorman, vest, shirt, bow tie, suspenders, pants, white gloves, and no pockets. When I worked the ticket door, if a person would hand me a ticket, I would make believe to rip it in half, but I actually slipped it into the lining of my tails. I did this to give my friends tickets to get in. What in my makeup, my genes, or my experiences would give me the audacity to do such a thing?

1960. Fort Gordon, Georgia. Aside from my Mormon friends, the platoon sergeant in charge of all of us was an avid ping pong player. I watched and learned and became good enough to give him a run for his money, which created a relationship that let me do pretty much anything I wanted. That is the way it worked then in all aspects of life: you scratch my back, and I'll scratch yours.

1960. My dad was working at Yonkers Raceway as a bartender, and I had nothing to do one night. I drove over, parked my car, and started to walk to the entrance. As I was walking, the speaker system was saying that there was only fifteen minutes left to place your bets for the daily double. I wanted to get my bet in, so I started to jog. I immediately stepped in a hole, twisted my ankle, and fell to the ground.

I remember hobbling in excruciating pain over to where my father was. He kept telling me to go to the first aid office, I kept saying no. He said at least they will wrap it in a bandage for you. Finally I acquiesced and went.

They wrapped it with ace bandages, wrote down all the facts of how it happened, took my name, address, and phone number, and I left, slightly less painful. I went through the rest of the evening at the track and went home.

The next day my ankle blew up like a balloon, and I could hardly step on it. A few hours later, the race track insurance company called to see how I was doing, I told them about the current facts, and they said they will call back tomorrow.

I called uncle Morty, told him what happened, and that I was sure I could get some money from the insurance company. He said, "What's the name of the company?" I told him, and he said to forget it, they don't give out anything, don't waste your time. The insurance company called again and were very concerned with how I was getting along.

I explained that I was still in pain, can't go to work. They said, "We will call back tomorrow." Called Uncle Morty again. "Morty, they are really concerned and worried. They will be happy to pay and get out of this."

"You don't know what you're talking about, forget it."

The insurance company called again, I brought up that I couldn't work and that I will be going for x-rays. They countered with how can we help, and we started to negotiate. I got them to pay me $500.00.

I had no knowledge of these things, and $500 at that time was not chicken feed. I called uncle Morty because I was so proud. I said, "Guess what? I got them to pay me $500."

Morty said, "You jack ass, you should have held out for more."

Now, how do you process that? A man I respected and loved, valued his opinion. He had blindsided me with a non-intelligent pro and con. Not easy, but a lesson well learned.

Go with your gut. You never know whether the advice you are getting is truly based on the adviser's intellect, ego, or impatience.

While decorating the apartment, I installed wood panels and a shelf system, I had an amplifier on one shelf, needing an FM tuner. I purchased the tuner.

My sister Karen and her husband Jack berated me for spending money on a non-necessity. I felt so guilty, I returned the unit at 75% of what I paid. I labored over letting them influence me, and never again let someone else's judgment make me react so insecurely.

Sony, the world class electronic giant, came out with a video recorder and player called Beta Max. I was the first in my circle to have it, plus all the paraphernalia that came with it. Of course, it became obsolete within a short period of time. But, everything has positives and negatives. I never rushed into a new gadget again. I waited to be sure it was a keeper, then bought.

However, it is very hard to stay in front of the electronic curve. It is a well-organized industry, with planned obsolescence of a product before it even comes out. They already have the next generations planned and ready to be released.

From the time I got married, Louise always had the nicer car, and I drove an old jalopy. I bought her a brand-new Cadillac, and after a while I started talking to myself. "Why do I not have a new car as well?" I bought myself a brand-new Cadillac.

A friend said, "Are you crazy? People will see that you have two new caddys. They will rob your house and kidnap your kids," etc.

One car was kept in the garage, the other in the driveway. One night I came home from work, and we were having the driveway blacktopped. They had a rope across so I could not park the car.

Hearing my friend's words, instead of the two cars being parked in front of the house, I parked mine six houses away. In the middle of the night, someone smashed into my car, and it was totaled.

Several years later, that same friend? TWO MERCEDES IN HIS DRIVEWAY.

Electrically, from all my troubleshooting and school and just common sense, I became so knowledgeable that one night I came home, and it was freezing in the house and the boiler was not working. I spent two hours taking apart all the electrical connections to find out where there was a break in the wire because the electricity was not going through. Finally, after tracing the wires all the way back to the source, I found the problem. Adam had inadvertently turned the emergency switch located in the kitchen off.

The barter system? I learned a new word for "up yours": barter. We were wiring a kitchen for a kitchen remodeling contractor. I asked him about cabinets, as I wanted to redo my kitchen. He figured out the price and said, "You do the wiring on this job, and I will supply the cabinets, even trade." I did my job. When the delivery never came and I pushed to get them there, they came in C.O.D.

Throughout the years with Louise, there were a lot of common sense calls that no one had the ability to see. When Laura (Louise's sister's daughter) was about five or six, she had this white blonde hair, white complexion, and bulging eyes, it did not appear healthy to me.If I hadn't said that she should be looked at, her condition would have gone on for years.

Same with Harry. He couldn't breathe in Florida. He had to sit down and rest continuously. I made sure he went to see a pulmonary specialist, and he was given oxygen to administer on his own, which made his life more tolerable.

Pearl was staying in our house, and had what they thought was a flu. After sleeping for three days, and omitting a foul odor, I said, "She is in a coma, probably a diabetic coma." Sure enough, she was hospitalized and diagnosed with and treated for diabetes.

Louise, one night after wine and shellfish, became faint and her eyes rolled back into her head.After all the tests and doctor's exams were negative, the neurologist suggested a medication for seizures that she would have to take for the rest of her life.

I felt it was an isolated situation and if it happened again we could always go that route. It never reoccurred.

Recently, a TV commentator lost control of her speech during a segment. She was diagnosed with a severe migraine, which means they do not know what caused it. I wonder if they examined whether she ingested shellfish with alcohol.

CHAPTER 14: LIFE IN THE FAST LANE:

When I was on the board at Tam O'Shanter, Max, my partner in the horses, was also a board member. He grew up with a bout of polio, was a champion handball player, a scratch golfer, and a man's man. He had dancing eyes and was a magnet to all who did not suffer from envy.

Max and I were on our way home from a board meeting at Tam O'Shanter when we stopped for a drink at The Lakeville Manor on Northern Boulevard in Great Neck.

We chatted for a while with a young lady named Kathy. When we left that night, I had Kathy's phone number. I was recently separated from Louise, my wife of eighteen years, and it took a few months to feel comfortable enough to call.

When I did, she was upset that it took me so long to call. We made a date for dinner. She was a very exciting, very beautiful, magnificently-figured, young, Irish redhead. A bright girl, she worked as a pharmaceutical rep. At that time, the position included a car, her own territory, the ability to work out of her home, and schedule her own hours and appointments. What this meant was that she really did not work very much.

We made several trips to Atlantic City, Las Vegas, Bermuda, and the Hamptons. Being recently separated, some things made me a little uncomfortable, but she pushed me into three mistakes that I made during this time. The first one was to test my commitment to the relationship. She kept after me to take her to the golf club, which I felt at the time was inappropriate.

Golf clubs in those days had very strict rules, such as no single woman could be a member. A single man had to submit the name of a companion he would bring to the club as a designated escort.

He was not allowed to bring different dates to the club. It was a very social atmosphere, with each member knowing the other members.

One night, I finally gave in. We went to the bar, which was fortunately empty, had a drink, and left as fast as I could, as I was extremely uncomfortable.

It seems, at least with the women I have been involved with, that instant gratification is required. Instead of waiting for a sensible amount of time and respect, they must satisfy their feeling of insecurity immediately. The next request, with the same pressure, was to meet my children.

We did go and have her meet them. It was a cordial brunch, but for me, it was not comfortable.

Wendy was at college, on a budget, had her car, a gas card, and received a weekly allowance. Of course it was never enough. I visited often, and when I was there, I would hand her a hundred dollar bill.

On one visit to Wendy, I took Kathy with me. When we left, she had noted that I gave Wendy the hundred dollar bill, and being an intelligent, well-educated girl, she made sense on many points, convincing me that it was not a good thing to do. I thought she made sense, as I had a friend with an older daughter who was single, living off her father, and who seemed to think that there was no need to find a spouse while she was being provided for.

After that conversation, I said "no" once in a while, which is a very hard word for me, but I thought it was in her best interest. (Wendy did not.) What I also did not know at the time was that Rich, her boyfriend, was actually living with her, and when they knew I was coming, they temporarily changed things around.

Finally, the third mistake with Kathy was asking me to take a trip to Bermuda with her on Father's Day, which she knew, and I did not realize—not smart.

That Father's Day, Wendy, Elyssa, and Adam made a very creative, fun, Saturday Night Live-like video as a Father's Day present; I still laugh when I watch it.

The relationship went on for almost six months. She was much younger and very passionate, something that the females in my generation were not. When I brought her home from our first date, she led me directly to her bedroom. When she stayed over, she brought a music cassette, provocative lingerie, and preformed a strip tease for me. As much as I enjoyed it, it was also a little intimidating.

During our relationship, we went to her friend's wedding in Richmond, Virginia. During the reception, she told all her friends that if we made it through the summer, we would be getting married. I had not been consulted on this, but I paid no attention.

That summer, we spent the weekend of the Fourth of July at a bungalow-type complex in the Hamptons. My friend Richard had a new girlfriend, and he was madly in love with her; they were staying at another friend's house in the Hamptons for the weekend as well.

We visited them, swam, went out to eat, and had a very nice day. His girlfriend, Linda, he later married and divorced, and then married someone else, and finally rekindled a friendship with Linda.

We went back to our motel and were fast asleep; our bungalow did not have a phone, and there was a knock on the door. The manager said there was a phone call for me in the office. I went in and it was Richard.

He said, "Mike, Linda had a Rolex watch that she had left on the dresser in the room where you and Kathy changed. We traced our steps, checked everywhere, and could not find it. The only conclusion we can come up with is that maybe Kathy took it by mistake."

I told him I would check and get back to him tomorrow. I said nothing to Kathy and went back to sleep. The following day, we were going back to the city. I suggested we pack our bags, put them in the car, and hang out by the pool.

While at the pool, I left to get breakfast and bring it back. When I left, I turned onto a side street, pulled over, opened the trunk and the bag, and sure enough, at the bottom of her suitcase, the watch was there. I put it in my pocket. On the drive home, I did not bring it up.

After I took her home and said good night, I never spoke to her again. She realized when she found the watch gone that I knew she had taken it. She tried to contact me, but I would not take her calls. Eventually she wrote me a letter trying to explain her actions, and she said that the temptation because of her modest past was overwhelming.

Years later, I found out through a friend at the golf club that she had been married and died at a young age from breast cancer.

August, 1983. Back in the singles' world.

I was attending another one of many singles' cocktail parties. This one was in October of 1983 in New York City in the lobby of the Olympic Towers. I was sitting at the bar, minding my own business, and watching the same cast of characters hovering, casing, stalking, and circling. The woman sitting next to me says, "Aren't you Michael Scheffler?"

"Yes."

"I know you."

"Okay."

"I used to work for you, and you fired me."

As I was listening, trying to recall who she was, my eye caught a glimpse of a striking image. As in a movie, everything switched to slow motion, and the words of the former employee were playing like a recording on slow speed.

My head turned behind me, at a pace as slow as one frame at a time, trying to see what it was that had attracted my eye. Frame by frame, a mane of long, blonde hair flowed to the back, then ever so slowly to the front, trailing each step of a statuesque figure wrapped in a well-tailored, winter white pant suit, which adorned a figure of model-like proportions. Her bronzed face and natural beauty was accentuated by the contrast between the blonde, the white, and the tan. The long, slow-motion, hypnotic fixation of my eyes then moved down her statuesque figure, where, in her hand, a brown soft leather briefcase completed the natural and embellished vision of my most cherished desires.

As she walked, every man stared and approached her, one by one. She carried herself perfectly, looked and acted with class. Then and there, sitting at the bar, no longer in slow motion, in real time, I said to myself, "That's it, I am going to marry that woman." I approached her when she was free of all the other interested parties and offered her a drink. She was very polite and explained that she had not had dinner yet, so I offered dinner. She explained that she had come with a friend. I said, "Bring her along."

She responded, "Thank you, but no thank you."

The evening ended without any further opportunity to communicate. When I originally started going to these singles' outings, I had befriended the people that ran them. They kept a record of all attendees.

The next day I made my calls only to find that she had indeed come with a friend and that no one had her information. I continued my pursuit, remembering that the friend she came with worked with her.

Obtaining the friend's number, I called, explained that we met at the party, and that I would like to call her friend but did not have the number. Her retort was short and annoyed, and she said, "I work with her. I'll ask her. Call me tomorrow." I called the next day, the same short annoyed response: "I forgot. Call me tomorrow." I called the next day. Same voice. "She is seeing someone right now. Not interested." Click.

I was determined not to let rejection, ego, insecurity, or anything else get in my way. I just wanted her to sit across the table from me over a long, leisurely dinner. If then she was not interested, so be it.

Her first and last name were known. She lived in New Jersey. She worked in the city.

In 1983, there was no information highway. In order to call information (411) or use the phone book, you had to know the area the person lived in. New Jersey has two hundred and fifty boroughs, fifty two cities, fifteen towns, two hundred and forty five townships, and four villages. Using a map, I started with the areas closest to New York. I struck out, over and over again.

Continuing my search to find Denise came up empty. There was a file in my office drawer listing all the months of the year and all the days of the week. When I made a call or gave an estimate, I would decide when to follow up, and then put that folder or note in the proper folder.

After spending so much time trying to find her, Thanksgiving and Christmas vacation were getting close. I put her in my Monday follow up. Each Monday I would try a few towns in Jersey and put it back.

On Thanksgiving I took Adam with me, to Cancun. We swam and fished and he was possessed by windsurfing. I had a twenty-four-hour bout with chest pain and discomfort, which I attributed to a chest cold. Knowing now that at some point I'd had a silent heart attack, that could have been the time.

For the Christmas vacation, we rented a condo on the beach in Puerto Valletta, the three kids and myself, rented a Jeep, went to the discos at night after leisurely dinners and sunsets in a charming part of the world.

The first morning I woke up there, I looked out at the beach and ocean, directly under my window, there were about ten people, men and women, slowly moving their heads, then their arms, then their knees.

It seemed like a haven for some cult, but it was just yoga.

1984. Back from vacation, refreshed and rested, I came across the follow up. Remembering again that her charming friend worked with her, I realized that if I could find out where she worked, I could find her. I then recalled that the friend appeared a little older and might very well have a child. At 4:00 p.m, I called the house. A young lady answered. I said, "This is the lighting company, may I speak to your mother?"

"My mother is at work."

"How can I reach her?" She rattled off the number. I called the number; they answered, "Federated." Wow! Federated Department Stores!

She must be a buyer. I knew lots of people in the garment center, even some top executives in Federated. All I had to do was find out what department she bought for. Called Federated again. I said, "Denise, please."

They connected me, and I hung up before anyone could answer. I was just confirming that she still worked there. I called again, and they responded, "Federated."

"Excuse me. What department is Denise in?"

"She is the administrative assistant to Mr. Dean."

Called again. "Excuse me, what department is Mr. Dean in?"

"Oh, he is the chief operating officer." Click. That narrows the field. What do I do? I knew that direct contact would probably result in a rejection.

With that realization, one of my salespeople (Joanne) was walking by my office. I called her in to tell her the whole story, since I found the investigation and pursuit fun. She left my office, and unbeknownst to me, she called Federated, asked for Denise, introduced herself, and said she was trying to find out whom to see about doing business with the local stores.

Denise said she wasn't sure and suggested she call Peggy Fleming. Joanne called, made an appointment with Peggy, called Denise back, thanked her for guiding her in the right direction, and in appreciation would like to buy her lunch.

Denise said it was not necessary, but Joanne was persistent, and a date was made. Since I knew nothing about this, Joanne came in and told me the story. We developed a plan; she would explain at the lunch that she was meeting her boss at the restaurant at two.

I would show up a half hour early and sit down with them. Everything worked as planned. I sat down, and Joanne introduced me as her boss.

"Do you live in the city?"

"No, I am looking for an apartment in the city. I live in New Jersey."

"Some of my friends own apartment houses in New York. I could help you."

"I would love that."

"I will call you tomorrow, and we will make plans to go see the apartments."

"Thank you. That is very nice of you."

"My pleasure. Where in Jersey do you live?"

"Parsippany. Have we ever met before? You look very familiar."

"Not that I recall."

When I called the next day, we had a very nice conversation. After a few minutes, she said her boss was calling and had to get off. She took my number and said she would call back later. She never called. It did not make sense; everything was very congenial, strictly friendship and apartment hunting.

The next day, someone else answered her extension

No call back.

The next day, a guy answered,I kept asking where she was and whether she got my messages. He gave me evasive answers.

Suspecting something was not right, I called Parsippany 411, got her home number, and called. It was the middle of the day; if she answered, I knew there was a problem.

Sure enough, she said hello. I said, "Hi, this is Michael. I tried to reach you in the office, and I suspect you have a problem. Maybe I can help you." She started to speak, and I cut her off with, "I am about to go into a meeting. Why don't we have dinner?"

"Well, I live in Parsippany."

"No problem. I will come there."

"Okay," she said.

"About eight, I will call back for directions."

Realizing that I'd gotten her at a vulnerable time, and fearful she would cancel when I called for directions, I had my secretary call, say I was unavailable, and get the info. Parsippany was a good hour's drive. I picked her up, and we went to the King George Restaurant.

She explained that at a luncheon with a colleague, there was a discussion where she divulged her boss's salary. She had probably been set up, as management found out and temporarily furloughed her. They were going to relocate her to another department. We had a lovely dinner. As time went by, we did not realize that we were the only patrons left in the restaurant. We left only because they wanted to close.

My theory was, because of her attractiveness, men were challenged in making her a conquest. So I played it cool, lightly lip kissed her goodnight (warm, inviting, lips), made plans for two nights later, and went home.

She was very receptive to the kiss and the new plans. I suspect that the evening probably could have ended more romantically, but my interest was in today and tomorrow, not just today.

Two nights later, for the first time in my life, I hired a limo and a driver, complete with roses and champagne, picked her up in front of the building where she worked, and had the driver go around Central Park.

Cocktails at the top of the six's,

dinner upstairs at Bruno's, where a singing piano player entertained us with professionally-rendered Broadway soundtracks.

When she first got in the limo, she asked if it was mine. I told her that it wasn't and that I had rented it and had never done that before.

Next was a weekend in Atlantic City with one room and two beds. We played baccarat together and won about three grand; I gave it to her. All along the way she continued to jab at me with remarks about my age and weight, saying:

"I never should have left my ex-husband."

"You drink too much."

"You eat too much."

"I'm starving."

"I have a headache."

"My father left my mother for a younger woman."

"You are never getting divorced."

Pointing out that we were fifteen years apart, forty two and twenty seven, was like her theme song. Although I was not overweight, she continually jabbed at me with comments about the younger men she dated who were all in good shape and worked out.

It was my opinion that Denise was a diamond in the rough that had bruises from being mistreated by men. My psychologist, who I was seeing on a weekly basis, agreed with me. Once she felt she could trust me, she would be more secure, and the rough edges would start to smooth out.

While we were first dating, I was seeing another young lady, who was very nice but not as pretty as Denise. My favorite restaurant at the time, The Doriental, was my focus group. I had the waiters and bartenders choose between the two women; they did not choose Denise. I attributed it to those edges that would eventually be polished.

Next came a ski weekend. When I picked her up to leave, somehow, because I was so out of sorts around her, I left her ski boots on the ground. When we realized they were gone, she freaked out, asking me, "How can you be so stupid? How am I going to ski? Is it an age thing?" Assuring her I would buy her new ones, all she could say was, "Those were my favorites!"

It was non-stop for two more hours. She kept on going.

At the lodge, Mount Haven, we were dining to the serenading of a piano player. I told him we were married twenty five years and asked if he would please play the anniversary waltz. We were on the dance floor when he announced our happy event. She was not happy.

She yelled to the band leader, "We are not married! I would have been married at two years old!"

She turned to me and asked, "Why did you do that? That was not funny."

There were so many insults and freak outs over the next few months, but I was so enamored with her, or the thought of winning her over, that I kept on pushing.

During our dating period, Denise had a wisdom tooth pulled. Several hours later, the pain was excruciating. The medication the doctor gave her was not working. I took her to my pharmacist, who gave her Percodan. After observing her dramatics, the pharmacist was in shock when he found out it was one tooth and not four.

Because of the Percodan, the sex was almost consensual.

Next up, in March of 1984, was a trip to my favorite place in the world: Acapulco. We stayed at the Las Brisas hotel, had a master bedroom with a king-size bed and a large veranda.

There was a private pool, a swing for two, coffee and pastries waiting for you when you woke up, views that would turn the most jaded into a romantic, the pool at the bay with the most luxurious views, and dinner on an outdoor terrace overlooking Acapulco Bay.

The weather was as perfect as you would create yourself if you could. Before we left New York, we started taking a daily dose of Bactrim to avoid any stomach illness. The sun apparently doesn't mix well with Bactrim, and by the end of the first day, we were trying to figure out how to reduce the swelling of Denise's lips.

If you hadn't realized it yet, please note that any illness or physical change to Denise is not a light-hearted mend. It is the most life-threatening situation that one could have. "Drama Queen" is too demure a title.

The focus on herself dominated most of the time, and the snide remarks toward me, the rest

About the third night, we went to dinner at Las Brisas. Denise got up to go to the ladies' room. On her way there, she slipped, fell, and was lying on her back on the floor, as if she were paralyzed, moaning all the way. The only repercussion was the pain in her back when it was time to make love.

We visited the Princess Hotel and had drinks around the outside bar. When we got back to the room, I realized I had left my camera at the bar. I told her I was going back to get it. She attacked, saying, "How could you be so stupid? It will never be there," and a nonstop freak out.

As I drove to get the camera, I was seething. I had enough. The continually degrading remarks, the continual drama, the continual sexual avoidance.

This broad was nothing but a pain in the ass. I got the camera, went back to Las Brisas, threw her plane ticket and two hundred dollars on the bed and said,

"Sayonara, baby."

Entitlement

Cause and Effect

164

.

CHAPTER 15: NEVER SPEED IN THE FAST LANE

"Sayonara, baby" closed the deal for Denise. After I said I was leaving in Acapulco, she then came around, apologized, begged me to stay, and acknowledged the relationship as mutual.

This was the pinnacle of the future. At the thought of me leaving, she professed love and need. Based on those words, my determination was reinforced, no matter how badly she behaved. The way she acted may have caused arguments, but my resolve to make her mine was undeterred.

Shortly after that we moved in together at North Shore Towers, although we held on to her apartment for her security. Her job was annoying her on a daily basis. I told her to quit, bought her a new car, and provided a social, romantic, and active lifestyle.

We spent time at the golf club, weekends in the Hamptons, visited Adam in camp, went apple picking, socialized with friends, traveled to weekend ski areas: Stowe, Mt. Snow, and Sugarbush. On the ski slope, Denise would keep taking lessons; now she was insecure about her ski outfits. I have always been fastidious in my clothing. I picked all my outfits from the outset. I never bought a shirt in the hope of finding pants that go with it. When I went shopping, all the clothes I selected were put on the counter: pants, jacket, shirt, tie, socks, shoes, handkerchief. Each outfit was coordinated and then purchased.

We went shopping and did the same. We bought her beautiful ski outfits. We always went shopping and picked out her clothes together. When we found a store that we liked for her, she would try on everything she liked. Whatever looked fabulous on her was selected.

Once in a while, in her anxiety to buy clothes by herself, she would take home everything the sales people told her looked great on her, and then try it on for me. If my opinion on an item was negative, she would become defensive and say that the salesgirl said it looked great. She always had the option, as in everything else, to overrule me, but she never did.

We were looking at furnished model town houses in Jericho. The place we were looking at was one of the last two units that were not sold in the project. I made the builder a ridiculous offer, and we owned a condo.

Before Denise, I was not very happy being single. I hated not being with my kids every day. I hated giving up my social life. I did not enjoy continually starting a new sexual relationship. I was unsure of what I was doing and feeling a lot of guilt. Prior to Denise and me becoming an item, the relationship between Louise and me was cordial.

I continued to pay the same bills I paid before, I gave her the same weekly amount as before. At one point I considered that the life I gave up for the one I was looking for was not worth the side effects and the possibility of any real improvement was not realistic. I had started to discuss with Louise the possibility of getting back together.

It may never have worked, but it couldn't get started because of "them." The people that I am referring to are the so-called friends that are now telling her how to live her life. They make a list of demands, telling her, "Tell him you will not get back together unless you get…" and a list of material things are spewed out.

It is a shame that a person that knows you for a short time tells you how to interact with a person you have lived twenty years with. It happens every day by almost everyone.

When I had this epiphany that I was going to marry Denise from the second I saw her, so did the reality of divorce raise its ugly head.

Louise became under the control of "them," and I wanted to finalize the legal separation agreement we had and convert it to the same terms in a divorce.

Each time we came to an agreement with our respective attorneys, I would show up for the execution of the agreement and something new was added. This went on continuously, as she was getting advice as well from her vindictive brother-in-law.

Meanwhile, Denise was feeding her desire for unhappiness, telling me every day:

"You are never getting a divorce."

"We are never getting married."

"I should move back to my apartment."

Finally, when all the terms were set, Louise's lawyer did not take any calls to set up a meeting from my lawyers or from me. I called my lawyer, he called her lawyer, no return call. I called her lawyer, no return call. After several weeks of this avoidance, I took one of my employees with me to where I knew her car was parked. (The car was registered to me.) He dropped me off. I took the car and stored it in a garage. Now, everyone was calling me after all their threats did not work. They acquiesced to meet, at which point I returned the car.

Both lawyers were decent guys, and not these "blood-sucking frauds" (which is a course given in law school and part of the requirement to pass the bar) called divorce attorneys. That situation led to the bad blood that existed for a few years. None of the evil, vindictive ways were that of Louise or her attorney. They were all orchestrated by her brother-in-law, but she followed his lead.

The papers were signed and presented to the court for final dissolution.

In our discussions of marriage, it was always assumed and agreed that Denise and I would try to have a baby as soon as possible. I had been to Europe twice and Denise had never been. Knowing that we would be having a child in the near future, I planned a trip to Europe.

We flew to London, took the train to Dover and the Hydrofoil to France, and then the train to Paris. In Paris, I rented a car and intended to drive through the French countryside and then on to Zurich, Marseille, French Riviera, and Italy. We stayed at the Inn at the Park in London, had tea and cucumber sandwiches, toured all the famous sights, and saw the show *Starlight Express*, which was so much better in London than in New York.

In fashion at the time were these black net stockings, which Denise wore with a black dress, and I thought that she dressed very nicely. To this day, I do not know what the English found so interesting about the stockings, but they stared and pointed.

Denise was not a seasoned traveler, and she was not inclined to take advice, at least not from me. We traveled with much too much luggage, which we carried to the London train station when we boarded the train for Dover and on to Paris. We were booked at the Hotel George V.

When we arrived, Denise became intimidated and insecure. She found the room they gave us inadequate, which was the same way she felt about any hotel room we have ever been offered. (Hotels, restaurants, and prescription medication are never accepted at a first offering, only the second.)

Understanding the process, I sat in the lobby until she was finished complaining to the desk clerk.

The outcome was there was no other room. Denise was convinced that they felt she was unworthy of the hotel accommodations and the fact that she did not speak French made them all pompous asses.

We toured all the famous sights, rented a car, and started to drive on a well-planned journey through the French wine country. As soon as we got onto a highway, Denise, again, freaked out. "The signs are in French. What do they say? Where are you going? I'm hungry."

All the restaurants were closed for their afternoon siesta, and the only thing I could find open were *le patissier* and *le fromager*, where we had ham and cheese sandwiches. She didn't like that, but she ate anyway.

The freak-out continued for about four hours, until we got to the town of Dijon. I parked the car on a normal town street, had a map, and toured Dijon by foot. If I said, "Turn left," Denise asked why. "How do you know? Have you been here before?"

She proceeded to find a policeman and tried to communicate. He was communicating with her body, but not in English. She had me so nuts that for about fifteen minutes I was not sure of which street I parked the car on. She was in full freak-out and hysteria mode, and she frantically asked anyone she passed if they spoke English.

This tour of Europe was intended to show Denise as much as I could in the time allotted. But I could not take any more. I drove to a Hertz office, which was closed. I wrote a note, slipped it in the mail slot with the keys, and headed to the train station with six pieces of luggage and no one available to help.

After the wine country, I had planned to go through Switzerland on our way to Monte Carlo. That was scratched, and we took the train directly to Monte Carlo. Denise was reading her French dictionary so that she would not feel so inadequate.

When we arrived at what I thought was Monte Carlo, it was actually a town directly before it called Beaulieu. We stayed at La Reserve, a magnificent French hotel overlooking the yacht-filled inlet.

We slept on mattresses that you needed a step stool to get up to. We dressed for dinner, and in the lounge, Denise tried to order a glass of wine in French.

The waiter could not understand her, so I ordered for both of us. One glass of wine, one Dewars on the rocks with a twist. The waiter had no problem with the order.

The next day, at the pool overlooking the Mediterranean Sea, I ran into a Lido golf club member. I went over and said hello. He was as nice as could be, and he thanked me for remembering him and saying hello.

We then drove to Nice, Eze, and Monaco along the Middle and Grande Cornice, stopping at Mt. Boron for gorgeous vistas over the Grand Cornice. Lunch was on a balcony forged into an ancient castle overlooking the entire countryside, where we met a couple from Turkey. From there it was on to San Remo, Monte Carlo, and the Palace, where we gambled in the Casino, said hello to the Hotel de Paris and its lounge, which was as elegant as can be.

The next day, Denise and I toured the historic sites in Nice. But the most interesting thing to Denise was all those little stores full of shoes and clothes and jewelry, where she spent most of her time.

Still attracted to the playgrounds of the rich and famous, I had read about a restaurant outside of Monte Carlo that Roger Moore was seen at. It was a Greek restaurant, out in the open, with donkeys, goats, and chickens running around.

In the Greek tradition, one can show passion, warmness, and joy by the smashing of plates, with the accompaniment of music and song, along with the chanting of "Opa!" at the sound of a smashing plate. Greek nightclubs recreate this tradition to the great pleasure of the patrons.

Being August, the celebrity entourage was not around. At the table in front of us, eight Americans were dining, and they were apparently there as part of a business trip. The more they drank, the more plates started to fly.

They were throwing them into a fireplace and yelling, "Opa!" They were laughing and clowning around, and when they were getting ready to leave, when they got the check, you could have heard a pin drop—even the animals were quiet. Apparently the restaurant charged them for each plate they threw. They did not leave happy.

The final leg of the French Riviera was a trip to Cannes, St Tropez, and another of my rich and famous locations, Hotel du Cap. I had rented a convertible in Beiliue, and we started to drive toward the three places above. As we were driving, the freak-out was playing again. "Do you know where we are going? The signs are in French. I'm hungry."

I wanted to have lunch at the Hotel Du Cap, but within a half hour of getting there, the freak-out worked, and there were two restaurants together on the Mediterranean. I pulled in, and the place was packed. August is Europe's vacation month. Not one person spoke English, and of course we had a lunch that we did not enjoy.

Onward to du Cap. Denise, for whatever reason, tried to prevent the trip to du Cap from happening, asking, "Why are we going?" and insisting, "It is too late. What is the big deal? It will be all French." While I was driving, she would pester me: "Watch where you're going," or, "You can't read the traffic signs."

In spite of all the negativity, we arrived at the hotel. At the entrance, smoking a cigarette, was Kirk Douglas. Inside, there were beautiful people having a grand old time around a magnificent pool overlooking the sea and a very comfortable bar and restaurant area. Everyone spoke English. It would have been really nice to have lunch there, but a drink and the memory will do. The only other place we got to visit was St. Tropaz, with the pebbled beaches and topless women and cafés with dogs sitting next to you in a chair. On the way back, we visited Picasso's Riviera studio.

On a romantic interlude to Bermuda, I was apparently getting more and more concerned with what I was getting into by marrying Denise, As soon as we arrived, she was insecure as the beach was inhabited with several romantic couples; Denise assumed they were all on their honeymoon. It made her very uncomfortable. Back in the room, as usual, she avoided intimacy. However, she wanted to get a massage to help her relax.

While she was out, I had a hysterical realization that by selecting her, I had screwed up my life. In an uncontrolled fit of rage, I threw a chair, which landed on the coffee table, smashing it to smithereens.

Embarrassed at my behavior, nothing like that ever happened again.

For Christmas 1984, we went to Vail, Colorado. Denise, Wendy, Rich, Elyssa, Adam, and I flew into Denver and took a small plane from Denver to Vail. On the same plane was Scott Hamilton and the current Olympic ice skating team.

When we arrived at the condo I'd rented, Denise made sure that she had dibs on whatever she needed first. We stayed for two weeks in a condo with one bedroom and one bathroom. That was my first taste of Rich, as he slept with Wendy in a sleeping bag without any concern for me being there.

Vail. Quaint, rustic, snow-packed streets, great bars, beautiful people, great clothes. We had lockers by the slopes, where we kept our skis and boots, and we skied every day.

Denise was insecure because all the kids were good skiers, so she took lessons every day and skied with the instructor.

We ate out every night at whichever restaurants were the best. As the beginning of the future would have it, there was friction between Denise and the others. At the time, Elyssa was sixteen and a vegetarian. After sulking over various issues previously, at dinner she ordered salmon and then she did not want it and wanted to order something else. The request was denied, and full-time sulking ensued.

Elyssa was difficult, and I guess that was the last straw. I told her that if she didn't eat it, she would be on a plane back home. The threat was too harsh for the crime, but it was a festered anger from walking on eggshells every time she would sulk, which was very often.

Denise's entry into my life certainly set off Wendy's jealousy buttons, at least when it came to what I might be spending on Denise and not her.

(After all, it's all about money.)

On March 17, 1985, in the afternoon, Denise and I were married at Tam O'Shanter. Adam was the best man, Wendy and Elyssa were the maids of honor. A good time was had by all.

The next day, we left for our honeymoon. Having had two prior unhappy honeymoons, Denise was determined to have this one work.

We flew to St. Thomas, took a boat to the United States Virgin Island of St. John. The beaches and vegetation at Caneel Bay are the attractions that have made the resort's reputation as a place to get away from it all.

Though many of the visitors are honeymooners from Middle America, you can still run across a pop singer, a film star, a politician, or a chairman of the board. Aside from the beauty, you can avail yourself of sailing, wind surfing, scuba diving, tennis, or feeding the mongooses that come begging at mealtimes.

Denise did make it work. She was pleasant and cooperative. The week we were there was the longest period of time that Denise was not unhappy about something. We visited all the other little islands, including "Little Dix," and had an event-free, relaxing time.

1986

Denise was an excellent artist, and during our beginning years, she went to an art studio in Roslyn. She was very happy with that arrangement, as she did not feel inadequate when she was creating art. I set up a studio-type area in the house, but soon that was all history too.

One night, at a restaurant that had a piano, she was inebriated enough to play, and she had an entire repertoire of beautiful songs played magnificently. She never played again, and we even had a piano in the house.

She took golf lessons at the club and hit the ball very well; as soon as she saw anyone watching her, she would pick up the ball and not play.

Denise, during pregnancy, was pleasant and not difficult to get along with. One could theorize that while pregnant, there was no need to feel insecure? We went to Lamar's and set up everything for what we knew was a girl.

After being two weeks late and several false alarms,

on June 17th, 1986, Amanda Ashley Scheffler was born.

Having never been in the delivery room before, this was initially not a great experience. Amanda was born and had swallowed her meconium. The delivery room went into action and pumped out her lungs. She was brought to the critical area of the nursery and placed in an incubator with all kinds of tubes connected to her.

The doctors could never assure us of what the repercussions might be. To say the least, we were both devastated. I could not talk about it without crying except with Denise. When speaking with her, I tried to assure her that everything will be alright.

Fortunately, as time went by, we could see that Amanda was progressing as any infant would. Aside from huge hemangiomas on her face and body, she was fine. Those were outgrown by three.

Amanda grew up infrequently disciplined because anything I would do or say Denise would reverse. She was a very spoiled child. She was Denise's toy, dressed in the best. No one could come near her without a doctor's note.

We did all the same things with Amanda that I did with the other kids, but Amanda had lavish parties with hired entertainment and Mommy and Me, housekeepers, nannies: Patrice and then Gayle.

Amanda brought to me a reason to accept my unrequited love relationship with Denise. I loved having another little girl and enjoyed every moment with her.

Entitlement

Cause and Effect

It was painful in some respects to watch girls grow up, as they all seem to have difficulty with their friends. They pair up and then change, and invariably, mine are left out in the cold. It has given me a horrible feeling of inadequacy, as there was nothing I could do about it.

CHAPTER 16: PASSAGES

During the Christmas vacation of 1986, we went to Sugarbush without Rich, as I was trying to convince Wendy that she needed to date others before deciding on her mate for life. Unfortunately, it did not work. Rich sent flowers, called, and it was over.

Wendy and Rich were engaged, so I planned an elaborate engagement party at Tam O'Shanter. We had dinner with the parents of the groom, Morty and Eileen. When wedding plans started to surface, I told them that I would give them twenty five thousand dollars to do with what they wanted in regard to the wedding—the choice was theirs. First they were going to take the money, then it was going to be for the wedding, and then it was a Saturday night, black tie affair.

Explaining that a Saturday night black tie affair would cost a lot more than then money I had committed to and that I could not afford more, they assured me that Rich's father said he would contribute to the wedding. As plans were being made, and we shared many dinners with Morty and Eileen, nothing was being said about what he would contribute.

Denise confronted the situation by asking him outright. His response was that he would pay for the rehearsal dinner. I had no idea what a rehearsal dinner was about, and I nearly choked at the nerve of this guy.

In order to facilitate the economics, I told Wendy how many guests she was allowed in total for her, her mother, and her in-laws. When she tried to figure it out, it came down that she would only be able to satisfy their friends and her mothers' guests.

I told her that whomever wanted to invite more guests would have to pay for them. No problem. Morty had six couples that he was going to pay for.

The wedding was at Tam O'Shanter, and it was beautiful. But I made two mistakes. One: the divorce from Louise ended bitterly, and I was still angry, so I refused to walk down the aisle with her. I should have been more sensitive to Wendy's feelings, not my own.

The second mistake: even though Denise asked for Wendy's permission and got it, she wore a white gown to the wedding. I was too naïve in weddings, and although there were no repercussions, I should have prevented her from wearing that gown. But I had no one in my life that would say to me that this is about your daughter, not you, Denise, or your ex-wife. I would have agreed.

The wedding was over; they were on their honeymoon, and there had been no discussion of Morty paying for his guests. When I called to ask him, he said he thought it would be a nice gesture if he gave the money to the kids instead. I told him unfortunately that I had paid Tam O'Shanter all but his portion and that he would have to pay them directly.

Morty was quite a character. He was a nice-looking man who never really worked. Somehow he was administering the estate of a nursing home-housed relative for his income. He questioned every single thing he would think of buying or ordering in a restaurant. If you were waiting to order, you would get very impatient as the waiter would be with him for quite a while. His son had the same traits.

When we rented tuxedos for the wedding, we all went to the same place. He gave the rental guy such a hard time that the guy pulled me aside and said, "You sure you want your daughter to marry into that family?"

After the wedding, I got my first lesson in Married Daughter 101. My cousin had invited all of us to his son's Bar Mitzvah. Wendy said that she did not think she would go, and I explained that they came to all our affairs and that I would like them to be there.

Rich said no way. He complained that it was an hour's drive on a weekend and there was going to be too much traffic. I was about to flex my parental muscle and tell her, "You have to go," but it dawned on me that I no longer have parental muscle. I did not like it, but I told myself that I was no longer the guiding figure for my daughter, so I had to step back.

In their first apartment and for their first family holiday dinner, Wendy and Rich made Passover dinner for Denise, Elyssa, Adam, Amanda, Rich's brother, Bruce, and his girlfriend, Denise's mother and her boyfriend, my sister, Marilyn, and I.

A year or so prior, Denise's maternal grandmother had passed away. Wendy was serving and in the kitchen. My sister arrived and went to light a cigarette. They do not allow smoking in their house, which is understandable. But not to my sister. She went outside to smoke and would not come back. I sat outside in the car with her and finally convinced her to return.

Elaine, Denise's mother, after one vodka, was on her way to la la land. She started to cry about the fact that her mother was not there. She wasn't just sobbing and not excusing herself, she was just monopolizing the entire room and dinner, which was not unusual behavior for her. After a while, I asked her to please go inside or whatever, and it just got worse from there.

After the planning of our wedding, Wendy's engagement party and wedding, and Adam's Bar Mitzvah, Denise went into business as a party planner at the encouragement of our therapist and myself.

She did a good job, occupied her time, and it gave her some extra spending money and independence. I seeded the venture, replenished funds when necessary, and built an office in the garage, and it seemed to keep her in check for a while.

In 1986, an opportunity arose that under the circumstances was unlike any other as a divorced man, my ex-wife let my son move in to my home. It was a dream come true. Amanda was six months old, and Denise, Amanda, and I were living in our house at the Hamlet.

He had received some bad marks from school, and Louise was complaining that she could not control him. She was also complaining that the car she currently had was falling apart and I made her a deal. I would buy her a new car if she would let Adam live with me. Denise was not pleased, but this was nonnegotiable. Amanda had to have the bigger room, even though she was an infant.

The house was under the control of Denise and Patrice, our live-in housekeeper. I enrolled Adam in middle school, where he met friends with higher academic goals then he was used to. I watched his grades, went to open school night, gave him rules about hours of study, and bought him anything he wanted.

Adam had contracted the measles shortly after he moved in. Denise, in conjunction with her mother, was freaking out. She said, "Send him back to his mother, and let his mother take care of him." In addition to worrying about taking care of him was the possibility of Amanda catching it. If she had said, "Let's find out what we have to do to protect Amanda," I would have been fine.

But the cry from her and her mother was for me to give my son back to his mother to take care of. No F----N way! That is my son you are talking about. Eventually they shut up, and all was well.

Adam stayed out of Denise's hair and she stayed out of his. He went on to high school, and I made his room into a very comfortable teenage boy's room. He went to sleep away camp during the summers and kept his grades adequate.

On his 17th birthday, he received a brand new Mustang convertible, which was white with red upholstery. We then went through the SAT prep courses, which he completed and took the test twice with not much difference either time. But again, it was adequate enough to get into college.

Getting into college, as with my other children, meant working with a college advisor, Jordan Cohen, who would tell us the safe schools to apply to, the reach schools, and the schools that were a possibility. We went through all the normal things: a car accident, minor altercations, girls, guys.

As a father I think there was nothing else I could have done. Adam was a little on the short side, and I continually discreetly prevented people from kidding him about it. I wanted him to have the confidence along with my teaching to be very secure, and I wanted him to know that he could be whatever he wanted in this world.

During the summers, when not in camp, he worked with my men, learning the electrical business. After we traveled to the various colleges, the choice came down to Tulane on a normal degree or Boston, where he would enter as a teaching major, and then, after the first year, switch to business.

Embarrassed to enter as a teaching student, he chose Tulane.While he was a freshman in the dorm,

I woke up one Saturday and decided to surprise him: Denise, Amanda, and I flew down, surprised him, and spent the weekend there.

Shortly after that, Adam had decided that Tulane was comprised of either nerds or druggies, and since he was neither, he would really like to transfer to Syracuse, where his high school friends were. I said I had no problem with it but that he would have to do all the paperwork. He did, and he got in. The drawback was that I had to pay for a dorm room and that he wanted to stay in the frat house. So I paid for an empty dorm room and a shared frat room.

I visited often, befriended his friends, and gave him whatever money he said he needed. I am sure all his friends were telling him that his stepmom was a MILF.

Tried to get him to go to Europe for a semester in his junior year, he was not interested. He later decided to take his final semester in Florence, Italy. The program consisted of living with an Italian family, going to classes, and exploring Florence, Italy and Europe.

Denise, Amanda, and I visited him. We met in Rome, stayed at the Grande, saw the sights, drove to Venice, stayed at the Danieli, drove to a few other little towns and back to Florence to the Grand hotel. We visited all the historic sites in Florence, including Michelangelo's Tomb, the Statue of David, the countryside, and the central market.

Denise then dragged me across the Arno River, on the Ponte Vecchio Bridge, for an entire day, through all the jewelry vendors on the bridge, until she could decide what she wanted.

As we went from city to city, Adam met groups of his schoolmates who were also traveling. In Florence, we saw his apartment and met the lovely people he was staying with. It was a great feeling for me to have given my children the ability to experience these things at a young age to enhance their education in worldliness.

Entitlement

Cause and Effect

184

CHAPTER 17: OPPORTUNITY KNOCKS

With the clock ticking on the tenure of my M-rated union mechanics, I had to get into the marketplace that would accommodate the soon-to-be A-rated mechanics. I needed a gateway to the big leagues, which I felt I had to do to survive in the union world of intensely high cost and capital combined with poor production. I needed a superpower to survive.

Joanne, the employee that set up the lunch date with Denise, was originally hired because she had connections to some of the real estate developers in New York City. As luck would have it, we would be at the right place at the right time. I was introduced to an executive of Helmsley Spear who was in charge of awarding major construction projects.

At the time, he had just awarded two major projects that were currently being started to another contractor. The electrical contractor that was awarded those jobs was also working at Leona Helmsley's estate in Connecticut. Unhappy that she had been billed for the work he did, she threw the contractor out of all Helmsley properties, leaving these two projects up in the air.

My contact at the company said that the work was mine if I could match the prices he had from the other contractor. I obtained both jobs for over one million dollars each.

One job was the Helmsley Hotel on 42nd Street, where we furnished and installed a state-of-the-art fire alarm system. The other was the wiring of massive air conditioner chillers in the Empire State Building.

Aside from both jobs being profitable, the contacts I made with the Helmsley employees and the other trades kept me at those properties for over fifteen years.

I had nurtured, cultivated, and developed relationships with all the buildings, building managers, assistants, and top level execs, as well as accounts payable clerks, brokers, receptionists, secretaries, etc.

The other accounts I had were primarily general contractors, which required bidding against heavy competition for a small profit and waiting a long time to get paid. At Helmsley, I was family, so my profit was real and payment was swift.

This sort of arrangement is what I needed to survive in Local 3. I studied the process, learned who the right people were, and who my Rabbi would be. Once the charting was done, I started entertaining. I took my contacts to the hottest shows on Broadway and the best sporting events in town. We frequented the best restaurants, attended golf outings and Tony and Tina's wedding. I provided gifts. Boat excursions, weekly golf games. Whatever it took.

Every Christmas, we made a catered affair with themes, hot bands, great food, and entertainment. It all worked well. Prior to the Christmas party, my car would be filled with presents. I had someone else drive. I would deliver envelopes to each building manager and gifts to each secretary, bookkeeper, and receptionist. This took an entire day. For the next fifteen years, ninety percent of my income was work from Helmsley Spear.

Denise never stopped bitching. "Why do I have to go out with these people? I don't know them." Or, "How much is this costing? You should be spending that money on me." The complaints never stopped.

Denise would meet me in the city, with a limo picking her up, and it was like she was doing me a big favor by going. In fact, she felt I should pay her for her attendance.

The Empire State Building rented me a tiny space in the sub-basement. It was just for me, a space between appointments to make my calls and whatever I needed to do before going back to Queens.

Eventually, though, Manhattan was where the major portion of our work was coming from, so I rented a bigger space on a higher floor and made this my main office, as it made more sense. We outgrew that pretty quickly and ended up with corner offices on the 67th floor with a large office for myself and beautiful western and southern views. For those fifteen years, I enjoyed a lucrative and stimulating relationship with the Helmsley organization. All the executives had one goal, and that was to not let me get near Leona Helmsley. The reason was that all the other contractors that had come in contact with the "Queen of Mean" got barred from the organization. Not for any reason—just so she can keep her crown.

We had storage rooms, foremen, and electricians at 60 East 42nd Street, 420 Lexington Avenue, 230 Park Avenue, 25 West 43rd Street, 140 Broadway, 22 Courtland Street, 350 Fifth Avenue, and One Penn Plaza. In addition to those locations, we did the work for The Helmsley Palace, The Park Lane, The Windsor, The Helmsley Hotel, 112 West 34th Street, 1350 Broadway, 1412 Broadway, and 1400 Broadway. And many more.

Wein Malcom, who was Harry Helmsley's partner on various properties, started giving us work at their properties, too. Tishman Speyer hired one of the Helmsley Execs, and that started a relationship with them. Same for Swieg Weiler, Gould Properties, Emmes Realty, and SL Green.

At some of the more remote properties, I was awarded some major plumbing contracts with the major decorators such as George Anderson, Mario Buatta, and others.

We did the electric and the plumbing. Working with other trades on all these projects, we had IBM, Radio and Television Antennas, studios, the Democratic Convention.

The plumbing company I bought for ten thousand dollars with a volume of under twenty thousand dollars annually was now doing two million a year. Laurelton Electric was now doing twelve million, and the non-union electric company was doing one million.

CHAPTER 18: WEST HAMPTON

1987

We enjoyed a rental at the yardarm in West Hampton for the month of August. We had a two-bedroom apartment on the beach and enjoyed it. We decided to spend our summers in the Hamptons. The following year, we rented a room at the West Hampton Bath and Tennis Club from the owner from June 19th to September 19th.

The entire atmosphere was my kind of thing. The people were friendly. The restaurant, Star Bogs, a few blocks away, was on the beach with a great bar overlooking the beach and the ocean. It became at least a twice-a-week hangout for Denise and me.

We became friendly with the bartenders, the waitresses, the owner, and the musicians. In addition, there was always a table or two of people who lived at the Bath and Tennis. I would visit each table and joke around with everyone. I felt like and was considered the mayor of our community. It was a lot of fun.

The people were for the most part the same as the golf club members: all successful, down-to-earth, nice people. The Bath and Tennis itself was at one point a major playground for the Garment Center rich and famous. The units surrounded the pool and cabanas. Beyond the pool was the beach and the ocean.

Back in the day, the restaurant and the nightclub were swinging with drinking, dancing, and partying, in addition to a singles' bar in the lobby that had a line to get in on the weekends. It was directly across the street from a marina, which housed over one hundred boats. The marina had a two-story, motel-like building with forty more rooms called the "Boatel," and six hard, true tennis courts.

The property had gone co-op in the early '80s. When the homeowners took it over, the expenses were not as presented; the cost was prohibitive. The people without depth lost their units and most of the rich and famous abandoned theirs.

The remaining diehards would sit at the pool and reminisce over how the powerful men had their wives in the main hotel and their mistresses in the Boatel, which was across from the oceanside, facing the bay and marina.

In those earlier days, some of the bachelors would also employ prostitutes to stay in their suites for the day. As the men were sitting around the pool, when they saw one person leave the suite, the next in line would take his turn. The guys who were there during this period were twenty years older than me, but they were such characters and each one was a man's man.

I enjoyed their company. In the Boatel, there was a woman who was selling her unit, number 905. It was the only one there facing the marina and water that had two rooms plus a kitchen and a bathroom. I bought the unit for seventeen thousand and five hundred dollars and paid monthly maintenance of nine hundred dollars. We furnished it, we used it; it was fun to have.

Every year, there was a meeting of the Board of Directors. They reelected members and searched for new ones. Not having any new ones willing to get involved, the same members were always reelected. In the summer of 1989, the older guys kept teasing me about becoming a board member. In 1990, I did.

The Board members were the nicest bunch of guys, but the agenda was controlled by two men, a songwriter, Jack, and a lawyer, Bob (similar to the Senate and Congress).

They were spending all the money they had on legal fees to the lawyer's firm to fight the developer, who they felt had not been honest with the disclosure of the co-op perspective. My thoughts and experience to that date with the legal system was that you usually win when you're wrong and lose when you are right, and in the final analysis, only the lawyers win.

The property had such potential that I wanted to work on improving it. I wanted to go forward instead of trying to recoup the past. As opportunities arose to make improvements, the president, Jack, was opposed to everything. I have found that people in general, and especially groups of people on boards, let yesterday take up too much of today. This man was no exception.

He no longer lived there, but he had a unit, like Bob, that he rented out. Therefore, he had no real interest in the property. The Board members were very congenial, and whatever the two of them said, they agreed to. Bob was bringing his firm big money from the lawsuit with the sponsors. Jack, the song-writing president, was enjoying a leadership jolt for his ego. They could never lose an election because there were forty units that were not owned, and they decided that this group of votes was their proxy.

The only future the Bath and Tennis had was to get rid of them. I became friendly with three other owners who were of the same opinion. Together we campaigned to oust their leadership. It was a very emotional, controversial, and bitter campaign. Some of the residents were natural troublemakers. On the eve of the election, I realized that they were two-faced, and for the first time, I saw the possibility of losing.

The next day, the first thing we did was render the proxy votes illegal. When the votes were counted, there were two people assigned to enter the results. One for them, and myself for us.

Being computer-savvy, and with my laptop, I entered all the votes. It was done so fast that no one knew whether I was doing it correctly or not. I am sure that I was, but I was accused of being the Karl Rove of the time and manipulating the outcome.

We overthrew the Board, we each became an officer, and I was treasurer. We recruited one more owner, who wanted the same as us. We now had the necessary five votes to decide all proposals to the Board.

Through our high-level executive majority, we refinanced the mortgage and had four million to spend on renovations. We changed all the wooden decking to a lifetime-lasting, state-of-the-art vinyl. We installed a new pool, hired a new landscaper to redo the entire property, and fixed up the units that were owned by the co-op.

We signed a lease with a very popular local restaurateur to run the dining room. We had an outside bar and weekend barbecues. We lit the beach, opened a long-closed upper deck, hired musicians for Saturday and Sunday at the pool. We had a well-known architect design and build a new lobby and restrooms. The parking lot was re-designed to accommodate more cars on a keyed entry system. We purchased a bus so that employees of the restaurant and hotel could park elsewhere and be shuttled back and forth, computerized the entire operation to point-of-entry accounting, and advertised the Marina to the point of establishing a waiting list. We advertised the hotel to the point of being full. We changed the operation from spring and summer to year-round and established a beach club membership.

We also purchased state-of-the-art chaise lounges, umbrellas, and towels. We bought a tractor to groom the beach, hired a dock master and a hotel manager. We installed a playground to attract younger people. We were making money on the marina, the parking, the beach, the restaurant, and the hotel.

As treasurer, I produced a weekly cash flow analysis, which was always positive. We were able to pay all the maintenance expenses and our mortgage without increasing anyone's monthly expenses.

While this was all in the planning stages, I bought another suite on the oceanside that was directly in the center of the property, with views of the beach, ocean, and bay. We renovated it by designing the space similar to the inside of a yacht, utilizing and creating space with all new built-ins. It was an architectural masterpiece (in my opinion).

The unit cost seventy five thousand dollars and fifty thousand for the renovation. The unit next to it, number 207, also became available from a long-time owner living in the south of France. I bought that for twenty five thousand.

Two more units became available, one on the bay and one on the ocean, both owned by the bank. I called the bank, which was asking too much for them, and I suggested that the maintenance they were paying alone would eat up any chance of equity.

We agreed on ten thousand each; they accepted. I was labeled by the crowd as the" West Hampton land baron." The double suite I used for us. The other units were rented by the hotel, and I made a profit.

I encouraged a friend to buy a unit on the bay side for one hundred and ten thousand dollars. He sold it in 2006 for half a million dollars.

Some of the owners asked about having a lobster bake on the beach. The manager said that the fire department would not allow it. I never take a secondary source for something I deem important. I called the fire department. All we needed was a permit and to provide for the cost of paying a fireman to stay during the party.

Everyone had lots of fun.

Somewhere along the way, a customer had a picture of this beautiful old Mercedes convertible. It looked like a fun thing to have in the Hamptons. Figuring it would be too expensive, I asked its value. It was a kit car, a brand-new, shiny replica of a 1928 Mercedes, and it cost five thousand dollars. I bought it, used it for five years, and sold it for five thousand dollars.

The West Hampton Bath and Tennis was back on top. During my tenure, I tried to become active with the local politicians. When they were building the theater in town, I donated the ladies' room in our name. The plaque with Denise's and my name should still be there.

I tried to get close to the Rabbi, but I got the impression that unless you were a big time money man he would not waste his time. Still, I did sell thousands of dollars in ads for their annual Journal. I did donate the parking lot lighting.

1995

On the Saturday of the Fourth of July weekend, I stood on the upper deck that we had recently fixed up and opened. There were over one thousand people on the property, the beach was full, the pool was full, and the barbecue was full, as well as the bar and restaurant. The live music was playing, people were dancing, and everyone was having fun. The property values skyrocketed.

We did a hell of a job. The only reason we were able to get it accomplished was that we were all businessmen, and not lawyers or dentists or politicians. The five of us never disagreed. This was a Board like no other I have ever seen, and I have been on several. No egos or penny pinching. It was just five guys that had the same goal and the ability to learn and grow.

I was very proud since I was the catalyst; without my involvement, it never would have occurred. That project was a gratifying experience.

Boating is a really nice, fun, and romantic thing to do. I started too late in life. I did the golf club first and then boating. It should have been the other way around.

Denise convinced me to buy a twenty-five-foot boat from her beautician. We docked it at a marina in the Hamptons, and I immediately fell in love. The only problem was that the sea tow guy and myself were on a first name basis. I had no idea about the channel, the buoys, the low water, or the tide. As much fun as it was, I grounded the boat more times than not.

Denise was immediately afraid of the boat, and she was there to criticize whatever I did—similar to driving the car. The only thing we did with the boat was invite company and take it out for lunch.

Finally, Denise said that she would be happier with a bigger boat and that this one was too small. I bought a used thirty-four-foot Silverton, which had two engines instead of one, which made running the boat a whole new world.

The boat was docked in Freeport, Long Island, on the South Shore. I was now docking the boat at the Bath and Tennis on the North Shore. But for the grace of God, I got away with the dumbest thing I ever did. With Adam, I ran the boat at full throttle, thirty-five knots, through the Long Island Sound, around Montauk Point, Northport, Shelter Island, through the Locks, and on the inlet to the Bath And Tennis. One hundred and thirty five nautical miles over six hours. No map, no knowledge of the buoys, the channel, low water, rocks, instruments, etc. How we did not get killed is again by the grace of God.

The slip was across the street from our units. The boaters were great guys who were anxious to help and anxious to teach. I took the boat out every chance I got and kept docking it in my narrow, congested slip.

Eventually, learning how, and in addition to lunch, we explored Montauk, Shelter Island, and Greenport, but never alone. Denise would only force herself to go because other people were involved. She was afraid of this boat as well. Whenever we would dock it, she would go on deck and frantically yell instructions.

The following season I got into the big leagues. I bought a used forty-two foot Sea Ray, which was immaculate, with suites and TVs and all the bells and whistles that came with it. Never did I ever dream that I would own such a luxurious yacht. We used it the same way, except we did a couple of overnight trips to Montauk, Block Island, and Newport. Denise was still afraid and eventually lost interest, so I would run the boat by myself or just sit on the deck. I started out by saying how much fun and how romantic a boat is, which is true, but you need to do it with someone that wants to be romantic and have fun.

CHAPTER 19: A NEED TO RANT

1990: Tens of thousands of Chinese students took over Beijing's Tiananmen Square. General Manuel Noriega surrendered in Panama. Exxon Valdez sent eleven million gallons of oil into the sea, and after twenty eight years, the Berlin Wall was opened to the West.

For the past three years, 1990 included, we had rented a house in Windham, New York during the winter. Windham had a great family ski area. I realized early on in my life that the key to happiness was family. I wanted to do anything I could to make it easy and desirable for all my children to be with me. They all loved to ski. The house we had rented could accommodate everyone.

It was a very rewarding experience. Every Friday night, we would drive two hours directly to our favorite restaurant in town. We were always meeting people we knew from the ski area at dinner. The quaintness of the area, and the ease of the skiing, kept us going back for a total of three years. We had a locker at the base of the mountain where we kept our skis and boots. We had our favorite lunch and dinner places. Skiing is a wonderful family sport: it creates family togetherness all through the years.

We outgrew Windham, and our friend Ellen, Bruce's wife, wanted to rent in Stratton, Vermont. She had me convince Bruce, who did not want to drive the extra miles. I did. We all rented there, and it was a much better ski area with a gondola and a quaint little town at the base. The restaurants were better, and Amanda's ski school was much more professional.

Bruce and Denise were made for each other. Whatever she didn't complain about, he did. As I did every Christmas, before and after, I was enjoying the preparation for my family to be assembled.

Denise, as usual, was preparing to fuck it all up (not that she plans it). But the love, fun, and normalcy of family intimidates her, and one way or the other, she has to be the center of attraction.

Thus began the memory of Christmases past. Denise withdrew into herself and decided that Elyssa would be her target. First, she complained about Elyssa's room being sloppy. Then she complained that no one helps her clean, a comment that was directed at Elyssa. Everything Denise did or said was out of order. I had laid out all the scenarios before the vacation and told her to come to me with any problem; I would take care of them.

Denise never did any housework because we always had full-time help. She decided to vacuum and attack Elyssa, saying that if she didn't do it herself, it would never get done. I explained all she had to do was ask and we would all help. Fortunately everyone understood "that's Denise."

Elyssa had a male friend join us for a day. When he left, she asked Denise, "What did you think of my friend?" Denise replied, "Well, he's brighter then you." Elyssa handled her, and we went on.

Elyssa borrowed a sweatshirt of mine. Denise saw her in it and said to me, "I did not know your clothes were up for grabs." Outside of her little digs and complaining about skiing, her boots being too cold, too hungry, and being in space, we kind of ignored each other. But you could tell that the volcano was going to erupt. She tried not to, but whatever that force inside her was, it was apparent on her face and attitude.

Denise never lived in the present unless she was drunk; her happiness was always tomorrow or yesterday. I could never get it through my head that no matter what I did I could not change that fact about her.

One more day passed, and you could see that Denise just wanted the day to be over so she could get Amanda out of ski school because Amanda was her friend, and we were the enemy. After she had a drink with lunch, the stage was set. Denise had to get Amanda from school, but as previously arranged, Elyssa had already picked her up.

Our friends, Adam's friends, Elyssa, Amanda, and myself were all in the locker room. Denise came in, said hello, and Adam, who was eighteen at the time, informed her that he forgot to tell her that her mother called this morning. (They speak at least twice a day.) His little slip gave her an excuse. She yelled, "How can you do that? What if someone died? I'll forget to give you your calls!" She went on and on and on, and everyone just shrugged. "That's Denise."

As we were walking out of the locker room, Adam's friend told Denise that they had seen Amanda on the ski slope and that she wasn't happy. She said that Amanda was crying because she wanted Adam to take her to her mom. Denise turned to Adam and said, "How could you torture my child like that?" and she threw Amanda's knit hat at Adam. Adam threw it back and said, "What are you talking about?" Denise took the knit hat and viciously hit Adam over the head about four times and walked out. Our friend Bruce went to Denise and said, "How could you embarrass him like that?"

Elyssa went over to calm things down, and Denise threw a bunch of four letter words at her, saying that Adam needs a beating. I had walked away after she hit Adam and decided to deal with it later rather than putting myself through any more humiliation. It didn't work. Ellen came and told me that Denise and Elyssa were having a problem, and that Denise was having a fit. I went over and asked Denise, "What did you do now?" I told her that when the day comes that my kids are embarrassed to come to my house, it will not be a good day for our marriage.

When we got back to the house, she poured herself a drink, and that was it. She was ranting, raving, and banging doors; she kicked me in the foot so hard I thought she did damage.

Amanda, who was four years old, followed her around and begged her and cried, "Please, Mommy don't fight." I had to just take it all, as any further communication would not turn out well.

As scheduled, Elyssa left for New York and Adam departed with his friends. I started to evaluate my life and my marriage, asking myself, "What do I get out of this marriage?"

A social companion? When I am being social, she is annoyed; anyone we go out with is "provocative," and everyone has more money or has more children. Or has a healthy mother. Everyone has more than she does, and they all provoke her.

A caring wife? It was New Year's Day; I was the one awake with the intercom near me so that when Amanda awakens, I would be able to take care of her and let Denise sleep. This was our marriage: I take care of Denise. I made every day as easy as I can for her. How many times do you think, within a year, that she did the same for me? That she lets me sleep, or makes breakfast and says, "I will call you when it's ready."

There was never a birthday, a Valentine's Day, or a Mother's Day or any occasion that was not filled with flowers, gifts, and surprises. If I ever asked her to pick up or drop off something in her daily travels, the response was always: "Not today."

A financial partner? On Monday, she would say she understands our financial situation and on Tuesday she'd tell me that her wardrobe is inadequate and that my kids are too expensive.

A sexual partner? To have the pleasure of a man and woman bound as one in a moment of sheer pleasure, rapture, and love: this didn't even happen once. Even laying in each other's arms was nonexistent.

Someone to share my problems with? No f—n way. I tell her a problem, small or large, and it either falls on deaf ears or is later used to attack me in some way.

There is nothing that Denise finds enjoyable while she is doing it, whether it is sex, golf, skiing, or dinner. After the fact, she thinks back and says, "That was fun."

My marriage to Denise was nobody's fault but my own. Denise let me know who she was from the very beginning. Her beauty and youth overwhelmed me. My own impression of my ability to change her was where I went wrong. I confirmed all my feelings with my psychologist, Bob, who championed my thoughts and pushed me in the direction I wanted to go.

Bottom line was that the decision was mine, and I made it. I believed and still do believe that exceptionally good-looking women, on average, do not live a wholesome, happy life. Many times I watch a movie on television that was made twenty years ago or more, and there is a beautiful young woman in it. I go online to find out what her life was like, and I would approximate that ninety percent had a very hard way to go.

Denise experienced a bad relationship with her mother, a bad relationship with her first husband, and a second marriage she probably never should have had. All of the dating in between was not filled with any sincerity, and with the insecurity and ego of each partner, I believe that she never experienced the security of true love.

Therefore, I thought that once we were married and she had the security of a child and my love for her she would trust me, my love, and our life together.

It just cannot be done, and once I found out that I was wrong, there was no turning back. I knew then, as I know now, that I would not have been better off leaving her, as it was hard enough merging my first family with my second. Whatever I might have gained from being away from her would not be worth what I would have lost in family life.

On our first date, I arrived with my Mercedes convertible. On our second date, I hired a limo. I was not trying to pretend that I was something that I was not. After those two dates, I explained that I earn well, but spend as much as I earn, and therefore there was no real financial depth.

But at that point, I was already totally taken in. I was in love with her from the second I saw her. There is nothing I wouldn't have done and didn't do to make her happy. And even with all she put me through, I was not prepared to leave, as the family as a whole is much better than the family in parts.

The ski boots I left in the driveway, in my anxiety, that she berated me for, even though I was buying her a new pair.

The anger over the anniversary waltz I had played.

The drama of her fall in Las Brisas.

The drama of her reaction to Bactrim.

The berating after I forgot my camera.

The insinuations of age.

The insinuations of physique.

After being out to dinner and drinks, we would come home. I would get into bed and put on the TV. She would go to the dressing room and take off her makeup. She would not emerge from the room until I fell asleep. If I managed to stay awake, she would have the proverbial headache, or tell me not tonight, or say, "I like the morning better."

She would do anything in the world to avoid intimacy, and that was not just with me. That was her pattern in the past, as well, as we had discussed.

Shortly after she had moved in with me at North Shore Towers, these avoidances created feelings of unrequited love within me, thereby decreasing my adoration of her.

The tooth extraction, where my druggist couldn't believe the dramatics of the pain she was displaying for one tooth.

The fact that she would not give her father a break, even though he was a loving, nice guy.

The fact that the trip to Bermuda was no more than a massage for her.

In the very beginning of our courtship, Tam O'Shanter had a very active bar. At the end of the golf round, we would all hang around the bar and have fun. Tam O'Shanter had a great membership of really down-to-Earth people, and for a period of time there, when I was at the bar, I was in the center of jokes going back and forth across the oval bar, and a lot of nice, clean fun.

On one of those occasions, Denise became intimidated because she felt that I monopolized the surroundings. Of course, she was drinking, and her anger was so intense that when we left to go elsewhere for dinner she got out of the car while it was moving and would not get back in.

I thought of just leaving her there, but I was afraid for her safety. Eventually she got in.

When we first moved in to the Hamlet, she complained that the other women did not talk to her because she did not have a child. I would throw block parties on holidays so she could make friends.

After Amanda was born, the Mommy and Me and the play dates did not happen often as the girls seemed to shy away from Denise. Could be because she complained about everything to everyone.

We had a birthday party every year for Amanda. For some of the parties, all our friends were invited. For others, the neighbors or school companions. Then and now, she embarrassed Amanda by yelling at her whenever her friends were around, which I kept asking her not to, to no avail.

In the beginning years, as a carryover from her childhood, when she got upset enough, Denise would go in her closet, curl up on the floor, and suck her thumb.

We were invited, along with a whole group of neighborhood friends, to a golf club dinner. Denise was intimidated by one of the couples, and she was taking it out on me. In front of the entire club, she threw an entire glass of wine in my face. That same evening, when we got home, I was angry, and she was drunk, and she went to hit me as she often did. I grabbed her wrists and prevented her from hitting me; she called the police. This was before O. J. Simpson's wife was murdered, when the police used their own common sense to resolve a domestic dispute.

When Denise was one month pregnant with Amanda, all I heard throughout the week was that I was not happy enough that she was pregnant.

We had a ski weekend planned at a bed and bath in Windham, and while there, I was informed by answering machine that my controller, my licensed plumber, and lead plumbing foreman, had resigned to open their own business.

My head was filled with every emotion you could imagine. I asked Denise to just leave me alone for a while so that I could digest what this meant to me and figure out what I had to do to limit the damages. She refused to understand in any way, saying, "We are on vacation. You should not be working. You ruin everything."

Father's Day, every year, was spent in the Hamptons. The kids would come for the weekend and stay over. There was not one Father's Day that Denise did not make about her. And she would spoil it for me and everyone else. She just could not stand that the attention was not on her.

On the way home from the Hamptons on Sundays, Amanda and I wanted to go to Matteo's for dinner because it was the neighborhood hangout. Aside from good food, you ran into all your friends and neighbors. Denise would always say no, that she would not go because her hair is a mess or her outfit is no good. None of it true, but she wasn't the center of attention at these surroundings.

One night, after Denise had been at her art studio, we were in Roslyn having dinner. Denise had a few drinks, and she got nuts about something. She called my son Adam, who was thirteen at the time, at home to tell him in her drunken stupor that his father is an asshole.

One day we were on the boat coming from lunch, and I did not realize that you had to reduce your speed to five knots while going under a bridge. One of our guests and a friend of ours was an attorney and one of his clients was the police department of Suffolk County, where we were. The sirens went off. My friend said, "Let me do the talking." The police boarded our boat, and he started to talk. Denise butted right in—she just could not stay out of it. The officer left after giving us a warning.

One Monday night, we went to Star Bogs in West Hampton, a few blocks from our place, as we always did for the lobster dinner. We went to the bar, and as usual, we had a few drinks. Denise decided she did not want to eat there because she felt like having a pizza. I drove around on a Monday night to all the places, and they were closed. On our way through Quogue, it started to drizzle very lightly.

Denise decided I should have my wipers on, and she leaned across the steering wheel to turn them on, causing me to swerve slightly. I was pulled over by the police car behind me. They told Denise to stay in the car, as they were putting me through a field sobriety test.

Denise jumped out, cursed them out, and yelled, and of course I spent the night in jail. They told her that if one more word came out of her mouth, she too would be arrested; that did not stop her. Fortunately for her, the officer ignored it.

Denise was insecure around anyone that might be more educated then her; she was so possessed by her insecurity that she never listened to anyone and then always wondered why she was not heard.

With all the therapy she had gone through, trying to not be like her mother, she was a carbon copy, if not worse. When the two of them were together, there was always a fight or a scene.

She still received jewelry for every occasion. She had the best clothes and the best vacations. Her own Mercedes, long stem roses, and more.

Her grandmother's boyfriend worked for me her mother's boyfriend worked for me. The expenses for her grandmother's and her father's funeral were mine. The expense for whatever family dinner or occasion there was also mine.

The fact is that Denise does not know what love is. She said that she loved me, and she probably believed it. But the truth was that she loved me because I adored her. If I had a need for anything from her, I was out of bounds, and if that made me adore her less, then she hated me more.

We took a ski trip with Amanda to Park City, Utah, and stayed at the Leif Erickson Hotel. It was great skiing, but Denise had to stop every five seconds to adjust her boot or glove or socks. It did not make it fun for me.

We were married for five years, and other than my little beautiful daughter, I had nothing but a terrorist with a vest bomb that could explode anytime and anywhere, in the presence of anyone.

I explained to my psychologist the unhappiness of my plight, but that I would not go through another broken family. He suggested that there were many married women in the world with the same feelings. He suggested I find one and have an affair.

Entitlement

Cause and Effect

208

CHAPTER 20: EXPANDING HORIZONS

January, 1991: Professor Anita Hill accuses Judge Clarence Thomas of sexual harassment

THE FRIARS' CLUB

The New York Friars Club was having a membership drive. Some of the Bath and Tennis people were members there. They encouraged me to join, which I did, and it was another great experience. During every lunch there, a celebrity would be around, and cocktails at five would be in a very elegant setting. The elegance was old but true; it was a very fun time.

At the height of my businesses, we would have a meeting there once a month to review each department's progress and the plans for the future. The purpose was to have the department managers want to be a part of a company that had these types of perks.

March 1991: FIFTY

I had two parties to celebrate, my fiftieth birthday, One at La Busola in Glen Cove and one at the Three Clock Inn in Stratton, Vermont.

April 1991: GARZA BLANCA

On the way to Puerta Vallarta, Denise and I stopped at the French Quarter of New Orleans for about three days. We stayed at the Royal Sonesta Hotel on Bourbon Street. I had been there fifteen years prior, and it was not as honky tonk then as it was during this trip. But, it was still New Orleans, with the music and the food and the quaintness. The morning daiquiris, the scones, the famous dinner restaurants, and a great feeling of comfort.

From there, we went to Puerto Vallarta. At the time, they had a hotel on the beach called Garza Blanca. It was a magnificent, romantic place, with a beautiful beach, reception and lounge area, and an open restaurant on the beach. On the mountainous side, cottages with private pools.

We went up into the mountains to a well-known place called Chico's for lunch. After a few margaritas and the view, Denise was feeling no pain. She drove the Jeep back to the hotel laughing and singing. That was the happiest that I had ever seen her before or since. We had dinner by candlelight on the beach; the rooms had the little green salamanders hanging around, mostly on the ceiling. Every night when we would get into bed Denise would freak out about them. Need I say more?

The place closed; I do not know why. I miss it. It was a very special place.

1991: JOAN RIVERS

We were awarded a Job on 62nd Street and Fifth Avenue. It was a penthouse apartment that spanned the three top floors. The owner was Joan Rivers. Joan was moving back to New York from LA, as her husband had passed away recently. She had very specific tastes. I took her to some lighting showrooms, we had lunch, and she was very adamant about her switches, receptacles, plates, and dimmers being exactly as she had in LA.

Denise and I were scheduled to go to LA in a month or so, and so I arranged with Joan Rivers to go to her house in Beverly Hills to see what she had so we could copy it. When we arrived, Patrice, Amanda, Denise, and I were escorted to a den that was loaded with memorabilia. There were photos of Joan Rivers with presidents, movie stars, and world-famous dignitaries

When Joan came in, she said hello to me, looked at Patrice (who was very young and African American), and said, "You must be the wife," and then turned to Denise and said, "You must be the nanny," and it was very cute.

From there, we went on to La Joya, Laguna Beach, Palm Springs, and San Diego. We visited her dad in San Diego. He had a nice home, a big piece of land, horses, and kids. He was a warm and friendly guy.

As the job for Joan was being installed, we visited her backstage in Atlantic City. Denise took her girlfriends to her television show, and they had the best seats there. The electrical installation was not going well because the head mechanic was enthralled with Joan, and he was more interested in being her friend than doing the job.

He was removed and another foreman was brought in to get the job done. The original head mechanic told Joan that he was being replaced and made her think that without him none of it would come out right. She called me at home and blasted me with four letter words that would make anyone cringe, emphasizing that I was f-----g her over.

I explained that I would not be good at going in front of a live audience and keeping their attention. That is what she was good at. What I am good at is running my business in a proper manner in which everyone is satisfied. That explanation satisfied her, and the job was completed. We were doing work for her for a few years afterward and then we lost track of each other.

1992: ST. BARTS

St. Barts, to me, is the most romantic place that I have been to. On our first trip there, we had lunch every day on the beach with lobster and champagne and topless women walking by.

We drove our dune buggy up to the mountains.A hotel there had a bar where you could capture the magnificent view. The clothing store in town, Bernard's, was owned and operated by two charming gay guys, and they had all designer clothes at discounted prices. We picked out and bought an extensive wardrobe for Denise. We rented a half share of a catamaran for the day. When we got aboard, the other half was a gay couple. This was virgin territory for me, but it was a lot of fun joking with them.

We stayed at the best hotel, with a room adjacent to a suite with a pool. You could not see the pool or the room, but you could hear the occupants in the pool and in the bed. That was it for me; Denise could not handle it, so no sex for me. Same exact thing happened in a Paris hotel.

On several occasions we spent time in St. Martin before or after St. Barts.

The French town of Marigot and Grand Case have the best French restaurants I have ever been to, and that includes Paris.

CHAPTER 21: A DEAL THAT COULDNT BE REFUSED

1993: Bill Clinton was elected president. The best song was "Unforgettable," by Natalie Cole with Nat King Cole, and federal agents besieged Texas Branch Davidian.

We planned a trip to Florida to go to Disney World prior to Boca. The trip was based around us getting into the Hoop-Dee-Doo Revue, which everyone said, "Do not miss." It is hard to get tickets. I booked the four of us for the show and four nights at the Yacht and Beach Club Resort. Denise, Adam, Amanda, and I left for Disney World. At the allotted time and place, we went over to the Fort Wilderness Island. The prior show was in progress.

We had reserved seats, and since there was a bar next to the theater, we went there rather than wait in line for an hour. We went into the bar and relaxed. When it was getting near to show time, we went outside. While waiting in line, I could see that there was a problem. The line was not moving and people were getting upset. I told my group to wait—I will be right back.

Went to the front, said I was already seated, and walked in, and I realized they were completely full and overbooked the show. Of course I was angry, but while anger might make me feel better in the moment, I was still being shut out of what we specifically came for. I looked all around the dining room and the only thing that I could figure was the serving trays they had on stands all along the side. I went out, got everyone, walked over to where we could see perfectly, and told them to wait. I brought over four trays and four chairs, squared off the trays into a table, positioned the chairs, and told everyone to sit down.

Several waiters passed us separately as they were serving and said, "Sir, you cannot sit there." I ignored them; however, no one was coming over to serve us. Finally, a manager came by and said, "Sir, you will have to get up, you cannot sit here." I reacted with, "You better get a f---n army, pal, because I am not leaving." Ten minutes later, another manager came over and said, "Sir, how may I assist you?" I said, "You can assist me by leaving me alone and by finding someone to serve us." He said, "Very well, sir," and we had a grand old time.

Denise even participated in the show. The only one that was afraid of my threat was me. I do not engage in any physical confrontations because the person I prevent from getting hurt is me. I shall not be denied. Never did I think that they would associate a name with the incident or even remember it the next day.

When we returned to New York, I felt I had to write and advise them that what they did was wrong. I explained that we ordered tickets months in advance, and were very upset at the way we were treated. In addition I would inform a shame on you program for their disregard for their patrons.

The letter was addressed to Michael Eisner; I was sure it would be tossed, but, certainly they would have no way of knowing what did happen in the dining room.

Thus, their response:

DISNEY, FORT WILDERNESS RESORT

January 20th, 1994
Mr Michael Scheffler
330 Doral Court
Jericho, NY 11753
Dear Mr. Scheffler:

Thank you for taking the time to write Michael Eisner regarding the recent fiasco you experienced at the Hoop-Dee-Doo Revue. When we were forwarded your letter, it was easy to recollect the incident you described. It is a situation that is nothing remotely resembling normal operating occurrences and certainly not an experience we would ever want to put any of our guests through. **Although I admire your ingenuity in expanding our dining room capacity,** I must apologize for creating a situation that made that necessary.

We obviously didn't provide you with an enjoyable Disney experience and therefore are refunding the cost of your tickets for the show. Although this doesn't change the experience you had to endure, we hope you will view it as a gesture of our genuine concern. Your check will be sent through our accounting department, please allow four to six weeks for it to arrive at your address.

Please feel free to contact me at (407) 824 2745 if I can be of any further assistance now or on any future visit at WALT DISNEY WORLD. Mr Scheffler, we strive to provide pleasant, efficient experiences for all of our guests and when we fail to do this, we are greatly displeased. Please accept our sincere apologies for the dissatisfaction we caused.

Sincerely

Mark J. Smith
Asst. Restaurant Manager
Pioneer Hall Complex

After Disney, we spent a rainy Thanksgiving vacation in Florida at the Boca Beach Club. With little to do in the rain, we went looking at all the beautiful homes in luxurious communities. Realizing that Christmas vacations were becoming very expensive, as the family was growing and more rooms were needed, it made more sense to buy one of these and have the family come there every Christmas and any other time rather than continuing to spend on our very costly Christmas vacations.

We bought a modest house in Addison Reserve. While it was being built, we met with the decorator and furnished it with built ins, furniture, and accessories. The place was magnificent. On the golf course with our own pool and spa. The community had elegant tennis and dining facilities, immaculately manicured landscapes: a nice place to call home.

Throughout 1995, the Florida house was built and decorated and became magnificent. The prior year we had been at a dinner party hosted by a new friend. It was so elegant and was topped off after dinner by an illusionist from Miami. He entertained us for about an hour. To celebrate our Florida home, I made a party with a three-piece band, the same illusionist, an Italian buffet, a bartender, and servers.

It was a Great Gatsby moment

DOUBLE JEOPARDY

Some of our friends planned their wives' fortieth birthday parties, but Denise had informed me not to do that for her because she could not face being forty. I decided to make a surprise ten year vow renewal, combination thirty-nine year birthday party instead.

It was at the Friars' Club in New York. They could only accommodate one hundred people, therefore I invited one hundred people. We had plans to meet a customer and his wife for dinner at the Friar's.

When we arrived at the club, the four of us took an elevator to the 2nd floor. When the door of the elevator opened, one hundred people yelled surprise. The surprise was perfect.

After an hour of drinks and appetizers, Wendy and Elyssa led her into the locker room, where a rented wedding dress was waiting. She changed, and I changed into a tuxedo. Up to the wedding dress, Denise knew nothing of the renewal of vows.

We escorted her into another room where all the guests were seated. I had hired a rabbi, rented a huppah, floral arrangement, and video equipment. During the ceremony, the video of our original wedding was playing on both sides of the room.

After dinner, when the cake came out to celebrate both occasions, I arranged for my daughters to present her with ten dozen roses.

The only thing that did not work out was that I had white heels and a white bra to be delivered with Gail, our housekeeper, who was bringing Amanda and those items. As Gail was about to be picked up, she called and asked if she really had to go. I said no, forgetting about the clothes, and that was the only imperfection of the evening.

After about two days of enjoying the aftermath, she was back to herself, accusing me of making the party for me and not for her.

Entitlement

Cause and Effect

218

CHAPTER 22: WHERE DID I GO WRONG?

Elyssa was definitely the recipient of the middle-child syndrome, even though she was the second child at that time. My work schedule, when Elyssa was born, was intense. As an infant, I never spent the same quality time with her that I had spent with Wendy. It was just a circumstance of life, but even so, I am sure it is difficult for a middle child to understand.

At some point, Elyssa became difficult; I am not sure when it happened. She never cleaned her room. She would sulk at the slightest suggestion of anything she did not like, while Wendy took the discipline that was given to her, stuck her finger up when you weren't looking, and did what she wanted.

Elyssa wanted to know why and why not, and she was emphatic about asking. At one point, Elyssa said a four letter word, and I washed her mouth out with soap. That was probably too harsh. Wendy said a lot worse, but always under her breath so we wouldn't hear.

One of the girls caused a fight in school, and Elyssa was the victim. I took her over to the girl's house and made sure the mother understood that this was not to happen again.

Elyssa was a Bat Mitzvah in a more financially-pressed time for me, but she still had a beautiful affair at the Oceanside Country Club. She studied at Temple Hillel as the other children did. Elyssa was loved and adored by everyone for her intellect, charm, and beauty, but these traits were displayed only for outsiders. The Rabbi was so enamored with her that they wanted her to continue her Jewish education in a Hebrew high school.

Entitlement

Cause and Effect

Elyssa was a little overweight. I tried to do whatever I could, being cognizant to be sensitive, to convince her to take it off for her health and appearance.

She was also on a weekly schedule with a psychologist for several years, which was something she wanted and that I was happy to provide. Being more intelligent than most of the people who surround you is problematic.

One Father's Day, we went to the club for dinner. At the bar there were peanuts, which Elyssa took. I said, "Do you really need those?" and that was it. She sulked in the ladies' room for the next hour, stating how she hated her father.

By the time of her Sweet Sixteen, her mother and I were separated. The party was nice but awkward for me, and I am sure it was awkward for her as well.

As she got older, she worked for me part time, as well as at a shoe store. She always felt cheated in the sense of not getting enough money. All the money she earned, as well as her charm and personality, she spent on her friends.

Elyssa was like me in that regard: she was very insecure about being loved. When she could, she bought love and affection by money and charm. The difference is that I continued that persona for everyone, my family included, she did not.

There were periods of time that she may have experimented with the wrong things. Although I am not privy to the exact facts, I pieced it together and fortunately a crisis was averted. I knew she was smoking, but assumed it was a phase that she would grow out of. I made believe I did not know to see if nature would take its course, and it did. She never studied, was out of school often, and still maintained decent grades.

Entitlement

Cause and Effect

Elyssa had a natural intelligence and was able to retain facts and vocabulary easily. She was very rebellious until she left high school.

With her good grades and excellent SAT scores, and the help of the college advisor Jordan Cohen, Elyssa had a choice of many decent colleges. She and I flew, in small and large planes, and drove around the country to examine the schools and make a choice. Washington University in Saint Louis was selected.

She also received a brand new car for her 17th birthday with a gas credit card to go along with it. She too had share houses in the Hamptons every summer between school years. In her junior year at Washington University, she opted to study for a semester in London.

We were spending Christmas vacation at the Acapulco Princess, and Elyssa was leaving from there to New York on route to London. On line for beach chairs, I heard a British accent. I befriended the family, of which the daughter was Elyssa's age, and introduced them. She immediately had a friend abroad.

In addition, I had relatives in London from my grandmother's side who I knew of and had never met. I notified them of Elyssa's arrival; they invited her many times to their home for dinner. The English family from Acapulco also took her out and had her as a house guest.

Denise, Amanda, and myself visited Elyssa and took her to Paris with us. Elyssa was never verbal about any relationship with a guy, and knowing Elyssa, you always had to walk on eggshells. I never pushed the issue.

The only thing I ever said to my children about their future spouse was when they asked if I would be upset if they did not marry someone Jewish. I said, "Marriage is such a difficult relationship under normal circumstances that the element of religion would make it that much more difficult." But the final decision was always theirs.

Elyssa had returned from Europe with a male friend. He was an equally intelligent young man of Indian descent and was very dark skinned; he had dinner with us many times. Elyssa had my full blessing.

Finances at this time were difficult. Aside from her car on campus, tuition, and her allowance, I took advantage of the supplemental college loans. Elyssa had several in her name, but probably no more than $15,000 total.

After Washington University, Elyssa traveled all through Europe with her friends. When she returned, she gave me a journal of her everyday thoughts and experiences. At the conclusion of this rewarding writing, she wrote the following, "This is what I've brought you, Daddy, from my time abroad. It is the only way that I can let you know how much all you've brought to me matters, also it keeps you with me in my time away. I thank you, I miss you, but most of all I love you."

The only thing that changed from then to now is that I am not as affluent.

(Is it or isn't it all about money?)

Through the years, there was something about a comforter that I did not get her, a payment on her Amex card that I was late in paying, as well as those college loans.

She was accepted to Adelphi for grad school, which I believe I had something to do with. I rented an apartment near the school for her.

She graduated with a Doctorate in Clinical Psychology and did her residency in a hospital near the city. I then rented her an apartment on 57th Street.

1988

Some of the nicest people I had the good fortune of meeting were a couple on a cruise: Elaine and Leon. The friendship blossomed, and we planned a trip together with our respective families for Christmas.

Wendy and Elyssa could not get as much time off so we planned a trip to meet Elaine and Leon for one week in Puerto Rico with everyone, and then Denise, Adam, Amanda, and I would join Elaine and Leon and their family on a cruise.

Elyssa, who was twenty at the time, needed clothing for the cruise. She and I went to Bloomingdale's in New York. We searched the racks and found many pieces that she liked, and many pieces that I liked. I have found that even though I may fall in love with a garment, in order to marry it, you have to see how it looks on you.

We took all the garments to the dressing room. There were two dressing rooms, one on each side of a large three-sided mirror, facing the mirror fifteen feet away was a couch where I could sit and signal my approval or rejection.

One by one, Elyssa tried each garment on, came out to the mirrors, and I gave my opinion about how it looked. While Elyssa was trying on and going back and forth, there was another young lady about the same age with her mother, standing next to her at the mirror doing the same thing.

Elyssa would come out and wait for the mirror, stand in front of it, and then I would say yes, no, or maybe. She would then go back in the dressing room for the next piece. The other girl had been waiting for the mirror, and then she would get in front and look at her mother for approval and then through the mirror would look at me. I gave either a thumbs up or thumbs down. She went with my opinion, everyone got a kick out of it, and we left.

When we got to Puerto Rico, we met the other family at the pool. Their son, David, was recently engaged and was in the chaise lounge. His fiancé was face down, sunning herself, when she turned over to be introduced. Guess who? The girl from Bloomingdales! Now, that was fun.

Denise, Adam, Amanda, and I and their family left on the cruise; the rest of the family went home. Adam hung out with our friends' daughter, David and his fiancé hung out with us.

Elyssa, having dated many but liking none, spent her summers in the Hamptons at a share house with college friends . She reconnected with an old college friend, Steve. He was a great guy, but was a little slow in taking charge.

After months of Elyssa telling me they were going to get engaged, I feared that she may be wasting her time. I kept asking, "When?"

Finally she said she was pretty sure it would happen on Valentine's Day. Valentine 's Day came and went, and I said, "What did you get for Valentine's?"

"A cell phone," she said.

I was in shock. A cell phone is a nice, practical gift, but not romantic for someone you are about to become engaged to. My subtle, unimpressed feelings of her gift must have resonated as shortly thereafter they were engaged.

As with Wendy, an engagement party of the same magnitude emerged. In planning the wedding, I was advised that the groom's family would contribute. When it came time to collect I was told, "His parents could not believe how much was owed for college loans, and they decided to pay those instead." I got screwed again.

No matter what my financial position was, I made sure all my kids had the same lifestyle. What I cannot believe is that at the time I actually felt guilty for her having those loans. Certainly if I were in the position, I would have paid them.

Entitlement

Cause and Effect

226

CHAPTER 23: SWEET SMELL OF SUCCESS

1995: DENISE # 2

Adam had met his future wife Denise (same name) at the end of 1995. The Florida house was finished. Adam, Denise, and their friends spent Valentine's weekend of 1996 there, and were all duly impressed with the entire facility.

1995: OPTIMISTIC ROMANTIC

Denise and I came home from a friend's daughter's Bat Mitzvah, and a rare opportunity to make love occurred. During this momentous occasion, Denise said something and (being a hopeless romantic) I thought I heard sweet whispers of love. But, no, she was quick to correct my selective hearing and inform me that she was saying, "I am not wearing my diaphragm."

On February 19, 1996, Jordan Robert Scheffler was born,

Thankfully there were no complications. Gayle was our housekeeper and nanny at the time; Adam was living in the city. Jordan had his own room and on March 10, 1996, three days after my fifty-fifth birthday, we made a brunch in celebration of Jordan's birth and bris at Tam O'Shanter. My two sisters responded to the invitation:, as follows

Feb 24, 1996,

Dear Michael,

We want to congratulate you and Denise on the birth of your son! However, since we would not feel comfortable attending the festivities of March 10th- We still want you to know that we love you very much and will always be here for you.

Your loving sisters, Marilyn & Karen

To this day I have no idea as to why. Were they judging me having another child at my age, or was there something else I did not know about? Either way it was just a continuation of unrequited love.

1996: THANK YOU MR. TRUMP

Helmsley Spear had a ninety-nine year lease on the Empire State Building. The owners of the property and the building negotiated the deal with Harry Helmsley and Wein Malcom. It was not a lucrative deal for the owners, so their estate sold it to a group of Japanese investors who were convinced by Donald Trump that he could cancel the lease on the basis of inadequate maintenance.

Trump started a lawsuit, and of course it was highly publicized along with the shots at the queen of mean, Leona Helmsley, who had recently received the bad publicity she deserved.

Helmsley and Malcolm were not about to give up their prized possession, however. One of the causes of the suit was that there was no state-of-the-art fire alarm for the building.

Helmsley put out a bid to furnish and install the alarm, and I was the second bidder. The job was let to someone else. The lowest bidder got cold feet, realized that he might have bid too low, and withdrew; I was awarded the job by default.

Every week there was a job meeting to review the progress among the building managers, the equipment provider, the mechanical contractor, and us. Trump escalated his suit. Helmsley panicked, and they wanted that alarm system in within ninety days; an impossible task unless we worked around the clock.

That is what we did: three shifts with forty men on each shift, paying overtime rate for two shifts. All at an hourly rate billed and paid weekly. This was my one-in-a-million chance, being in the right place at the right time. It was a very lucrative project

That same year, a social acquaintance, Jay, was filling my head with talk about what a great businessman he was, and saying we should go partners. I was always looking for another place for backup for when I could no longer juggle the finances of the electrical business and have the security that would carry me through my retirement years.

He had an electrical device that automatically cut the electrical power at the source when anyone came in contact with the circuit. The inventor showed it, and I believed in it, and other electrical suppliers all had interest, but we never were able to move it further.

Next, he took me to Brooklyn and Queens, where two bakeries made this large-sized, fresh, soft pita bread that was absolutely delicious. His idea was to open a store with the bread rolling off the baking line and the customers taking the bread and filling it with all healthy salad ingredients that were at the salad bar. I thought the potential was unbelievable with the focal point of baking the pita bread in full view of anyone passing by.

I searched locations, got the cost of the equipment from Israel, did pro formas, but it was all talk on his part, so that died.

The next thing was a stock brokerage company; this was in the early stages of conversation. Jay called me one day, and his millions were tied up for the moment, so he wanted to borrow fifty thousand for a short period of time. I gave it to him (with no signature or note).

He did not return the money, but the brokerage business went forward, and my share of twenty five percent was funded by that money I had lent him. The partnership consisted of Jay, his two accountants, and me. It was called Whitehall Wellington.

He took Class A office space, hired brokers, the two accountants, and himself. For the first year it did no more then cover expenses.

We had meetings once a week, and whenever Jay was fearful of the two accountants fighting him on a decision, he briefed me on it and certainly slanted it to get my vote.

In the middle of not getting anywhere, he leased space in a huge building in Roslyn, Long Island, with an option to buy.

At the same time, I had been trying to get a balance sheet, financial, anything so I could see what money was coming in and out, so that maybe I could get a handle on how we could turn a profit. Jay had been putting me off for months. He kept saying that if the sheets got into the wrong hands, it could present problems. Eventually I told him to take the names off and just give me the numbers. I still could not get anywhere.

Finally my frustration at his concealing the numbers from me caused me to get upset and raise my voice. That was the end of our friendship. Somewhere along the way we had a good two months, and I collected about forty thousand dollars.

Then Jay called for a meeting. He said he wanted to buy the building. We would all put in money and buy it. The accountants were in agreement. He knew I was against it because the handwriting on the wall for this type of brokerage business was that its life expectancy was short. At this meeting, I could see that he set up the accountants to vote in his favor. I opted to be bought out. I was paid out one hundred and eighty thousand dollars, and the business closed a year later. I am sure they all lost money, but who knows.

IN ORDER TO SUCCEED YOU MUST BE IN POSITION FOR BOTH THE GOOD AND BAD STREAKS

On the heels of the Fire Alarm project came another. I won an award for another project within the Helmsley organization for approximately six million dollars. This was not a T and M job. The job was awarded to us by Helmsley, and Tishman was the construction manager. Tishman had concerns about our ability to produce and finance a job of this size. They sent their electrical contractor, Forest Electric, to speak to me.

We negotiated a finder's fee for me of 1.2 million dollars, and they did the job.

"Que Sera, Sera (Whatever Will Be, Will Be)"

At the end of 1996, Denise and Adam were ready to get engaged; the one problem was that Denise has juvenile diabetes; supposedly childbearing would be improbable, and her life span could be short lived.

He discussed this with his mother, then his sisters. They all recommended he move on as the sacrifices he would have to make were too drastic.

He came to me and my advice was, "If you love her and this is what you want , go for it. None of us know what tomorrow may bring no matter how healthy, or anything else, what exists today, could be gone tomorrow."

They had two engagement parties. One in Cleveland, her hometown, and one at Tam O'Shanter, my hometown.

The wedding was held in Cleveland. Her parents told me what to pay for and I did. No problems.

During the wedding, the band was taking too many breaks. Adam came to me and I straightened it out.

They married, have a boy and a girl, and seem to be living a healthy life.

1997: NEVIS

With Jordan as a toddler, Amanda, Denise and I spent a week with friends at the Four Seasons in Nevis, West Indies. While exclusive and beautiful, other than golf, there is nothing that would make me want to go back. Jordan had a good time as the golf course was overrun by goats and monkeys.

1998: ST. BARTS

We made a trip with friends to St. Barts and St. Martin.

1998: US VIRGIN ISLANDS

With friends again, St. Thomas, St. Croix, and St. Kitts.

CHAPTER 24: THE BEGINNING OF THE END

THERESA

In 1991, I had placed an ad for a project manager. One of the responses was from a young woman. She had previously worked for another Local 3 contractor, and she was familiar with the whole process, reading prints, etc. I hired her. She was very knowledgeable about the business, the union, and payroll. She became a key employee who I trusted completely. We became good friends. Little things happened along the way that should have set off an alarm in me, but I guess I did not want that alarm to go off.

She was very friendly with one of the electricians, Helmut. The first thing that caught my attention was a fifteen hundred dollar item that was a bonus for Helmut. The payroll was done by hand then and Theresa was in charge of that process. At the end of the month, while going through the bank statement, I noticed that there were two larger-than-usual checks for Helmut. After further investigation, I discovered that Helmut was paid that bonus twice. I was disappointed in Helmut. I liked him and would have thought that he would have let us know. I chalked up the fact that it was disbursed twice to an honest mistake.

Another alarm: I kept getting expensive Mont Blanc pens as gifts, and I kept losing them. One time, Theresa pulled one out of her bag, and I said, "Isn't that mine?"

"Oh yes, I have no idea how it got there. I must have taken it by mistake."

The alarm sounded, but I tucked it away. Who knows what else was done over the years that she was there other than the finale?

Back in the sixties, during the growth of Laurelton, it was very hard to get experienced electricians. I had a method that I am not sure if anyone ever copied, but it worked like a charm. I put an ad in the paper for an hourly rate twice as much as the market at the time.

We received loads of calls. In the beginning, I would set up appointments every half hour for them to come in. I learned that only twenty five percent showed up, wasting my day waiting for people.

Next ad, we set the appointment all for the same time. They were out in the street waiting to get in. My interviews lasted a minute or less, and all of the interviews were finished within an hour. What I did was have them fill out an application stating their work experience and rate of pay.

In reviewing the application with the applicant, they were asked how long it would take to do a certain task. If they knew what I was talking about and answered with the correct time, I would look at their last rate of pay and hire them for a dollar more per hour. Very rarely did anyone ask about what was offered in the paper. If they did, I told them that they had to be with us for five years to get that rate. In those ads, there was always a newly-arrived foreigner, and I could always use helpers that we could train. Some of my longest-tenured employees have come up this way.

One person I hired, Antonino Genovese, only spoke Italian, but he quickly learned English and the New York electric requirements. A good mechanic, I went to his wedding, and he went to mine, plus all the affairs for my kids.

He became Local 3 when we were unionized, and at that point he was earning a hundred thousand dollars per year.

Not a high liver, he had a home, and in 1995, since he had been working with me for nearly twenty-five years, I would guess his net worth was between one and a half and two million dollars.

In 1995, after several others failed, I was able to make Tony the "super" of the shop, which meant he was the connection between the union and me. During this period, his weekly expenses started to slip out of control. I would never question him. The payroll was submitted to me by Theresa. I would approve it, and that's all I knew.

In the mail one day, there was a card for Tony from a male erectile dysfunction clinic. It registered with me that he was possibly fooling around. Why else would this come to the office? I would not think so; I knew his wife and his family, and they were very traditional, but it was not my business.

That year, at the Christmas party, I also noticed that he was a little friendlier then normal with Theresa. At the time, it didn't faze me.

One day, an employee, according to Theresa, could not cash his check, so she made out a check to cash and replaced it. Somehow, days later, it came up in conversation with that employee, and he had no idea what I was talking about; meanwhile two checks were cashed. He only received one.

Theresa received her annual bonus in the form of not charging her for the electrical work in the renovation of a house she owned. The labor and material costs were so high that I was getting very upset with her. Tony was overseeing it. Finally I started to put together all the little instances over the years and realized that I had a problem.

At the time, we had several hundred men in our employ. Every week, we had a job meeting with all the project managers in my office. We would review each job, checking on the progress manpower, material, etc.

Based on the project manger's report, men would be shifted or added. From the union's ranks, Tony was the super of the shop. He was the man who would call the union and order men, and he would tell them what job to go to.

Denise's mother had a boyfriend, Bob Jaffe. He was a recovering alcoholic and a harmless con man, and he never worked in his life. To improve her mother's quality of life, I gave Bob a job running errands, picking up checks, going to the bank, getting lunch, etc. He was taking home about four hundred dollars per week.

Theresa went on vacation to Europe with her husband. I was signing payroll checks, and noticed that one of the men we had recently laid off had a check made out to his name. Curious as to why, I looked further and the previous week the check was made out to his name with a middle initial. That couldn't be, because the computer has the name information stored. In order to change it, you have to go into the system, and then all of the checks would be changed, not just one.

Matching the foreman's payroll request forms, the checks issued, and the men on the job, I started to piece the whole thing together, but I had to be sure of who and what. I called Tony in and I let him know that I was looking into this problem. The next day, I called Theresa's cell phone, checked her messages, and there were ten messages on there from Tony In his accented broken English. "We got big problems. Call me." Then, "It's an emergency, big trouble." He was frantic.

In her desk, I found the payroll reports, the union reports, the withholding reports, and it was all right in front of me. Each week at the job meeting, I would question the progress and the completion and the need to hire, switch or remove manpower.

The major input was Tony. He had to tell me where we needed men, and then, on my approval, order them from the union, submit payroll sheets for them, and deliver their pay. Theresa entered the new employees in the computer. I would approve the payroll. She would issue the check, and I would sign it. We would then send Bob, Denise's mother's boyfriend, to the bank to cash the checks. The stubs and the cash were delivered to the job by Tony.

I had been paying net checks, union reports, and government reports based on nonexistent employees. The correspondence from the IRS and the union questioning the existence of these ghosts, was in the folder in her desk. I pulled all the evidence, hired a temp to go through the bank statements and cancelled checks, and copied all of them. I could not believe that Tony could possibly do this, especially to me.

A friend recommended a private investigator, a former New York City police detective, Jay, and after putting together all the evidence, and after interviews with each employee, we uncovered many things, including the fact that Tony had purchased a diamond ring for Theresa through another employee, who had a connection for diamonds.

Erectile dysfunction, Christmas party, expenses very high, jewelry, a few other little things that meant nothing until now. And it dawned on me that the only way Tony could do this was if he was in love. Knowing that Theresa is a vixen and a pathological liar, she must have used sex and faked love.

As I kept investigating, I stopped counting at where I thought it started, over $400,000. Theresa and Tony were having an affair. Somehow she got him to turn against me and justify his actions. It was, I am sure, a fabulous tale.

When the payroll checks were signed by me, they were put in envelopes to be delivered to the job sites. The office payroll was called in to the bank to be cashed. Bob picked it up and delivered it to Theresa. Each week the money for the ghost employees grew, starting at $3,000, and at the final count it was $9,000 per week.

My guess is that most of that money went to Theresa. I do not think Tony was in it for the money. He was smitten. The detective interviewed the entire office staff and further found cars, boats, and real estate in Tony's name and used by Theresa.

Theresa, having spoken to Tony, called me from Europe just to see how things were and tell me when she would be back. She tried to get me to say something. I made like everything was fine. I already had all the papers, checks, and proof to go to the District Attorney.

Theresa was holding firm and telling Tony not to worry, as she knew I was not going to lose my confidential business connections and my family because of her penchant for lying. And whatever she would claim, whether true or not, would have jeopardized my relationships.

Meeting with Tony in a diner, I showed him what we had, and played the tape of his messages to her. I showed him the payroll reports in his handwriting and signed by him, and asked what he knew about it. "Not a thing," he dummied up. He was fired.

Theresa is a pathological liar, but not a good liar.She returned from Europe secretly a few days earlier then she had told me. Her son, Anthony, called and asked for his mother. I took the call, and found out that she'd returned from Europe and was supposed to be at work.

I suspected that after we closed she would be there to clean out her draw of an envelope that contained all the information on the ghost employees

The correspondence from the IRS and the Union with regard to the same. I had copies of everything, I could have set a trap, but I was between a rock and a hard place. What good would it do? There was nothing I was going to do about it.

Sure enough, the next day the folder was gone. The detective, Jay, tried to interview Tony and Theresa. Tony would not answer his calls; Theresa came in to the office. He interviewed her while I went outside, but she gave up nothing. I instructed him to get the keys to the company car, phone, and office keys that she had as well.

Jay was positive that Bob was in on it too, but he too held firm. And if I confronted him, I would have had to deal with Denise and her mother. The money was gone. Tony was gone. Theresa was gone. During the course of this relationship, Theresa's son, Vincent, was born. I am sure that he is Tony's son, and he is probably still paying. Over the next five years, Theresa worked for various electrical contractors and each time was let go for either kickbacks or theft. Then she disappeared. There is no record of her through her Social Security number, divorce records, union records, or any search websites.

Her two sons, Anthony and Vincent, are on Facebook and the Internet. There is nothing on her. Her ex-husband remarried (I think), and is on Facebook and the Internet, but she is not. The kids do not even mention their mother or father in their profile. She is either in the witness protection program, jail, or rehab.

On March 1st, 2011, I hired Jay to look into where they both are in the hopes of recovering some of the money. He took my deposit and disappeared.

1999: LEONA

Leona Helmsley was having a relationship with a younger real estate broker, to his financial gain as well as hers. He convinced her to sell all her buildings. Within a short period of time, all the years of cultivation were over.

In order to stay afloat, I had to chase after and take jobs just to keep the cash flow going. Only now I did not have the profitable Helmsley jobs to bail me out.

I had been introduced to a salesman, Vic Alicanti. He had a portfolio of good accounts. I had been warned not to trust him, but as usual, I had to see for myself. He did well for us. He sold a huge renovation job, which though hard to get paid, was a good job.

In addition to other jobs with general contractors, he obtained a job from Macy's for one million dollars, with the probability of a second phase that could be several million dollars.

These were all capital intense, slow-paying jobs. I was drowning in cash flow. I had always had a large check coming from Helmsley, but now had to wait for money from general contractors, which was torturous.

My union payments were $60,000 to $70,000 a week. I sent in the payments at a reduced amount so that my weekly check would be manageable until the cash flow got better. To make matters worse, now that Tony was gone, the union forced me to take one of theirs as my Super. He was more destructive than constructive, and he caused me to lose money on several jobs

We billed a progress payment to Macy's of $500,000. All payments need the engineer's approval, and he reviewed the request, confirmed the completed portion, and signed off on the bill.

After trying to collect the check and being stalled, Macy's told us that their capital improvement budget year was coming to a close and that in the next sixty days the new year would begin, and they would pay the invoice then.

Prior to that, I had started a relationship with a factor, and was getting advances on some of our other progress billing. The delay of the $500,000 was devastating. The factor, after several weeks, finally advanced $250,000 upon executing a bond to guarantee it. Adam and I were required to sign, along with our wives. At my request, everyone signed, and we got the $250,000.

Macy's continued to jerk us around. What I did not know was that Alicanti and the Macy's exec had an agreement to partner in their own electrical business to procure the additional job coming up behind this one and more. The payment of $500,000 was never going to be paid.

When the sixty days went by, they danced with us, until finally they called in the engineer to reexamine the progress for that payment. And, lo and behold, he came in with much less percentage. And they still did not pay it. The factor would not advance us any other funds, on any job, and threatened to call in the bond.

I was stuck and desperate and had always been able to survive the storms, and maybe in retrospect, I should have filed bankruptcy. Instead, I had to stay alive long enough to get Adam's name off the liabilities. I used whatever resources I had, and with the lure of high interest, borrowed $250,000 from friends and family.

In the past I had a great relationship with the union officials and controller, as I had with my bank managers and vendors. I had leeway, and they always worked with me.

The union had a new management team. Previously they were electricians and business people who grew to management positions. This group was a financial management team. Their purpose was to invest the many hundreds of millions they had in retirement funds.

Alicanti's plan was for me to be out of business and take over, as I heard from a trusted employee. I was unaware that Alicanti and others were also stoking the union fires. Having no relationship with the new union management, they started taking a hard line with me.

They audited my books, and with the back payments due, I owed them well over a million dollars, and they wanted it.

The union called me in with my attorney. Fearing that I would file bankruptcy, they noted their position was to not allow that to happen. They would file lawsuits, liens, and would not cooperate with any such filing. I wasn't planning to nor did I have any intention to file bankruptcy. But they were pissed and wanted their money, so I had to figure out my next move.

AMANDA

In the middle of my 1999 financial Tsunami, Amanda was turning thirteen, and all of her friends had beautiful Bar and Bat Mitzvahs. Amanda's was booked at the Bath and Tennis in West Hampton Beach long before the disasters started to occur.

Because Denise was a party planner, and Amanda was a pre-teen, the only thing they had been into for the past two years was this affair. There was no way I could alter the festivities and break her heart.

Friday night, April 30th, 1999, she read her Hoftorah as the first Friday night Bat Mitzvah held in this brand new West Hampton Synagogue, presided over by Rabbi Mark Schneir.

Amanda, who was tutored to read Hebrew, did it beautifully. After the services, there was a smorgasbord of food and drinks.

Saturday night, May 1st, there were three buses, delivering all the kids from Jericho. The kids were escorted off the buses by a unit of United States Marines, who also escorted all the guests as they arrived. The theme was a cruise. When you came in, you received a passport leading to your table and the evening festivities. From there, everything was decorated to appear as a cruise ship. There was two hours of cocktails and appetizers and a reggae band.

The kids had a separate room set up with all the electronic games and a gambling casino with craps tables and blackjack tables with prizes they could buy with their winnings. The kids also had their own food buffet. During the affair, there was the photo montage, a candle-lighting ceremony, the hottest DJ of the time, and four young dancers to keep the crowd dancing.

Amanda's siblings made up a spoof-type song for her and sang it for the crowd. Afterwards, there was another room set up with cigars, liquors, after-dinner wines, and a calypso group. The following day there was a brunch for everyone. It was the talk of the town. Mother and daughter were very pleased. Outwardly, so was I, but it was hard for me to enjoy it, as I knew what was coming down the road.

ADAM

Adam was personally liable because of me for $160,000 in payroll taxes, the $250,000 bond, and $350,000 due to American Express for material purchases and miscellaneous personal guarantees to vendors.

It was time to get out. I paid American Express in full, worked with the union to assign receivables of concluded jobs, paid the $250,000 in loans plus the interest.

Hired an attorney to fight Macy's, the factor, and the bonding company. I negotiated with vendors where Adam's name was involved and hired a bankruptcy attorney for Adam.

The $160,000 to the state was being negotiated, but Adam had sold his condo at a large profit, and the state took their $160,000 at the closing. After paying off all the above, Adam was still out $160,000 for the condo, $20,000 elsewhere, and equally liable for the $250,000 bond.

We had receivables of $1,627,525.00. I assigned them to the union, as I knew once the sharks tasted the blood in the water they were not going to pay me so quickly.

EMS,our formerly non union company, which Adam was the owner of had been unionized with all M-rated men, was in a great position to do union work. They continued to do so, and I went back to non union work out of Laurelton. However, my three good men had been unionized, and although they continued to work for me, they were paid out of EMS.

We had the union EMS company and Laurelton Electric. In order to reduce my personal overhead, I decided to sell everything and move to our home in Florida. I felt I could run Laurelton from Florida and start a new business there and come up to the Hamptons for the summer.

I spoke to Denise, and we decided to sell Jericho, boats, toys and move to Florida. It was not a sad decision; it seemed like an exciting idea. Wendy tried to make me feel guilty, that I was leaving my family in NY.

Adam and I now had the opportunity to be profitable in both union and nonunion situations. We moved to the building I owned in Queens. It was just Adam, a secretary, and me.

Verderame Construction, owned by the senior Verderame and run by the two sons, Anthony and John, had the bulk of any work in the Garment Center. The two brothers did not get along. Anthony ran everything from the office. John supervised from the field. They each sold their own jobs, and each distributed the work to their favorite contractors.

The only way to get the work was to be in their offices every day at 6:00 a.m. Anthony had his electrician there, and John had me. John would organize himself for the day and give me a list of jobs he wanted to be done. They were tough to do business with. They were very demanding and were not warm people. The only one I could get close to was the father; he had no input on the day to day operations by choice, but he enjoyed my benevolence for dining and golf.

One day he called and asked me to meet him for lunch. I had no idea why. He wanted to know if I was paying off John to get the electrical work. I could not believe my ears that a father was thinking his son was stealing from him. I am sure that Anthony put that thought in his head.

When the father died, Anthony got most of the inheritance. He was a lazy guy anyway, so he completed his existing contracts and moved to Florida. John formed his own company.Adam and John were tight.

John and the Verderame Organization were a great learning place for Adam to have a successful business. John was all business and no life. The combination of the two of them was a formula for success. John was hands on, a one-man operation, with little overhead and high profits and a lot of money in the bank.

Adam had learned from me how to handle John, and seventy-five percent of his business was with John.

Entitlement

Cause and Effect

246

CHAPTER 25: CAPTAIN GOES DOWN WITH THE SHIP

TRYING TO RISE ABOVE THE OBSTACLES

All of the toys were sold with the exception of two Hampton condos. We were moving to Florida after the summer in the Hamptons. At the end we would ship one car and drive down in the other.

Adam's Father in law called and was concerned whether Adam had the business acumen to handle New York .I assured him he did, and that the only phase of the business that would be difficult was the cash flow.

When we were ready to leave I gave Adam my Florida car. A three-year-old Mercedes convertible . I also gave him another 15,000 for working capital

Before we left, about fifty of our friends gave us a farewell dinner roast, with costumes, skits, videos of me captaining the boat when I was learning, and a good, fun time for all.

Adam was on his way to his in-laws in Cleveland for some gathering. I called his father-in-law, informing him that I was giving Adam $15,000, and if he could match it, it would be a great help for Adam's working capital.

Apparently, his in-laws were outraged at my request. Adam, who had been growing more and more distant as the financial problems arose, was outraged as well.

I did not see the problem. His father-in-law had been a stock broker all his life, and as a product of his experiences, he probably did not understand.

After stopping at Disney World, we went on to our home.

Organized in Florida, I had the proceeds of the property sales. To be sure I invested wisely, I put it all into AT&T. Private school for both kids and the cash flow projections based on my current income had the expenses working on paper.

. His father-in-law called and was concerned that Adam may not have the business acumen at this point. I assured him that he did, and I would only be in Florida to handle any problems that may arise.

Adam had moved in to my friend Cliff's Manhattan store, for a year or so, rent free. When he had to leave Cliff's place, he moved his office in with John Verderame, who was privy now to all that was going on between Adam and me. Adam now had a lot of prompting from John Verderame, who hated his father. Additionally, Wendy's husband, Rich, who had no respect for his father, and Adam's in-laws, who were not products of business, were whispering in his ear.

"Why do you have to pay the lease payments for your father's car?" etc. Adam had no respect for me and found me burdensome.

About a year later, Adam and John were not getting along. John wanted to own Adam. And at this point, John was his major customer. I met with John; he told me that without him we would be out of business. He was laying the groundwork for something but never really established what he really wanted.

Adam moved to his friend's office on 36th street, and John was history. He needed more money. I did not know that I had about $35,000 in equity in a life insurance policy. He advised me of it, and that money I gave him too.

In negotiations of the multimillion dollar case against Macy's, we settled for a release from the bonding company and of all the personal guarantees. I signed over a life insurance policy of $250,000 to Adam to cover the $160,000 he lost

Adam was now made whole; he was completely repaid for any monies I had cost him. I was disappointed that I did not carry the suit to term, as I believe we had a great case, but my only goal was to make my son whole.

RESET

Moving to Florida was not an easy task for Amanda, as she had all these established relationships and had to start over.

In Florida, after being unable to get Amanda or Jordan into academically-acclaimed schools (it's all about money), they both went to American Heritage private school. It was not scholastically satisfying to me.

The reputation of the public high school in Boca, Spanish River, was excellent. Amanda transferred there, and I drove her to school every day. I switched Jordan to Donna Klein, where he would be educated in the public school curriculum and get a Hebrew education as well. I was very happy and proud that I was providing him with that opportunity.

Amanda did not have to give up any friendships; her Long Island friends came down often enough. She made new friends and kept the old. Amanda's Long Island friends would come down to the Boca Beach Club during Thanksgiving, Christmas, and spring break. As we often did, I would drive her to the Club about forty minutes from our house. Because it was not cool for a parent to be visible, I waited in the car for about four hours for her to be ready to leave.

One weekend, while Denise and I were in New York, Amanda decided to have a party at the house without telling us. She let some of her friends know about the party. Unknowingly, when kids find out there's a party and parents are away, they believe it is open house and hundreds show up.

We found out as the security office called my cell phone and advised me of what was going on. After getting Amanda and the housekeeper on the phone, and getting security to get everyone to leave, I had found out that boys had slept over, had been drunk, etc.

Investigating, to find out what the truth was, I called the boys' homes and talked to their parents to inquire as to how all these events took place.

Although I found out that Amanda did what any other kid would have done in the same circumstances, I felt that the deceit had to be paid for. So beyond Denise's objection, I delayed Amanda from getting her driving learner's permit for three months.

On Amanda's 17th birthday, June 17th, 2003, she got a brand new Audi A4 red coupe.

When we first moved to Florida, I took an office and controlled my part of the business via cell phone, fax, and email. In Florida, I put an ad in the paper to buy a contracting firm or hook up with someone with a license. An elderly gentleman responded. He had a corporation, Pioneer Electric, which housed his license, and for a monthly check of $1,000, he turned it all over to me.

The housing market in 2000 was strong, and everyone buying a house wanted to spruce it up. I obtained mailing lists for all the new Boca Country club developments. I sent out well-presented, oversized post cards for the installation of landscape lighting and went on the estimates. I was good at laying it out and pricing. I decided my niche there was landscape lighting, and a profitable entity was born. In addition, we did some commercial work with people I had known and to whom I was introduced.

DELAYED COMPREHENSION

As an entrepreneur, you are an automatic risk taker, as such you know that the other shoe can drop at any time. We settled in Addison Reserve, still hopeful that all would work out.

I get a call from an IRS agent who was very nice; he said they just needed some business records. He needed my fax number to send his request. When Vic Alicante obtained a contract with George Comfort and Sons, it was with the condition that ten percent of the job of two million dollars would go back to the general contractor and the owner.

It was built in; each time they made a payment I had to give back ten percent. They wanted it in cash. I said, "Endorse a check, and I will get you the cash." They did not want to do that, and so we continued as agreed, with checks made out to some contracting company, which I carried as commission.

One day during this project, the general contractor's payment were very late. I held up a part of the job until they paid. Not unusual, standard operating procedure.

Getting a haircut and a manicure in Manhasset, I received a call from Alicante. He sounded high on something, and he said, "What did you do?"

"What are you talking about?"

All he kept saying was, "What did you do? What did you do? I have to see you; we have to talk."

Telling him where I was, he came over, again high on something. The conversation was, "What did you do? What did you do?"

Assuming he was talking about the fact that I held up the job while waiting for payment, I kept telling him, "Don't worry; it will all work out. They will pay, and we will continue."

He was so stressed and high that I figured his condition was making him overreact. He continued, "What did you do? What did you do?" That was 1995, and nothing further was ever said, and we went on.

Back to 2001, the IRS faxed me their requests from their fraud department for any checks made out to this company, payments, contracts, arrangements, and correspondence. These was the people I was giving the checks to. It registered now; they were probably made aware of being investigated in 1995, and the investigation did not get to me until 2001. That is what Alicante was talking about.

His people were either fishing or thought that I had informed the IRS about their operation. Now, I gathered all the checks and info, and I am not sure if I am culpable in any way. I hired an attorney. It cost me fear, aggravation, and money. Their interest was not in me.

PLAY IT AGAIN, SAM

March 7th, 2001. I reached the sixty-year-old milestone. I never really complained about being sixty, although it is a rude awakening. But, after much consideration I would like to do it again.

With the exception of Amanda, who was in college, we all went on a cruise that took us to the Pacific. Each family had to pay their own way, and they created a very well-done birthday video tribute to me.

TAKE NO PRISONERS

One week after the September 11th terror attack, Denise's brother Steven was getting married in New York. We were scheduled to fly up, but under the circumstances, we drove instead. We checked into the hotel and dressed for the rehearsal dinner.

When we got to the restaurant, Denise and her mother were upset because they were seated away from the other family and the bride and groom. Denise just couldn't let it go. She and her mother attacked the bride-to-be on the eve of her wedding and of course made her cry. Amanda and Jordan witnessed the whole thing. There is no one that escapes the wrath of Denise.

REMEMBER THE GOOD STREAKS

From 2001 through 2003, money became more and more difficult. I had a substantial amount of equity in the house. I wanted to move to an apartment or rented house and put the proceeds from the house in the bank.

The AT&T stock tanked. I kept putting more money into the business. I was never able to keep up with the payments for the three union mechanics I was using.

Denise was only willing to move if we bought another house. We looked and found that there was nothing that would make a substantial difference. We put the house on the market. The fact that I did not have an equity position in the Golf Club was damaging.

Our market of buyers was reduced immensely. On the advice of the brokers, we kept lowering the price, but there were not even any nibbles.

Christmas of 2001. When the kids came down, we all went to South Beach on a rainy day. Wendy and Elyssa bought some clothes, and Denise bitched and sulked to all of them that she could not buy anything as finances were difficult.

Whenever the kids did stay at the house, they were very respectful to clean up after themselves and their kids. However, not a time went by that Denise did not say, "I have to do everything; no one helps me." Elyssa learned to ignore her, but Wendy would fight back.

As time went by and things were not as lucrative as needed,Adam became more difficult and more distant. He wanted to leave the business. Eventually, after enough whining, I said, "Fine, just give me time to figure out what I have to do, and go."

That stopped the threats. He wanted me to move back to New York and take care of my own things, since the little things I had asked him to do for me were an annoyance. If I asked him to make a deposit for me of a customer's check at the bank downstairs from his office, he would say,

"Don't make this a habit."

Chapter 26: THE DOMINO EFFECT

Denise, Amanda, and I made several trips to New York for family or business. On one of those trips Adam sat Amanda down and gave her an earful about having my men on his payroll. She did not understand what it was about, but she did repeat it to her mother.

Denise, being fueled with the above started to realize, as I was telling her, that the ship might be sinking. She tried to find out from Rich if I had any equity with him. He happily told her that in his opinion I was broke. These conversations planted the seed in her brain to bail.

The school year was over; it was time to go to the Hamptons. She wanted to put it off for a few weeks. No reason; she just wanted to. The kids would not acquiesce, so we left as planned.

Soon after, and I have no idea if this was premeditated or not, Denise lost the diamond stone from her engagement ring. It was uninsured and purchased in 1984 for $20,000.

Earlier in the year, Denise started therapy again, and I had a thought that the reason could a have been to supporting her thought of bailing. The physical encounters between us were few and far between, as she was never really interested. For me it just wasn't worth the effort. I felt she was thinking of bailing, but I had so much on my plate that I just ignored it and let the chips fall where they might.

We left for the Hamptons. Having recently arrived, Amanda had a bunch of friends over. At Denise's suggestion, we took them out to dinner.

When the check came, she went into, "Why do we go out for such expensive dinners," etc.

That complaint was only lodged in front of others. Whenever we went out, it was her choice to eat in or eat out, and she decided what restaurant to go to. Never did she offer to make dinner or lodge a complaint in private. She was just bolstering herself up for the courage to initiate her departure.

All my mail was delivered to the Hamptons for the summer. Every day when I came back from estimating, some of my mail had been opened. I assumed Denise was looking through it for whatever her paranoid reasons were. I did not care as there was nothing I was trying to hide.

As things started to develop, I realized that her not wanting to leave for the Hamptons until weeks after the kids were through with school was because she had a fantasy that she could end up with her therapist.

She was under the impression (because someone told her) that in separation or divorce that I would have no choice but to support her in the lifestyle I had given her. There was nothing hidden with money. After eighteen years of marriage, everything was open; there were no secret accounts, but in her less-than-intelligent reasoning, that was not her problem.

None of those theories worked out for her, but there we were. She publicly advised the world that she was leaving me. She called my kids and told them. She treated me pretty badly in front of all our friends and neighbors.

She took Jordan, who was seven at the time, and from day one she told him not to tell me where they went or what they did. She went back to Florida and put more energy and initiative into divorcing then anything she has ever done.

She hired a lawyer, found a group of single women, went online and started dating. I tried to talk her out of it, to no avail. I stayed in the Hamptons. I was more humiliated and embarrassed than upset. At the end of the summer, I drove back to Florida. Both condos were under contract with substantial equity. The house was up for sale, and I was not moving out.

When I arrived home I unloaded the car from all of our clothes from the summer. Somewhere along the way I scratched my leg, leaving a scab of dried blood. It was a very uncomfortable situation. In front of my children, in my own home, I felt like I was on the outside looking at my life. After unpacking I went to my office, off the living room.

Denise got a phone call, started whispering, took the phone outside, and covered her mouth as she spoke. I felt so many emotions that I could not put them into words. When she came back inside I was seething, and an argument ensued. As she turned and walked away. I threw a tiny, empty, bean bag clip holder from my desk, and it lightly landed on her behind.

As if she had planned this with her therapist, she immediately called the police. When they came in, they each had their hands on the handle of their guns. They made me back up to a chair and sit while they made sure I wasn't armed. She described that I threw this thing at her. I saw how serious the police were handling this. I was sure that unless I did something they would arrest me. So I said, "Officers, the only reason I did that was to defend myself, as you can see by the blood on my leg, from the impact of her kick."

When Denise heard that she freaked out. She screamed as many four letter words that were ever vocalized at one time by one person, she ranted for about three minutes in front of Amanda and Jordan. She certainly did not ingratiate herself with the police. They informed us that we could not stay in the house together. One of us had to leave for the evening.

Denise decided she would take Jordan and go. She left, the police left, and I could not control myself. I exploded into loud, painful moans and a sea of tears. When I composed myself, I told Amanda to call her mother. There was no reason we both couldn't stay there.

We stayed in the house together for several weeks. Denise kept advising me to get a lawyer, as her attorney did not want to deal with me. He wanted to deal sleazebag to sleazebag. As always, I wrote my feelings at the time:

> It is so hard to comprehend, that after twenty years of history—especially since the one who suffered most was me— Denise could do this. To give up a full family and extended family life. This has to be a mind-induced action from others without intellect, perceived in insanity and ignorance. If this same focus was put into the marriage as the divorce, we both could have been very happy. She speaks about the age of women I will date, that they are not to be younger than my daughter. She wants me out of the house. She demands more and more money.

> Although I believe this will probably be an opportunity to enjoy whatever time I have left, the motivation of Denise leaves me mystified. The way she is convinced that the children will not suffer. She must have been discussing this with her therapist for some time.

Finally, the tension and discomfort were too much. My sister was going to Paris for the next two months, and I moved in there. I had difficulty keeping up with the payments; prior to this, nothing had changed.

But she was after me for money, for everything and anything. The settlement of the condos and the sale of the house had not yet occurred. Adam had stock that she was the guardian of; she forged his signature and sold it.

Amanda needed money. I met her at an ATM machine and gave it to her. She went on her way, and I went on mine. I stopped for gas on the corner. While I was pumping the gas, Denise pulled up, jumped out of the car, and grabbed the gas hose and pointed it at me. I jumped in my car before she could pull the trigger and took off.

Denise had hired one of these bloodsucking Boca divorce attorneys. He was the first of a long list.

As always, through Chuck I was able to get attorneys who were professionals, who cared about what they were doing, and who did the best they could for their client. A very rare thing in that profession. Usually categories of people, professions, etc. are tainted with a few bad seeds; the legal profession is the exception. This category houses the scum of the Earth, and only rarely can you find an honest good one.

This divorce was simply a person bailing out of a listing ship. The anger, the rage, the need for money that is not there to give became the daily banter. How can someone be so irate, knowing the money is not there? She seemed to have the same characteristics of a drug addict.

Financially unable to maneuver, being attacked physically, mentally, and legally by my charming ex-wife and my son Adam, it was hard to keep my head up

Adam was giving me a very hard time. Denise was trying to plead poverty and telling me to cooperate with her by giving her money. When I told her that I did not have it, she said, "That's not my problem."

On September 10, 2004, I wrote the following memo to myself:

> *Well, where am I? Do not know, but time to start answering the voluminous amount of emails accumulated from "her." The thing is, I can probably clarify my position in a few sentences. What lies! What deceit! What did I ever do other than pushing the financial envelope too far? I seem to have run out of steam.*

My sister was returning. I moved to an apartment. The house in Addison was never sold and went into foreclosure. Denise rented a house in a country club. Amanda and Jordan, at her convenience, were not her children but her friends.

When she went out, she discussed her every dating experience with each of them. Private emails and photos that should have been locked away were left out in the open. Jordan went to the first of several different schools. Amanda was away at college.

Denise could not get what she wanted financially from the first two sets of lawyers. Finally, the third was smart enough to understand what could be done and what couldn't. An agreement was reached.

When the agreement resulted in dollars and cents, she was unhappy, and he was fired. In addition to the cash settlement, from the condos she was getting $1750 per week plus $1000 per month from my social security

Meanwhile, all I did was spend as much time as possible with my son and daughter. And all she did was berate me on a continual basis. I do not believe throughout this whole period I was more than a week behind in my alimony payments.

I made her send me an email when she would complain that I was behind. It was for $344. That is what I was behind from a payment of $1,750 per week.

After she was dating for about a year, and after being rejected by any substantial available men, Denise settled in with Steve. He had a son and daughter, who at the time were fourteen and eighteen years old, respectively. The son lived with them, and the daughter was in college. Steve was divorced and supposedly had money in the past, but not anymore. The son was troublesome, and Steve was a pot head. Denise and Steve would smoke pot together and thought that Jordan did not know. Neither one of them worked; both were living off of my money.

They bought a house with two mortgages and got caught deeply under water. The house was foreclosed on, and Steve went bye-bye. Of course that was the second house she lost because of me.

After the continual emails, phone messages, threats, and continual bashing of me to anyone she knew, I sent the following letter, in 2004:

> Let me advise you that I have no remorse or anger with regard to our marriage. As it was only for the fact that I did not want to break up a family for the second time that I stayed at all.

Entitlement

Cause and Effect

I tried to be "Pygmalion" and take in an unhappy, incompetent individual. I thought if I provided love, adoration, comfort, and a family then the frog would turn into a princess.

It was certainly farfetched, but at the time I had complete confidence in myself and my therapist, who also thought you were a diamond in the rough. That diamond remained in the rough, as even in so-called better times, there was never a moment that you would allow me any happiness. The only time you were ever at peace with yourself was while you were dancing, painting, or pregnant. The rest of the time you took out your miserable existence on whomever was around you.

There are volumes of despicable lies and accusations that I have catalogued and recorded from your emails and phone messages. When my children are old enough they will understand the misery of a person that you are.

Most parents want to give their children a better life then they had. You wanted to show them how you had to grow up with a crazy mother, and then you became her. Now, after all your threats and your vulgarity, after your attempts to defile me and my life to anyone who would listen to you, now you say, 'Work with me.'

This is a perfect example of "the world according to Denise." You have burned every bridge in life that you crossed, and they were bridges you never would have even approached had I not brought you into my world. You would never have had a child; no one would have put up with you long enough. Just like your two prior failed short-term marriages.

You took my temporary business problems that any entrepreneur risks and can fall prey to and used them to try and hurt me with my children and the world.

Entitlement

Cause and Effect

You never kept a promise in your life; you always took without giving, and you exaggerate or outright lie whenever it suits you. Just like now when you say you can't get a job; more lies. You are probably applying for positions that you are not qualified for.

You think if you received your alimony any sooner that you would manage, yet you could never manage. The reality is you get your money on time. Just another excuse to blame someone else for your inadequacies. You have the nerve to say we were married a long time and I should have some heart. You read the volumes of pages, and you talk to the people who told me they had to run away from you. How you bent their ear for all the terrible things I did to you.

Had you in any way behaved like an adult, or showed any appreciation for all the things I did for you and your family, had you tempered your outrageous dramatic displays, or not tried to insult my fatherhood for your own selfish interests, I would have cooperated with your needs to the best of my ability. But the "world according to Denise" just does not work that way. You get out what you put in.

For the sake of our children, I do not speak to you, and I will not answer your emails. As far as I am concerned, I will mail your check every Friday for as long as I am able to. Beyond that, you do not exist.

Anger is an emotion best spent as an investment; you have nothing worth investing in so, I would not waste even that emotion on you. One cannot invest in something that has no future; you live only in the misery of whatever you can muster.

These words are just for myself to put in writing, I could go on for chapters, but it would not phase you a bit."

Entitlement

Cause and Effect

The letter prompted a new set of attorneys and a Motion of Contempt. She sued me for not talking to her, for legal fees, and for not paying on time.

We were before a Magistrate in Palm Beach court. I defended myself; Denise had two attorneys with her. This magistrate as opposed to any other, is the only one that actually sat behind her desk and listened and judged based on the facts. The Magistrate ruled on the case as follows:

Legal fees were deemed legally non meritorious and were denied.

For not paying on time, the court ordered payment of arrears totaling $620.00.

For not talking to her, the magistrate wrote the following:

> As for the former wife's assertion that the former husband has closed all avenues of reasonable communication and that he has failed to participate in shared parenting as contemplated by the parties' separation and property settlement agreement paragraph 4 and Florida statutes Chapter 61, this court finds the former wife's assertion is without legal merit. The former husband explained quite calmly and rationally that the former wife's communications with him are manic and harassing, and are in fact, over the top.

> By her own admission, she will call the former husband during Jordan's visitation, ask their son to pass the telephone to his father, and then will ask him where the support monies are. This conduct is inappropriate, manipulative, and ill-advised.

Unrebutted at hearing was the former husband's assertion that the former wife will send him 10-15 emails in response to his one. The Court is persuaded by the truth of the former husband's assertions based upon the former wife's conduct in court.

Literally speaking she could not keep her mouth shut. She was rude and attempted to interrupt the former husband's testimony repeatedly. When her own legal counsel attempted to restrain her and redirect her, she was unable to follow this good advice and direction.

She was histrionic.* All of this makes the former husband's letter and the sentiments therein at least understandable, and in his mind can be understood to justify his unwillingness to engage in communication of any nature whatsoever. That being said her request for relief fails."

*Histrionic, as defined by the dictionary is, "Constantly seeking a reassurance or approval. Excessive dramatics with exaggerated displays of emotions. Excessive sensitivity to criticism or disapproval. Excessive concern with physical appearance.

"A need to be the center of attention (self-centeredness). Low tolerance for frustration or delayed gratification. Rapidly shifting emotional states that may appear shallow to others. Opinions are easily influenced by other people, but difficult to back up with details. Tendency to believe that relationships are more intimate than they actually are. Making rash decisions."

Entitlement

Cause and Effect

266

CHAPTER 27: SON NUMBER ONE

During all of 2003 and 2004, Adam was letting me know of his displeasure on a daily basis. He refused to pay the union for my men, making them very unhappy.

In December of 2003, he informed me they no longer are on his payroll. I understood his frustration, but I do not understand why he did not say, "Let's sit down and figure out a way that we can make this work."

His emails became more adversarial based on the money he had laid out for my men. In April of 2004, emails were exchanged in which I asked why he was so belligerent. One of his answers was the fact that I hurt him and his family financially. I responded with, "I would be glad to discuss that with you with a third party."

Any conversation with my children about something that bothers me is unheard. The reason is they are so intent on being defensive that they never absorb my complaint in the first place.

Listing in an email, all the funds he lost and all the funds I gave him back. In fact, I probably gave more then I owed.

April 29th, 2004, his response (paraphrased): "Like I said, it is pointless to go over each and every issue. There has been so much money back and forth that it would be impossible to figure out. Who remembers if the money you gave me went to repay what I laid out for you for lease payments and insurance; let's move on. I am satisfied that I have been reimbursed for all I lost.

What we need to deal with now is the current funds I am owed and the reason for your current anger."

At this juncture, I was renting an apartment in New York and sending Adam emails, as he never went the ten blocks from where he worked to where I lived.

I sent him an email explaining why I was pissed off. He responded by email with the following:

> *1. Start typing so I don't have to waste time figuring out what you wrote.*

> *2. Lose the exclamation points if you even want me to read what you wrote.*

> *3. It is a shame that you could not separate this disaster which you created from our bond as father and son. Now, you have basically destroyed everything.*

After agreeing that the money aspect is moot he added a "Small list" of current peeves:

> *You had no right involving me with your company.*
> *I had to deal with your irate employees.*
> *I had to deal with how you run your business and with your lifestyle."*

In my response, I wrote:

> *I really find it distasteful for me to explain the above to you. Those words are not yours. You were taught better than that. They are the whisperings of others. The only purpose to this writing is for an inquisitive child or grandchild to try to understand what went wrong.*

> *My businesses was administered as I learned. I was a product of my experience, with an inadequate cash flow.*

The cause of which created an occasional bad choice of job selections so that the flow of money continued.

The reason for this is that I did not know any better. I took over a business with three men and an overdrawn balance of thirty thousand dollars in 1966. I immediately began to build a tremendous, successful business. The more business I did, the more money I needed. My accountant at the time, instead of guiding me into the world of finance and being proactive, kept telling me you can't do it with mirrors. That was his total advice.

Being an eternal optimist, I kept doing more and more business. After years of working seven days a week, I was drawing the same menial salary and sending my in-laws, who were living in Florida, a weekly paycheck for many years.

The same accountant was whispering in my ear. He kept telling me how nice it was of me to send them a paycheck. That most people would not do that. I felt it not only my obligation for taking over the business, but also it gave me pleasure in being able to assist in their quality of life

Inadequate finances, historical nature of the business cash flow, imperfections as a business man, inadequate advice, taught me how to survive with mirrors. The successes grew; the numbers grew.

Your mother and I went to Acapulco, and I came back a new man. Rested, full of new ideas and more ambitions. I decided right then and there that no matter what I was no longer taking a menial salary and my rewards would come first.

Yes, I paid my bills slowly and drove expensive cars, went on vacation, sent my kids to nursery school, camp, college, cars, trips abroad, impacted their lives with surroundings, friendships, and experiences they would never have had.

You are who you are today because of my blood, sweat, and tears and your history as my son. But the road got slippery, and you lost your footing.

As I write all this it brings back so many wonderful memories of experiences I have had and lives I have impacted, people I have helped. I would not have changed a thing and walk proudly in to the final and happiest part of my life. I hope I am able someday to put it all in writing.

How dare you defile my life; you of all people who benefited most by it. The words of the whisperers run so rampant within you that you cannot think properly. You think I am angry; no, anger does not obliterate a father's relationship with his son. No, not anger.

Pain! Pain! of yesterday, Pain! of today, and no longer willing to endure the Pain! of tomorrow.

You have done everything possible to cause me pain in the past several years. In the very beginning of the rebuilding process, you threatened me on a daily basis, telling me that you wanted to quit, knowing that would leave me without the ability to earn a living for my family and myself. Then as you realized that you could do well in this business you tried and succeeded to separate yourself from me.

Finding any assistance I needed by your presence in New York a burden. Callous, hurtful remarks as to all phases of my life.

You showed complete disregard for me as your father and communicated with me during the working day only. Never once in your life showing an emotion of love even before these problems. You were respectful, on occasion, while you were being paid very well with all kinds of perks. Forgetful that you were handed a business with accounts, tools, material, office equipment, and a new and easier digital way of doing business.

In the end, if you ever acquire any unselfish emotions with regard to me, do not feel guilt, feel sorrow. Feel sorrow for yourself and your family at the loss of the most important tool that ever enhanced any of your lives, ME!

It appears you believe that when the chips are down, you, or the company that is an offshoot of my life's work, have no obligations to me. I believe that as long as you are in the electrical business, we have an obligation to each other. You have said that the circumstances that occurred which temporarily bruised you was an attack on you and your family.

The final outcome of the whole situation will probably put you in a better place, with better abilities to succeed. As life's strongest education is what is learned from struggling and or failing.

If my emotion was anger, then I believe we would have a future, but "anger is an emotion best spent as an investment." I have already made my investment in you, and lost.

We separated our businesses completely, and we had no communication.

CHAPTER 28: TRANSITIONS

2004: Amanda had a serious boyfriend, Mike, for the first time. As I heard stories about him, my radar was going off in my head. Nothing I could put my mind on directly, just subliminal things.

Amanda had been going to Tyler Hill sleep-away camp for the past ten years. Now at 17, she became a counselor in charge of ten-year-old kids. She persuaded the camp to hire her boyfriend, Mike, as well. At visiting day that summer, Amanda was saying that Mike was not being treated well by the camp directors. While Amanda complained how unfair that was, my radar understood that where there is smoke, there is fire.

The day after visiting day, Amanda called and said that the camp fired Mike for no reason. She asked if I could talk to them. I called the camp to find out why. They were reluctant to get into details, but it appeared that he wanted to do things his way and not theirs. I told Amanda that they appeared to have good reason and there was nothing I could do.

Amanda said she was going to leave camp with him. I told her that she could not; she had an obligation to the kids and the camp. There were only three weeks more, and she cannot leave.

Amanda called her mother, and between her mother and grandmother she was told, "Don't worry, honey. You leave; don't listen to your father."

Mike was on his way back to pick her up. I called him on his cell phone and at first nicely told him not to pick her up. I was not allowing it. He promptly told me that it was her decision, not mine.

After giving him a stern warning; he proceeded to pick her up. I called Amanda and forbade her from leaving. She called her mother, and with her mother's blessing, left.

Wendy was also encouraging her by letting them stay at her home. I had sent them all an email previously, saying that there is something not right with this kid, Mike. I asked them to keep an eye on the situation.

Amanda was to start college in Tallahassee, at Florida State University, that fall. In our recent divorce settlement, I gave Denise an additional $15,000 for Amanda's first-year college sundry expenses and one year's worth of lease payments on the car. When Amanda disobeyed me, I told her the car is going back.

Her mother, without taking a breath, took the whole $15,000 and bought her a car. I was stuck with the Audi, which I would have given back to Amanda after an awareness of her stupidity.

It was very upsetting that she turned her back on me and was not able to be responsible to her obligation. I remained angry for several months.

Mike followed her to college, interfered with her when she was out with her roommates and friends, and became insanely jealous if she even spoke to anyone else. So, eventually Mike was history, but not easily. He stalked her and in general was feared. It continued through college.

After all the badgering by Denise and Adam, I tried Match.com.

Online dating is a very difficult procedure. First, everyone has a warped sense of who they are. Second, they have a warped sense of what they want. Third, everyone lies.

The market, which is exactly what it is, was based upon the attractiveness of the female. If she was very attractive, your net worth had to be above a fixed number. As the attractiveness went down, so did the number.

Not one of these older single people were interested in any real relationship. It is all about money. In addition to money, everyone had major baggage; a lot were so nuts, that it was a complete embarrassment to be with them. The total reality of the situation is that both men and women are on the dating site but know not what they want.

They all believe, men and women, that no matter how financially secure they are, that they will meet someone with lots of money, and take them all over the world while keeping them on a pedestal. That is the bottom line. Unless they can find that fairytale, they are content being alone. They just don't know it. I had enough, and was not very hopeful of finding a relationship.

Rita and I were introduced by some very good friends. I was attracted to her from the very beginning. She was good looking, in good shape, enjoyed having fun. She loved casino gambling. We went to the Indian reservations, Atlantic City, and spent the summer together in an apartment I rented in New York and a weekend share house in South Hampton.

Even though my heart condition plus my libido made sex difficult, she was aggressive enough to make it work. She was living in the basement of her son's house, did not work, had no other social life, and no other ambition. But I felt there was enough there to work with, as life was getting shorter.

Not wanting to remain single, I wanted to change reality. She was a woman whose appearance was young while I no longer have what it takes to maintain a relationship with a younger woman, financially or physically. She is a woman who is attractive enough to satisfy my shallowness, and a woman who is basically loving and sweet. It was a good choice.

She maintained the youthful misnomers of jealousy and sexuality as a means to happiness. Making love was her satisfaction to being loved, as it was with me in the past.

We had a social life of dining, dancing, and meeting old and new friends. She enjoyed the experiences so much that she wrote a journal recording her daily events.

When the summer was over, she moved in with me in Florida. Truth is, she was never right in the first place, but in my desperate attempt to defy reality, I wanted her to be right. She had no friends, no social life, no ambitions. While I was working I felt that I had to entertain her, and I could not do both.

We had a trip planned to Vegas and San Diego. The Saturday before our ten-day departure we took a ride to Sawgrass Mall, where we ran into Denise, her boyfriend, Steve, Amanda, Jordan and Amanda's boyfriend, Mike.

Denise's very dramatic reaction to that was to start screaming at me. I ran away to avoid a scene, and she chased me around the Gap store. She made a scene confronting Rita, saying, "How can you be with a man like that?" I kept running around the circular clothing racks looking for a security guard.

That evening I was supposed to pick up Jordan, then Rita, then my sister (Marilyn) and have dinner. Because of the dramatization by Denise, I did not know whether I was picking up Jordan or not. By the time I was aware that I was, it was too late to be able to pick up my sister.

Leaving to get Jordan, intending to come back and pick Rita up. I realized by the time I got Jordan I could not do it all. I called my sister, Marilyn, to see if she wanted to meet us or wanted me pick her up. She chose pick up.

I called Rita to meet me at the restaurant, a twenty-minute ride. That was the only way the whole thing could possibly come together, and that it did.

Feeling very pressured, finally I picked up Marilyn and got to the restaurant. Rita was waiting outside. During dinner Rita sat on my left, Jordan on my right, and at times my arm was around Jordan.

Apparently my sister (after a few drinks) found my affection for Jordan suspect, so at the end of the evening while I was in the bathroom she questioned it with Rita. This caused Rita to be offended.

When I arrived home after I dropped off Marilyn, she privately berated me for my behavior and neglect of her, for not picking her up, and because "Saturday night belonged to her," and Jordan had no part in it. I could not recover from that. We were going away in thirty-six hours for ten days, what is Saturday night?

Every night is Saturday night. It was another nail in the coffin. It was all downhill from there. I now was offended by everything. I was not verbal about any of it, but my lack of affection was apparent.

We left the next day for Vegas. I was still not feeling any affection. We were supposed to go to San Diego for five days on Saturday to stay with my friends. That was cancelled. When we got home, I picked up Jordan for dinner, and it was too late to go back and get Rita. She fended for herself. The next day I left to go on some estimates, and as I suspected, when I got home she was packed and gone.

This is a memo I wrote at the time:

> This has been a year of emotional and physical turmoil, more intense than any I have ever encountered. Although I think the worst is over, the individual experiences with friends and family have been mind boggling to say the least.

CHAPTER 29: DAUGHTER NUMBER ONE

Sometime in the nineties, Wendy and Rich bought a house in Long Beach Island and renovated and decorated it beautifully. You were not allowed to come to the house without scheduling a visit far into the future, as they had guests every weekend.

Rich would not go anywhere else on a weekend, and like myself, he was upset about his kids being in sleep away while he was there. However he decided to keep Alec out of sleep away. As stated prior, Alec, like any kid that could have the opportunity, should have. The benefit of that experience is a life-enhancing education

Wendy and Rich would screen all their calls, you could never get them when you called. They would call you when it was an opportune time for them. Additionally, you were not allowed to forward any email without permission.

In 1996, when none of the cracks in my armor were showing, the house in Florida was furnished and the house in New York was being redecorated. Life appeared good, prosperous, and happy there was no indication of the looming disaster that was in the embryonic stages.

That Father's Day, Wendy got in touch with her very talented creative side and presented me with this beautifully written and framed poem.

A FATHER'S DAY POEM

by Wendy Aronwald

September 64, a little girl you had
It was then you took on your role as "Dad"
At the time you didn't know the kind of job you would do,
So I wrote this to tell you how proud I am of you

Entitlement

Cause and Effect

Kew Gardens was the place we lived at first
Whenever you went out, into tears I would burst (not to
mention throw up),
I played with Silly Putty and watched Bozo the Clown
But I enjoyed it the most when you were around
Because of you, lima beans I will eat; let's not mention the
chewing of the meat
When Elyssa came, jealousy made me sleep on your floor,
But I did protect her from that crazy garage door
31 Rosedale Road would be our next home,
There's so many great memories, but I can only fit one in this
poem
You would come home from work and scare us all by shutting
every light,
We couldn't see down the hall
Weekend mornings were always a scream
Running all over and breakfasts of strawberries and sour
cream
"Family day" on Sundays, we were out the door no matter
what we did, it was never a bore
We went on many vacations that were always fun (still do),
Whether we were skiing down the slopes or basking in the sun
Whenever I had a problem you would listen without a care,
and you would always come up with a solution that was fair
To make everyone happy, you would go out of your way
If you could accomplish that, it would be a successful day
i.e., Wendy wanted pizza, Adam Burger King, and Elyssa deli
You would make sure we would all satisfy our belly
Whether I was driving "WENDY 17" or swimming in the pool
Everyone thought my dad was so cool
Right from wrong I was always taught The few times I did
wrong I was always caught
At Laurelton Electric when I was working off the books

you never scared me with one of your looks
One day at Hartford, I called you depressed you drove up to surprise me,
You really are the best (Hartford has great fall foliage)
When it comes to funny guys, there is no other than my dad
who I always refer to as my big brother
We've had some whopper fights when I thought we'd speak never
But it only made our relationship better than ever
Still, to this day when I'm sad or uptight you're the only one who could make it right
When we spend our time together and it's time for goodbye

I still want to grab onto your leg and hysterically cry
I thank you for everything that I have in my life
because of you I became a good student, a happy mom and wife
So look in the mirror and shout out loud "I am a wonderful dad and my daughter
Wendy is proud!"
HAPPY FATHER'S DAY! I LOVE YOU.
P.S. Brooke Shields, so what, I'm not as tall, I threw her off your pillow, and I could rip her off your wall!!!

Beautifully done. As a Dad, it doesn't get any better than that.

This was written in 1996, the only thing different about me from then to below is the fact that there was a diminishing cash flow.

Eight years later, in 2004, Louise, wife number one, and mother to Wendy, Elyssa, and Adam, moved to New Jersey to be near her children.

She decided that she wasn't going to rush finding a new job. She wanted to enjoy her children and grandchildren, get used to her new surroundings, and then get a job. Prior to that, she needed a new car and could not afford it. The three siblings equally paid the monthly loan payments on a new car for their mother. About $75.00 each, per month. Each one could easily afford the payments.

Now that she wasn't rushing to go back to work they were concerned as to how she will manage, at which point she advised them that she had a few dollars put away.

Wendy related this story to me as if to say her mother duped them and made them pay for the car when she had some money in the bank. Why they would be upset and not proud to be able to help their mother, I do not know.

Meanwhile I was being harassed, badgered, defiled, and humiliated by Denise's continued need for an immediate fix for mismanaging her money. She became angry that I could not give her that week's alimony at the exact time she wanted it. She said that is "not her problem," and threatened that she would tell Wendy that I had a Diner's Club credit card in the name of Wendy Scheffler. It was not a secret, the card was in my name, but the primary holder was Wendy. I was in possession of that card for twenty-two years, since she was eighteen. That was the only card I had left, because I made sure to keep it up to date, as it was in her name.

Diner's Club never knew Wendy Scheffler was Wendy Aronwald; they assumed she was my wife and dealt only with me. The card was used all through those years for Wendy, Elyssa, Adam, Denise, and myself as well as their school, auto, clothes, business, etc. As always I was sure to keep it current.

At the time of this discovery, I owed Diner's Club ten thousand dollars. I had an agreement with them to pay it off. There was no record of it on Wendy or Rich's name. Denise of course emailed Wendy and without even discussing it with me. Wendy called and berated me in a manner that would not be tolerated by anyone. "My poor husband suffers to pay all the bills on time and you have the nerve to ruin our credit."

Again it was never in her married name or associated with her social security number. The letter that Denise sent, with copies to each, was so scathing and defiling that you would have thought my children would have been offended, that this woman, who was the benefactor of a magnificent life that I provided could possibly have sent this to them.

In this very difficult time for me, not one of those three children was interested or ever saw where I lived.

One of the things that always stuck in my craw, from years past, was a discussion I had with Wendy. She wanted a new car. I told her I could not buy it for her because Elyssa was turning seventeen, and I would have to buy her a car just like you.

Her response was a serious statement of just because you did it for me, you do not have to do it for her. I never could understand the fact that she would question that. At the time I partially chalked it up to youth, but now I can see it was a pattern.

There were also times that many of my acquaintances had negative feelings about Wendy, but I was never able to get a clear understanding to what it was, and I did not see it.

After the Diner's Card story, the first thing that occurs is that Elyssa jumps in on the Wendy credit card drama. "How can you do that? The repercussions," blah, blah, blah.

Not, "Gee, Dad that must be how you came up with some of the money in a timely fashion for us kids to get all those wonderful perks and opportunities." From that point on my relationship with each was that of an "inconvenient former patriarch."

Meanwhile, Wendy's father-in-law Morty and I were both single and living in Boca. His live-in girlfriend worked nights as a hostess. He had no one to play with at night. We became bar-hopping dinner buddies and went place to place where all the singles went. It was good for both of us; he needed company and knew everyone, therefore I met everyone.

Someone, either Amanda or Denise, told me that Morty ran into Denise one night and made plans with her and her friend for dinner the next night. In all our dinners together afterward he never said a word.

In 2005, on two occasions Rich and Wendy came down to see his father (fifteen minutes away) and never even told me they were in Boca. When I found out through Morty, I asked Wendy about it, and received the following:

"Rich told me the day before he was supposed to come that we would probably be meeting Morty in Ft. Lauderdale because he didn't feel well enough to drive to Key Biscayne. Then he told me that he had spoken to his father and we were going up to Boca because we had nothing to do in Ft. Lauderdale all day. We actually dropped hints about seeing your apartment (so that we could see you) but it didn't look like Morty was getting it and we didn't want to take the time away from him, so we did not want to push the issue."

The second trip was never addressed.

Morty, Rich's father, had divorced his wife and somehow kept their Florida home. He had a younger, attractive girlfriend. In a trip to New Jersey, he was staying with his son Bruce and Bruce's wife, Bonicia.

Morty had a skin rash on his face, and Bonicia was pregnant; she was nervous and after a week asked Morty to please find other arrangements as she feared for her baby.

Morty never again communicated with Bruce, Bonicia and their children. Morty's daughter lives in Tampa; one holiday he was to go to their house; an argument about bringing his girlfriend. ended that relationship. The only family he was now talking to was Rich and Wendy.

A pattern emerges. And until his death, no communication.

Jamie, their daughter, my granddaughter, was having her Bat Mitzvah. Morty, Rich's father and Jamie's grandfather, was not invited. They did not want to make Rich's mother or brother, Bruce, or his wife or the daughter, Laurie, uncomfortable.

The grandfather was not invited. To this day I could never understand how any child can think in those terms. I found that very hurtful, not because of Morty, because of their lack of common decency. I realized that their disrespect was not limited to me.

Morty died unexpectedly at seventy-five. The funeral was in New York, and I did not find it necessary to call Rich to offer my condolences because I was sure he just plain didn't care. Anyway, I sent the following message with a basket of fruit to their home during the Shiva:

> *My heartfelt condolences for your loss of Morty. I had the privilege of spending time with him at a more relaxed time in our lives. He generously provided me with an entry into the singles' world probably unsurpassed by any one. I do not think there was anyone worth knowing that he wasn't friendly with*

and knew their entire history. His presence around all the hot spots of Boca will sorely be missed, the impressions he made in those same institutions is a legacy few have, or will achieve.

All these circumstances were cementing Wendy's quest to rise as the matriarch of the family. How dare I not call her husband. They were not talking to me. They held a memorial service in Boca which I attended and they walked past me without any acknowledgement.

Later on, Wendy wanted to make peace, on the condition (as usual) that none of the past was discussed. Just go forward. I agreed, but stated that I was disappointed. She could not understand why I was disappointed and that's where it stood. The following letter was written, never sent:

> *It is interesting that you would question my disappointment. I do believe you were here in the city of Boca, and never advised me of same? I guess the delay in writing is the realization that it is futile. I have never known you to ever be anything but defensive in any attempt at constructive criticism.*
>
> *From 2003 through 2005 was about the most difficult part of my life. I had lost my main business in New York. I was in the process of getting divorced. I was paying forensic accountants and divorce lawyers and I was being threatened, harassed, and humiliated by a crazy person every single day.*
>
> *None of my remaining assets were converted to cash. My income was still not adequate for my expenses.*

I had not had a place I could call home for two years and in the middle of all this I had to find time to have the depressed, insecure, normal feelings of divorce. That was the lowest point of my life.

So, what was it I did to you, for you to seize an insignificance to lash out at me without any regard or compassion?

Did I not give you enough money ?

Did I not remember all your friends' names?

Did I not get you into a good enough college?

Did I put you on too stringent of a budget in college?

Did I not make you a nice enough engagement party?

Did I not take you and your friends on nice enough vacations?

Did I not make you a nice enough wedding?

Did I lose your respect because I came late to Jamie's birth?

Did I not prepare yours and Rich's surprise birthday party properly?

Did I take too long to get to Hartford when you sounded down?

Did I not provide a luxurious enough lifestyle?

Did I give you, on your seventeenth birthday, a Toyota not expensive enough?

Did I not have the right to be upset when you purposely left my wife out of Benicia's shower?

What was it that I did to you, to not know compassion?

What was it that I did, that lets you think that you can treat me so poorly?

Was there some entitlement that I missed?

What can it be that far less giving parents are treated better by their children? Maybe it's because I land on my feet, would you feel more compassionate if I could not eat at my favorite restaurants? Or if I was destitute in general?

It appears it is not just me that this selfish disrespect is directed. You found your mother guilty of making you pay 1/3 her car payment and your father in law not worthy to be invited to his Grandchild's religious celebration.

It was an honor to help pay my parents' bills and your mother's parents' bills and each with pride. I do not need you to pay my bills, never did, and never will. So don't worry, that pride you will never bear. In the possibility that someday you may see that you would want your children to behave better then you, you should have them read this, possibly emotional decency skips generations.

Life has many bumps in the road! Can you imagine any of your children treating you like you did me? But I guess wherever I failed as a parent, you shall succeed, I surely hope so. I wouldn't wish the dividends of this upbringing on anyone. I am sure I will not have to be concerned, but please do not even consider memorializing me as in the phony hypocritical farce you presented for yourselves in Morty's name.

The letter was never sent, and as usual we reconciled without discussing the cause and effect of the problem. But, in 2008 I took the last disrespectful action from Wendy, and we have not spoken since.

CHAPTER 30: HURRICANES

FRANCIS

As in the Good Witch and the bad Witch, for me there were Good Hurricanes and Bad Hurricanes.

In 2004, After experiencing the tsunamis of divorce, financial ruin, disrespectful children, a materially addicted, terminally dumb, ex-wife, a simple Hurricane was just a drizzle

Hurricane season exploded with tumultuous weather affecting South Florida, causing severe blackouts in the Palm Beach area.

This created an opportunity for the furnishing and installation of standby natural gas and propane generators, which has been one of the products of my knowledge and experience throughout my career.

I met with an inspector in the building department on Australia Avenue in Palm Beach County and asked what licenses I would need to conform with the county's requirements. He explained that I would need licensed and insured electric and plumbing contractors to obtain permits for each location, and the only license required of me would be an occupational license, which I obtained.

As a one-man operation, I sold, and had the electric and plumbing contractors install, over one hundred home standby fully automatic generators to very satisfied customers. They all had the proper permits and final inspections.

In 2005 The hurricane season followed up with devastating hurricanes such as **Katrina, Rita and Wilma**

The following year, Wilma hit and devastated the electrical integrity of the area. In the midst of the winds and storms and blackouts, I personally serviced those customers in need of help to restart or make minor corrections for continuous operation of their generators. I had not worked with my hands in forty years.

Among those customers were senior citizens, ambulatory, oxygen-dependent and stroke victims. My mechanics were tending to their own family needs. I happily resolved all the mechanical problems

These blackouts made the generator business boom. I proceeded to hire salespeople to handle the influx of business and advertised in the newspapers and on radio.

From the last quarter in 2005 through May of 2006, we sold over 600 generator systems, valued over $8 million.

Sandy

My sister, Karen, and her husband, Jack, lived in a community in which friends of theirs Sandy and Bill had also lived. I had met them years earlier when I was with Denise.

Sandy's husband passed away, and my sister thought that Sandy and I should meet again as two single people at the appropriate time.

In October of 2005. that time came, and all four of us met for dinner. The evening was okay. I did not get any vibes of interest on her part, so I just let it go.

Several weeks later, my sister called to ask why I hadn't called her. I said that I did not think she was interested. So I called. We met for dinner on her way to the airport and had a very romantic, interesting evening.

Having been separated and divorced for over two years at this time, I was not finding the market out there too attractive, and I welcomed her interest in me and responded in kind.

In my sister's eyes, I lived a very high life, and currently things were going my way. My finances were not then known by anyone; she probably thought I was in good order, as I usually do not offer information.

However, I was so elated with the generator business. I would tell people it was like standing at the craps table with all the numbers covered and rolling nothing but numbers.

On Valentine's Day, I bought Sandy a beautiful gift, flowers, and cards. There was no real reaction. I had no idea if she liked the gift or not. My sister said that she loved it. I learned later on that Sandy was not able to show appreciation.

In March, Sandy made me a surprise birthday party for my 65th birthday at La Vielle Maison, a restaurant I had mentioned that I had never been to and wanted to go. It was all charming. Her kids, all living in New York, sent me a bottle of champagne and a card thanking me for making their mother so happy.

After many months of Sandy and I enjoying "happy hour" at my sister's, we spoke about me moving in with her, but she said she would not do that unless we were married. My sister kept pushing me in that direction as well.

We had planned a long weekend in the Bahamas for Sandy's birthday in May, at my sister's suggestion. (Which I assumed was discussed with Sandy) It would be a nice surprise to get engaged at dinner on her birthday.

I was anxious to get on with my life, for family unification, social continuity and a mutual partnership in a mature relationship

I felt that Sandy and I had the feelings for each other and enjoyed the same goals, so I was for it. I put down a deposit on a ring .

In the Bahamas, I presented a birthday card, birthday gift, and proposal. Although I was led to this path by her and my sister, and she knew this was coming, she rejected me on the basis of already having a relationship without the need to marry. I had no problem with that arrangement, but I was absolutely humiliated and could not understand.

Probably her kids talked her out of it. She did not seem to offer any consolation for my obvious, confused, embarrassed, and humiliated feelings. It took me twenty four hours to get past it.

CHAPTER 31 "GOOD OLD BOYS"

Realizing that the potential of this business was long lasting in sales and service contracts, I wanted to be as independent as possible. I wanted to get licensed in Florida to eliminate the need for an electrical subcontractor.

The most expeditious way to do that under Florida law would be to have a "qualifier" as part of the firm. After placing an ad for a qualifier and interviewing several applicants, I decided on Gordon Meyers, a Florida-licensed electrician. Meyers informed me that his license was currently inactive; however, he had a friend by the name of Michael Wood who is a professional specializing in the expediting of licensing and would be able to get the necessary approvals within a few weeks.

In October of 2005, and upon mutual agreement, I paid Michael Wood a deposit of $4,000.00, and was assured that within a few weeks we would be all set. Meyers and I came to a mutual agreement of $1,000.00 a month.To begin upon receipt of the license, about November 9, 2005. Meyers requested an advance of his first payment of $1,000.00 for the first month and was issued a check for $1,000.

Wood came back informing me that the Department of Business and Professional Regulation (DBPR) required a bond in the amount of $25,000.00 to activate Gordon Meyers' license. I deposited $25,000 with the bank and secured a bond.

Generators was the business to be in, at that time, selling millions of dollars' worth. I built a real organization and felt like king of the world, as I truly believed I was doing a good deed and servicing the peoples' needs. I was building a future for my kids and was meeting nice, interesting people.

My thoughts on proposing a generator to someone was to explain that it is an insurance policy that you hope to never need. Therefore, do not buy one that will power the entire house, but just the areas you will need to be comfortable in case of a blackout.

We designed a proposal that listed groups of items people might like to power if they lost electricity. Each group had a price. Salespeople who had no experience with generators could ask which grouping the customer wanted, and the price was right there. I was the only one in the business locally selling in this manner. The competition was selling by the square footage of the house. Ninety percent of the time they were trying to sell a unit too large and too expensive, unnecessary for an emergency. Therefore we obtained the lion's share of the business.

We were on radio daily and the newspapers weekly. The leads came in, and the sales people went out. Invariably there was the customer who wanted the whole house done no matter what the cost. So sales came in daily from $10,000 to $100,000, and each sale came with a 33% deposit, which enabled me to pay for the generators COD and collect the second third on delivery so the money was there for advertising. Sales people were paid their commission on each payment made on the same day they brought in the check.

The office was my apartment, with secretaries, accountants, installers, etc. My lifestyle did not change at all. The money that was coming in was going right out to finance each project.

The various counties of south Florida were feverishly trying to establish their parameters for the installation of generators, as they were bombarded with permit applications. These circumstances were well publicized in the local newspapers.

At one point they actually ceased issuing permits. By the time they were able to revise the code requirements to today's standards the back up of permit applications was beyond their control. The customers were understandably concerned, however, they were not interested in the reasons for the delay; they wanted what they wanted. Therefore, on August 25th, 2005, I sent a letter to the customers who had generators on order.

I explained why there was a delay and gave them a choice of accepting the new requirements, which would delay their installation, at no additional charge, or we would refund their deposit. Everyone accepted the new requirements.

In January 2006, I contacted Michael Wood regarding the qualifier license and inquired as to what the holdup may be. Wood responded by informing me that he had spoken with the DBPR and would have an answer the next day.

On February 07, 2006, I was still not in receipt of Meyers' license and had not received any word as to what the delay may be. I again contacted Wood, who informed me that he was attempting to overcome a glitch in Meyers' application process. Because of his prior bankruptcy, Meyers' application file had been flagged and was being submitted to the Electrical Licensing Board for review. I was never aware that there was a prior bankruptcy.

On March 23, 2006, Wood informed me that the Board approved Gordon Meyers' application to qualify for Pioneer Electric.

Upon obtaining certificates for liability insurance and workman's compensation, we could begin pulling permits. Wood then requested and was paid the balance due to him.

We contacted our generator supplier, Generac, and ordered all the generators for new contracts we had in-house. After several delaying answers and correspondence I was advised by Generac that I would have to pay for each order in full with placement of the order. This was not possible, as the contract was written so that the customer's payment would be based on delivery of the generator. Cash flow was predicated on paying as they were shipped and collecting as they were delivered. Had I paid in full before they would build and ship, I would have had to lay out three million dollars for at least ninety days, an impossibility. Prior to this, I purchased and paid for over $1 million worth of generators from Generac in the previous manner, the way we did it in the past.

Because there was a considerable and unreliable lead time, we placed the orders. As Generac notified us of what was ready to ship, we wired the funds. This was after conversations and correspondence with all parties concerned to explain that I could not abide by these terms, and we had established a pattern over the past year which was working very well.

They would not budge. I started searching the country for suppliers that had inventory and purchased them COD. However, this was not nearly filling the demand. What I did not know was that Generac had prior knowledge as to what was going to happen.

We had over one hundred generators paid for in full at Hunter Crane storage yard in Delray Beach, waiting for long-submitted permit applications to be approved. Our customers were getting anxious, as they had paid substantial deposits.

Hurricane season was approaching, and they were not seeing any progress. In order to diffuse their anxiety, we installed the required concrete pads for the generators to be placed on.

We delivered generators to their homes as fast as humanly possible. These delays, which were not just by us (they were with the entire industry in south Florida), were unavoidable due to the delay in permitting.

The customers were getting more anxious. By then it was April, and hurricane season starts in June. No one wanted to be left in the dark again. It was becoming more and more difficult to placate some customers.

Two Major competitors filed bankruptcy, the only other one of significance was a "good old boy" with long time affiliations with the license board the DBPR, and the police department

An investigative reporter named Sheppard from NBC was assigned the investigation that was orchestrated by the "good old boy" and an opportunistic employee of my firm. He led Sheppard to some disgruntled customers. When he had his report ready, he contacted me to make an appointment to come in with the TV cameras and interview me. I passed, and sent him the following letter on May 8, 2006.:

> *Mr. Sheppard,*
>
> *Until recently, I was not sure that this whole situation was not a hoax being perpetrated because I am apparently inconvenient competition. Apparently, this is not a hoax.*
>
> *I have been an electrical contractor in my own business since 1966. I am 65 years old. I ran a residential division and a commercial division. In addition to our ongoing customer base, we serviced an average of five new residential customers per day, six days a week for forty years, and approximately 50,000 customers over this period. There is not*

one unsatisfactory report in the Better Business Bureau over that 40 years.

Fortunately, I still have associated with me a gentleman who has been in my employ for over thirty years, Mr. Calvin Lewis. In all the interviews that were conducted by you, he was never interviewed. The only people you interviewed were those that could give you a more interesting story. Not a fair and balanced journalistic point of view.

When south Florida had power outage problems, I used my knowledge and experience to provide people with an easy way to have temporary power which would be providing a solution, in many cases, to life-threatening situations. That proved to be true.

During Wilma, we had many people installed, and they successfully endured the hurricane with their generators in operation. Some of them were dependent on electricity for oxygen; one gentleman had recently had a stroke. One woman a paraplegic; others are elderly and incapable of doing anything other than relying on automatic standby power.

In the infancy stages, there were some problems; some of the generators did not work automatically, and five different generators did not start. When we serviced them, we found the problem was a defective starter inherent to the manufacturer in each. The manufacturer guided us to a parts department in Palm Beach, which had a recording on their phone stating they were closed during the hurricane.

We had new units in the warehouse from which we stripped the parts and made sure everyone was in operation. These people, who are forever indebted, and quite possibly whose lives we may have saved, were never interviewed.

During the first day of Wilma, I personally went to the homes of the Cassidys, Schultzs, and Strochaks to start their generators manually and restore their electricity. Generators were ordered, paid for, delivered, and stored. We obtained surveys and hired propane and natural gas licensee contractors. These people were never interviewed.

We were waiting for our own qualification, which I was professionally advised would be forthcoming. It was not. We then obtained other qualified contractors to proceed.

Customers who felt they waited too long requested to cancel their orders and were refunded their money. What did I do wrong? From what I understand, there are several complaints with the DPBR. I do not have a single complaint in our office that has not been satisfied that I am aware of. If you have access to these complaints, I would be happy to address them one by one, and if we have not satisfied the consumer, I would be happy to do so.

Very Truly Yours,
Michael B. Scheffler

He ignored my letter. They aired a report that we made installations without permits, received deposits with no intention of delivering product, and were defrauding the public. The fact that most of the customers had received their generators, which were valued much more than their deposits, was not a sensational enough story. They would rather utilize their power with scare tactics and run with their biased, unsubstantiated story.

Subsequently, the story was picked up by the local newspapers and the Department of Business and Professional Regulations (DBPR), causing devastating cascading events—both in business and personally.

I was not overly concerned because there was nothing then and now that was done improperly. We never installed any generators without obtaining the proper permits, nor did I present myself as a general contractor. There was never intent to defraud, harm, or injure any of our customers, employees, or vendors. And there are paper trails to prove it.

The cascading events started with the manager of the bank I was affiliated with, with whom I had a good relationship. She called, and we set up an appointment for me to come in. When I arrived, the meeting consisted of the manager and their security officer. Without any interest in knowing the facts the security officer closed my accounts, threatened and humiliated me, and personally diverted $40,000 of my funds.

Next was Meyers' license to qualify the firm, which was finally issued on May 3, 2006, and which would satisfy all the requirements of the DBPR. I thought that meant that as long as there was no "Customer Harm" this entire catastrophe would be over.

On the same day of issuance, May 3, 2006, Meyers submitted his letter of resignation, which nullified the company qualification. The DBPR requested that I meet with them, which I did on May 15, 2006.

They explained that they had several complaints and that I was not operating with the proper licensing. The DBPR stated that in order for me to sell a turnkey product where I collected for and paid the licensed subcontractors, I would need a general contractor's license, or a company qualifier's license.

The law states that if a qualifier resigns, you may proceed for up to sixty days before obtaining a new qualifier. Without that, I would be subject to both civil and criminal charges.

Cooperating with their request, we provided a list of customers we had sold generators to and informed them of the location where we had stored an additional sixty-five generators that were pending delivery. They visited the storage warehouse and verified that these facts were true.

The investigator in charge, Michael Greene, seemed to understand that we would work with him to resolve any improprieties that may have occurred.

He advised me that criminal charges would apply only based on "Customer Harm." As they suggested, I prepared a new contract in which the customer would hire their own subcontractors. I submitted the contract for customer approval and advised them that I would either refund the deposits or rewrite the contracts to their satisfaction.

In the two weeks that followed, I returned over $500,000 in deposits and continued to write business in the manner in which the DBPR suggested. Meanwhile, we had over $200,000.00 in approved credit card deposits that we were waiting for our processor to deposit to our account.

We were processing our credit cards through Innovative Bank, which had a $15,000 security deposit and was requesting $15,000 more as our volume was high. That was paid. I then informed our account manager that I was sitting with almost $200,000 in credit card deposits and asked how he would like me to handle it. He advised me to process all of them, which was done on April 21, 2006. All were approved but were never funded to our account. There was no response or explanation from anyone in the company.

Entitlement

Cause and Effect

300

CHAPTER 32: BAD THINGS HAPPEN TO GOOD PEOPLE

There is a tranquil beauty in welcoming the day in south Florida. The rising sun, the breeze from the ocean, the cleanliness of the surroundings, the exotic foliage, and the sea breeze aroma all give you the sense of being at a vacation resort. The closer to the ocean, the higher the euphoric appreciation. This particular day, June 1st, 2006, three months past my 65th birthday, I woke in West Boynton Beach, still south Florida, but with only a fraction of the amenities offered closer to the water.

Sandy was going to New York for her granddaughter's graduation on an early flight from Fort Lauderdale. We took her car, as mine was too small for the luggage. I dropped her off to check in, parked the car, and went back to escort her to the gate. We said our goodbyes and I headed back to the car. It was still early, about 7:00 a.m. My next appointment wasn't until 10:00 a.m.

Taking a casual ride on US 1, I stopped at a Denny's and enjoyed a rare, unrushed few minutes as I dined, drank my coffee, and scheduled the order in which I would go about my business responsibilities for that day.

From there I went to Coconut Creek, an area between Fort Lauderdale and Boca, west of Pompano Beach. I was to meet with my business attorney, who I recently retained, and Florida's Department of Business and Professional Regulation investigator, Michael Green.

Green and I had met twice before and spoke on the phone two or three other times. The purpose of this meeting was to finalize a business plan that we had previously agreed to over the phone. The prior day, Green had called to ask me to come in to tweak it and put it into writing, which we scheduled for 9:00 a.m. the following day.

Thinking it would be in my best interests to have my attorney with me to dot the I's and cross the T's, which is something I never had the patience for, I called to advise him. He had an appointment and could not make it until 10:00 a.m.

When I called Green back to reschedule. I explained the need to reset the appointment, as my attorney had a prior engagement. Green put me on hold. After a few minutes he came back, trying to talk me out of an attorney, and he was annoyed that the time had to be changed. However, the new appointment was set.

Arriving on time, my attorney a few minutes later, we were kept waiting in the lobby. Sometime later, an official-looking gentleman arrived and was immediately buzzed in. A few minutes later we were escorted to the supervisor's office.

In the room was Supervisor Cheryl Biesky, Inspector Michael Green, the official-looking gentleman, my attorney, and me. I had met Cheryl at a previous meeting; at that time she was dressed similar to the other employees in jeans and a casual shirt. Today she was dressed to the nines.

There were the cordial hellos and introductions, and that was it. The unknown gentleman stood up with his badge; he had a gun attached to his belt. He notified me that I was under arrest, and read me my rights. He had me empty my pockets, give everything to my attorney, placed my hands behind my back, and cuffed me.

Feeling like a bad dream, I asked Green, "What is this about?" He did not answer.

I was then escorted toward the front door, the detective on my right, my attorney on my left.

Entitlement

Cause and Effect

The director and investigator were behind. My attorney, so far mute and clueless, asked if he could have a minute alone with me. The detective put us in an office without windows and stood guard at the door. My attorney was to receive a $5000.00 dollar retainer that day. He had the check with my other personal items, but it had not been signed. That was his concern. I signed it with my hands cuffed behind my back. Not an easy task.

My attorney was to get me a criminal attorney. I asked him to use my cell phone (which he also had) to find my daughter Elyssa's phone number, and have her coordinate between the attorneys and myself so that I would be informed as to what to do.

He understood. We walked out in the same formation. They continued to escort me to the front outer door. The office was a store front amongst other unoccupied stores of a strip mall with a large, shopping center-styled parking lot, empty with the exception of some scattered vans and cars.

When we exited the front door, the scattered vans and cars came alive. All their doors sprung open. Rushing out of each of the vehicles orifices were TV cameras on tripods, news anchors with microphones, and newspaper photographers with their cameras. They all circled around me, pushing the microphones in my face, yelling questions and statements as the cameras were rolling. The only thing I thought to do was bury my chin in my shoulder.

This was all happening as I was being escorted to a squad car, as if I was starring in a Law and Order episode. My head was pushed forward as I lowered myself into the back seat.

The interviews that appeared on all the TV news reports that evening were than filmed with the detective and the well-prepared director for her fifteen minutes of fame.

I was in a small cage in a very cramped area of the back seat, my knees up to my chin, my arms behind me and cuffed together for what seemed like an eternity. I was taken to a substation in Pompano Beach.

I was photographed, fingerprinted, booked, and placed in a cell four feet wide by six feet long with one other inhabitant, a young, emaciated, sparsely dressed man who paced the area floor for the entire six hours I was there. Finally the cell door was unlocked. My feet were cuffed at the ankles, my wrist was cuffed to my cellmate, led to a waiting prison bus, already occupied with prisoners gathered from other substations. The Pompano shackles were removed, the prison bus shackles were installed, and I was led to a caged-in section of the bus, seated and cuffed to the seat.

As we drove away, I looked out of the window at the cars passing by as the drivers were trying to get a glimpse of a prisoner, just as I have often done in the past. The bus headed to the Broward county jail. We arrived, the prison bus shackles were removed, and the Broward jail shackles were installed. I was led, in chain gang fashion, to another, bigger holding cell with about forty inhabitants, one toilet, and one sink.

Several hours later, I was chained again and brought to the shower and changing section. I was given an envelope to store my civilian clothes, led naked to a shower. All your cavities and crevices are inspected, prison garb is issued.

Next, I waited several more hours to be interviewed by a nurse as to any medications I required. Then, chained again and marched to the bullpen area, a huge room with a dozen cells bordering one side. Each cell had two bunks, one toilet, and one sink.

The experienced perpetrators immediately claimed their cells and bunks and lined up for the phones. The phones required a line for each, and depending how tough a cellmate looked determined who was told to hurry their calls or not.

The phone could only call the local area code, 954, or collect. I had no one to call in 954. Whoever I tried to call collect had their answering machine on. Finally I reached a business contact who had the same area code. I asked him to have the attorney let me know what is going on.

Thursday night at ten o'clock, I was eleven hours into day one. I was led in chains to a cubicle, two feet square, with a head-sized circle of glass on the opposite end. My attorney was on the other side of the glass. The area was so confining that I was starting to hyperventilate with claustrophobic anxiety. He informed me that the criminal attorney would be there in the morning at my arraignment. He never reached my daughter, as he did not know how to use the phone. I am sure had he asked anyone in his office, they would have showed him how to use it.

Back to the bull pen with no medicine, and only the floor to lie down on. I lay on the floor, catching cat naps through the night that never ended. I was awakened at 4:00 a.m. for a morning feeding. At 8:00 a.m. I was shackled, chain ganged, and led to a huge auditorium with a closed circuit TV to the courtroom and judge.

After an hour, my case was called. I had no idea what to do, but a voice in the courtroom acknowledged "not guilty." Bail was set at $7500. With a sigh of relief that at least I knew something of what was going on, we were then led back to the bullpen. I waited for my release, and waited, and waited, and waited.

Friday, twenty-two hours into day two, nothing, no news, no communication with the outside world. My daily medications for my heart, which were carefully listed during the interview with the nurse, were never provided. Nothing to do but wait, no way of reaching anyone, no one to ask about procedures or expectations, no pencil, no paper, just waiting. Cat naps on the floor again, waiting and waiting and waiting. Visits came at all hours from threatening sheriff deputies, warning anyone if they step out of line they will be there forever.

Bail is posted twenty-four hours a day; inmates were being paged continually as they were being released. Each time I heard the P.A. system go on, I prayed for my name to be called.

Saturday at about 6:00 p.m., eighteen hours into day three, my name was called. Instead of being released, I was disappointed to find that I was called with others to be moved to more permanent quarters. I was given a blanket and pillow and was informed to wait in the open area for my cell assignment.

This area was half the size as the last with two bunks in each six foot by ten foot cell, one sink, one open toilet, and one TV in the center room, which was controlled in the same manner as the phones. This area was not as intimidating as the other, and some of the nicer prisoners would try to make small talk. Of course they would address me as "Pop."

One of the young inmates came over to me, noted he had seen me on TV, and marveled at the amount of money that was associated with my arrest. He almost asked for my autograph, but walked away saying to his friends, "Hey, you know who this is?"

The only way that I could endure what I was going through was to compartmentalize my state of mind.

It is a sophisticated method of multi-tasking, which is how I lived my life in order to keep that proverbial cup three quarters full. My reasoning concluded there was just nothing I could do, and there was nothing I did wrong. I just had to wait to get out and learn what this is all about. I sat and watched TV, composed and patient.

I marvel at all the critics of George W. Bush's reaction to the news of 9/11. That is the way any rational person would react. Absorb the situation, don't show panic, learn all the facts, and when the facts and alternatives are known, act on them.

Finally at about 10:00 p.m. I was called out and sent to the release area. I was given my clothes and personal belongings and exited through a maze of doors. Each locked behind prior to the next one opening. I was trying to figure out how to get home. I had no wallet, no money. Sandy's car should have been at the parking lot where I left it, but I had no keys.

When I arrived in the lobby, to my very happy surprise, Sandy was there waiting for me. Not only did she fly right back from New York when she heard about me being arrested, she was waiting about four hours in the lobby. The two clerks in the lobby processing bail and releases were enjoying whip cream pie, compliments of Sandy. Had she not done that I might still be there.

Entitlement

Cause and Effect

308

CHAPTER 33: FOLLOW THE MONEY

There are receivables of five hundred ninety three thousand five hundred and seventy two dollars and fifty cents ($593,572.50) that I have been trying to collect with little success.

The DBPR then issued a cease and desist order, putting me out of business without the ability to deliver the generators in stock or collect monies due for generators previously delivered. Even the electrical and plumbing contractors who had my deposit money used this as an excuse to not to return any of it!

Having been arrested and charged in Broward County, I retained a prominent criminal attorney. He assumed that the state would combine the Palm Beach County and Broward charges into one package in Broward County. He quoted his fee and was retained. Instead of keeping the case in the white collar crime unit, Palm Beach wanted a piece of the action and arrested me there as well.

My attorney, David Bogenschutz, neglected to tell me that his practice excludes anything north of Broward County, and that in Palm Beach County I should retain the public defender, whom he would guide through the process. In fact, he was hardly accessible to either me or the public defender. However, he is a stand-up guy and is worthy of his reputation.

There were two or three other generator companies in the same situation, but they had the required licenses. Due to the delays in permitting and the customers demanding their money back, those firms filed for bankruptcy with millions of dollars of deposits which were never to be returned to their rightful owners. All of this was substantiated in newspaper articles.

Since we had proof of the purchased generators, issued purchase orders, had paid deposits to subcontractors, and had filed and paid for permit applications, there is not a single human being who, after verification of all the above, could or would think that there was ever an intention to do anything other than good honest business practices.

The situation could have been remedied. Instead, with the politically motivated actions of the DBPR, The state attorney and the incompetence of the code writing department, seventy-nine customers were unable to retrieve a total of $500,000.

There was no crime committed here. The infraction of the general contractor and qualifier licenses was nonsense. The prosecutors just wanted the glory of the NBC story to rub off on them; all other laws were followed, and all requirements, permits, installations, etc. were well executed in accordance with all other laws.

Again, the following could be easily verified with checks, credit cards, and bank statements: a total of $853,596 was refunded to customers. Over $100,000 of deposits were given to subcontractors. As previously stated, that money is not being returned because the subcontractors feel they can take advantage of the situation. Over $500,000.00 of receivables is being sought through legal means, as these customers as well are trying to capitalize on our misfortune. All the above information can be one hundred percent verified and substantiated by documents, witnesses, and testimonials.

Although I have been in business since 1966 without a blemish, not one official or prosecutor ever asked for or cared about any of the facts. The statements I sent to them, with the facts listed above, were never read and were just ignored. I believed in the system of innocent until proven guilty, and was sure this would be resolved intelligently.

Over the next two years there were status reports, court appearances, and very little public interest now that it was not a media magnet.

There was no other choice but to accept a plea. 110,000 down and $1,750 per month restitution. In addition nine months of incarceration The nine months was supposed to be spent under house arrest, but the state's attorney in the presentation to the Judge, omitted that little item. When we objected the Judge said He will accept the plea as presented or not at all

We agreed that I was to turn myself in to the Palm Beach court on Tuesday, Jan 8th, to begin serving a nine-month sentence.

Other than Bogenshutz on the criminal side, I tried to obtain a civil attorney to handle all the cases I have for the money owed and the wrong done to me. No one would even talk to me without a minimum of a $25,000 retainer. The one lawyer who I did hire with a $15,000 retainer did nothing. He did not return calls and had a total disregard for time-sensitive issues. Therefore, I am suing him, pro se, as well as the parties for the listed amounts on the following list:

Generac: $6,000,000.00

Wood / Meyer: $6,000,000.00

Subcontractors: $615,000.00

Attorney: $55.000.00

Receivables: $32,850

Total: $12,702,850.00

Settled and received prior to these suits: $54,200

The legal system is designed without regard to justice and geared to be able to file enough motions of procedural insignificance so that the case can outlive the plaintiff and defendant. I do not expect to prevail.

The judges do not have any love for anyone acting as their own attorney. Realizing this, I was trying to position myself, as any reasonable businessman would, to settle for less than it would cost to pay a lawyer to defend the case. That does not seem to be happening.

The one attorney, who was a mensch, responded as a professional. I had read about him in the paper when he was being awarded a $100 million-plus case. I sent him my information. He may have been the only person who has read the facts, as he says he read them with interest. As he sees it, I was taken for a ride.

There is an article online by Professor Berman, who attended Princeton and Harvard Law School and who was chair of the Harvard Law Review. Professor Berman is a specialist in plea bargaining and sentencing. He writes the following, verbatim, on his blog:

> "Attorneys are strongly advising their clients, regardless of their innocence, to take the pleas. This eliminates expensive court appearances and is a "sure thing." There are more innocent people on probation in Florida than is statistically acceptable. Florida boasts a 96% conviction rate. I certainly wouldn't brag about that. It would make me look a fool. If we are not convicting the innocent, shouldn't the rate be lower? Florida prefers to convict the innocent rather than allow the guilty go free. Isn't this unconstitutional?"

The Duke Lacrosse case decisions were made without any regard to the law and the Constitution. Law enforcement, as in that case and many others like my own, displays a tragic rush to accuse with no regard to the humiliation or life-threatening dangers imposed on the one accused. While the process is supposed to be innocent until proven guilty, the attitude of the legal system, law enforcement, the public, and the media is: Guilty. Who cares if it is not true?

The bottom line is they did not care. They needed a scapegoat. If anyone wants to investigate suspicion of wrong doing, it is a no brainer. Just follow the money. Had they accepted my invitation to do that, this whole chapter would have been a road untraveled.

Entitlement

Cause and Effect

314

CHAPTER 34: EXTORTION

I moved in with Sandy sometime in the summer of 2006, as my apartment was the hub of the generator business. It was a good time for me to be invisible.

We were a good fit. We made trips to New York, where I had a small apartment in a Queens luxury building. Sandy had a town house in New Jersey.

We spent time at my place and hers. We went on cruises for the holidays with Jordan. We took Jordan to the Keys.

Sandy, prior to us being a couple, had rented an apartment in Paris for the summer. My sister and brother-in-law did the same. She was very anxious for me to join her. However, I had the sense not to, as the criminal charges and negotiations were hanging over me. If it was discovered I that I was vacationing in Paris, the Florida press would have presented me as living in the lap of luxury.

During this period, my Florida business was shut down, and my New York business, which I had neglected during the generator surge, had to be rebuilt. Money was difficult.

After years of motions of contempt, forensic accountants, and a revolving door of different lawyers representing her, Denise finally agreed to meet with me and a professional mediator.

In that mediation we agreed on all the financial and parental terms. Denise was satisfied with the new agreement, but requested to think about it overnight and said she would most likely execute the agreement the next day.

That was the last civil discussion. Denise, on someone's guidance, she got a hold of a sleazebag lawyer. Those are easy to find. Between them, they figured that if they could not get money from me, they would be able to extort money from Sandy.

They filed a new motion of contempt, subpoenaed Sandy for her records and me for mine. In response, I served her with papers to produce all her financial records.

In her papers, I found one item that was not deleted, as obviously others were. Addison Reserve had returned our bond of $25,000, which she kept, but never acknowledged. Legally fifty-percent was mine. This while she was crying poverty on a daily basis. And taking me to court for $344. In addition, the bank statements had whiteouts and various questionable entries.

At the deposition, they tried to find money between Sandy and me because someone had planted a seed in Denise's head that I was filtering money through Sandy. After being unable to find anything, they went to plan B: a master plan for extortion.

Their plan was to have the judge find me in contempt. That meant that the judge says that you owe back payments of X amount of dollars. You must pay that at a reasonable rate while also paying the original agreement payments. They accomplished that. The court, the judge, and the system could not care less if you can afford it or not. I had a pending motion for modification before Judge Smith that showed every facet of proof to my financial condition. It sat in her chambers never read

Their next move (I say they, but of course the sleazebag is orchestrating this) is to file a motion of commitment to have me incarcerated. Their plan was that they assumed Sandy would pay whatever was required to keep me out of jail, including the sleazebag's fee.

Sleazebag at this time had a brother who was a sitting judge in that court system. Therefore Judge Smith did not listen or talk to me. I could not win a point. At one hearing I said, "Your Honor, please just read this two-page statement."

"I do not have time for sport reading," she responded. Between Florida's favoring the wife, the judge sucking up to his brother, and the ranks of lawyers promoted to judges, the legal system is controlled by a pompous bunch of nepotistic snobs.

Expecting to be incarcerated on the motion to commit, I had Sandy drop me off. The relationship between attorneys and the court does not preclude, admonish, or react to anything the attorney says, even if it is a bold-faced lie. The attorney said I was not paying the court-ordered contempt payments.

This was not true. I explained to the Judge that I was not paying the current agreement payments, but was paying the contempt-ordered payments. Although her lawyer tried to offset it, the judge asked Denise to confirm what I was saying was true.

Fearing to lie, or just confused, she said yes. Had she said no, the judge would not even let me show proof. They would have taken me into custody. The motion to commit was denied.

Denise left crying. She screamed at me in the street while I was waiting for Sandy to pick me up. Her disappointment that I was not incarcerated caused her to fire her lawyer on the spot.

One week later we went back to the mediator to sign an agreement that we had made one year prior. Sleazebag tried to have the court overturn the mediated agreement. He figured that when he had me incarcerated, he would have Sandy pay his fee as well to secure my freedom.

Failing that, he then sued Denise for his fee. I am defending Denise in court as I had agreed to when we finalized everything. The case is sitting idle for the past five years.

Before going to court on the order of commitment, I had prepared a motion for contempt against Denise. Had she continued the extortion process, I would have claimed all the actions she was doing with the kids were in opposition to the law.

Any judge, based on my experience with the court, would give Denise an opportunity to purge by no longer doing those things, not involving the kids, and not harassing me with emails.

It would be impossible for her to abide, and thereby I would file a motion of commitment. So far that has not been necessary.

Some of the points of the brief:

> There is no mother-daughter relationship, but rather it is friend and confidant. There is conversation of dating, sex, and their father. The live-in boyfriend would continually smoke marijuana in and out of the house in the presence of the children.

> My ex-wife defiles me to the children and whoever would listen, including the bank manager of where I do business. She insinuates to the children and others that I lie about everything, even though there is nothing to merit those accusations. Yet, as they say, if you throw enough stuff against the wall some of it is going to stick.

> In March of 2007, my ex-wife and her mother jointly and independently informed the children that they should not have anything to do with me until such time as I was paying her original weekly amount. My 11-year-old son was brought to tears.

Attached is a tiny sampling of the three thousand-plus emails and phone messages she sent me. All are available upon request. Please note that in each case, these statements were made in the presence of the children, which is in total violation of the court-ordered agreement.

"I have told Jordan the truth about your Social Security check."

She believes the amount I receive is a lie, even though I have produced all proof to the court and her.

After being badgered and badgered regarding the money due to her, I asked via email what I owed her. On December 7, 2006, she said, "Alimony paid to date has balance owed of $344."

On September 27, 2007, she emailed Amanda and copied me. "He makes more than enough to support himself, you, and me. See you in court, and I don't care if you rot in jail."

On October 23, 2007: "What happened to you is your problem... You think that because of the lousy $3,000 you gave me that I am not entitled to more."

"Jordan will have to live with you an older father who cannot provide him with a fun life. I am afraid for my children; I feel sorry for my children. It's pathetic. You will be very sorry too."

On October 23, 2007 she said, "I have informed Jordan of the truth. You have lied to him, and I will no longer sugarcoat your actions."

On October 29, 2007: "It is apparent that you are no longer a father. You have let our daughter down, and our son as well. Listen to me very carefully: They take driver's licenses away from deadbeat dads, and they end up in jail. As far as I see it, you deserve at least that."

"I will see you in court, and you can count on the fact that I will subpoena your girlfriend Sandra to see her records and how you are filtering money through her you pathetic piece of —"

On October 29, 2007, she said, "When and if Jordan spends time with you, it is your responsibility to pick him up and return him home. I will never do what I did yesterday again." (Once in four years, out of necessity, I asked her to meet me halfway.)

"It would be my pleasure to think of you as a dead man."

November 6, 2007: "Do not plan on seeing my son. He has no father. Don't call him, don't contact him, and I will get sole custody. WATCH ME."

January 5, 2008: "I have contacted my lawyer. I am getting an emergency hearing; you will not pay restitution before me. You are a liar, you have money, and I will subpoena Sandy when this is all done."

On January 29, 2008, she said, "You are disgusting and despicable. You came up with money to stay out of jail; don't give me the crap that it came from Sandy. Oh please, stop feeding lies to my children. Stop it immediately. See you in court with your ankle bracelet."

"Sandy must be a desperate woman."

When my son is with me, the phone does not stop. Every half-hour, just to exercise and display control, she calls. Each time I arrived to pick up my son to spend the weekend with me, he was sent with a message to ask for his mother's check. Each time he arrived at home he was interrogated as to where we went, what we did, who I was with, what restaurant we ate at, how much money I spent, etc.

Entitlement

Cause and Effect

321

Each week my son would say to me, "Mommy told me not to tell you this but…" I assured him that he did not have to tell me anything, and with regard to me he was free to advise her of anything he desired.

During the entire separation and divorce procedure I have been subjected to harassment, annoyance, physical and mental abuse, accusations of lies, and impugning my being. This has been completely discussed in words and in writings with our two children for the sole purpose of discrediting me in their eyes. All of these are violations of the "Final Judgment of Dissolution of Marriage" dated June 23rd, 2004, on Page 1, #3; page 2, #4; and Page 4, #11 and 13.

I humbly request the court to hold DENISE SCHEFFLER in contempt of all the violations listed. In addition to the attached exhibits I have and will present, if requested, approximately 3,000 pages of email over the past five years, in addition to taped messages left with the most outrageous accusations.

If Denise decides to ever go back to court, this will be filed.

Entitlement

Cause and Effect

322

CHAPTER 35: INCONVENIENT INSIGNIFACANCE

January 5th, 2008. I came to New York to complete some unfinished business before turning myself in to the Judge on January 8th 2008 to begin serving a nine-month sentence that we had pled for house arrest, but never had it confirmed. So I was a little apprehensive to say the least.

Sunday, January 6, 2008. I had arranged with Elyssa to meet her, Steve, and the kids for brunch in the city. I was in my apartment in New York, that Sunday at about 9:30 am. Wendy called to say she would be coming into the city to pick up Jamie, would I like to go back with her, and we all could have brunch. I said I did not think so because I have too much to do, but I will call her back at 10:00 a.m. Elyssa called, told her the same, she said Steve would drive me back this evening if I wanted, I said I will review my papers and see.

At 10:15 a.m., Wendy called, I said okay, and she said she will call when she leaves her house.

10:30 a.m., Wendy called, she is on her way. I tried to convince her to pick me up but she had to pick up Jamie and her friends and had to drop them at the Short Hills Mall at 12:30; she would meet me at 85th and Park at 11:30.

At 11:30, I called her to see if she was there and she was. I was in a cab and would meet her at the Holland Tunnel, which was how she was going back from 85th and Park.

At 11:47 she called and asked where I was. I said on the Long Island Expressway on my way and would be there in ten minutes.

She snapped at me, "I don't understand. Why did you not leave before?" I explained I had a lot to do and she snapped again, "Do you enjoy inconveniencing me?" I hesitated and then disconnected the call rather then enter into a confrontation.

She called back and asked if I hung up on her, I said no, and she said, "You know what, Dad, I love you and I am leaving, goodbye."

I arrived at the meeting place (after she left) at 11:57. I think with no traffic, one could get to the mall very close to 12:30? I went for breakfast, and Elyssa called a half hour later and came in for bunch on the condition that the situation with Wendy that just occurred would not be discussed; nothing was. I went back to Queens at 3:30 by cab.

At this final portion of my life, the one person I held in higher esteem was Elyssa. I thought that her intelligence, psychology education, and general emotional concern would lead her to the understanding that all these events in my life that have transpired would create a need in me for an awareness, compassion, discussion, and just an acknowledgement of love.

Elyssa, however, was never intellectually close to me again. I attributed it to the fact that she was happy with her relationship with Wendy and Adam, and felt that keeping me at an arm's length would not jeopardize those relationships.

However, as circumstances prevail, I no longer accept that excuse. The selfishness and total ambivalence amongst the three of them is so predominant that I wonder if maybe I am not their father.

Wendy left me in New York without any regard to my fragility as to possibly being confined to prison. Elyssa prefaces our brunch by limiting our discussions, as if brunch required a doctor-patient oath of secrecy.

Later on, I sent Elyssa in the body of an email: "The attached summary is being sent to attorneys, civil rights advocates, and the like.

Considering your talent for writing, I would like you to critique it and advise if any changes are required. With love, Michael B..."

The response was, "A please would be nice. It appears to be all run on sentences; correct it and send it back."

Well, if I was to do that, I would not need her to correct it. In similar words, I informed her of that. She responded that she would get to it and get back to me. She never did.

A friend did it for me in one hour, and I never heard another word about it from Elyssa. What should have been an honor and pleasure to do for me instead was another inconvenience.

Florida school semesters end in early June. Jordan wanted to go to New York before camp to be with his siblings and cousins. I requested that Amanda, Elyssa, and Wendy work out a time period for Jordan to go to New York. As his camp was not until the second half of the summer, I said he would be available from June 15 or later. Elyssa responded that on June 15 her kids were still in school, and Jordan would be bored.

Wanting to book flights and pickups, I said, "Okay then, solve the rest for me."

The response was, "Why do you talk like that?" I was at a standstill until they could respond, which they did eventually, through Amanda.

Because I am no longer an enabler of entitlement, I am no more than insignificant and inconvenient.

On Father's Day, 2008, one of my three phones was not working. Having received two insignificant Father's Day cards and no phone calls from Wendy and Elyssa, I checked my voicemail that night.

Both had called me at 1:00 and 1:05 to leave an obligatory message.

In the middle of July, I noted, "Elyssa is moving into the same circle as her sister. It has been almost four weeks since she called."

When Elyssa returned from Europe, as noted earlier, she presented me with a beautifully-written journal of her experiences. At the end she wrote:

> *I can't wait to see all of you, my family, who mean so much to me. This is what I have brought you, Daddy, from my time abroad. It is the only way that I can let you know how much all you've brought to me matters. Also it keeps you with me in my time away. I thank you, I miss you, but most of all I love you.*

If I changed since then, I grew intellectually, became more mellow and respectful of her acknowledged intellect. What changed was my financial circumstances.

ADAM

After three years of not speaking and years of bad blood, Adam and I reconciled. Shortly thereafter, while visiting with him in New York, I mentioned that I was planning on starting a generator company in New York.

Having had success with generators in Florida, I had a gut feeling that the northeast coast was prime for a devastating storm or heat wave where electricity would be lost as the weather patterns were starting to cause blackouts in and around New York.

Adam jumped right in to say he would be interested in being part of it. I formed a corporation, made him an equal partner, let him set all the conditions, and we were in business. There were recent blackouts in Staten Island and Long Island and New Jersey.

I designed, printed, and mailed oversized postcards to the areas affected. With the outages not being fresh in peoples' minds, I only received a few responses. I sent Adam an email with the first response. I included the person's name, address, and phone number. I said, "Meet with him and see what he wants on the generator. Check if there is an existing panel to satisfy his needs, or if we need to reroute to a new panel. Pick a place for generator with footage to electric, natural gas, or propane. I will price it and send to you."

His response was, "I thought we discussed the way you speak. Where is a please and thank you?"

With Adam visiting the site, I then proceeded to propose a system and negotiated two sales: one in Staten Island and one in Long Island. The jobs were sold with a minimal profit. I wanted to have some immediate references so that if there was another blackout we would be in a great position to take advantage of it. The intention was for my men to do the electrical work, which would have been helpful to me, but Adam's men did Staten Island. He subbed out Long Island to a friend.

Both jobs came in at no better than a break even. Adam, who took it upon himself to respond to a few of the initial service calls, decided to call me up and angrily demand that I come up to New York to take care of these things. As usual, with total disrespect.

A few weeks later, I was coming in for Father's Day. I was trying to keep expenses down, so I noted that Adam's wife, Denise, was going to visit her father in Cleveland and would be leaving her car at the airport. I was coming in, and she was going out. I mentioned to Adam that it would save me a car rental if I could use her car. He hesitantly agreed

The day before I arrived. He called to say "I wanted to return the car to the leasing company. Do you really have to use it," blah, blah, blah. I did not take his car.

The plan was for me to go to Wendy's in Long Beach Island for Father's Day.

Adam had just closed on a $1.7 million house and was redoing the floors himself. He said he would not be there on Father's Day. When I arrived with Jordan, Adam was there, and his other car was at home in his driveway. At the end of a cold few hours, he left. Never did he pursue any further communication.

 I sent the kids gifts, and left it at that. The only other thing that existed between us was liability insurance; he had a policy for his company and mine was named without any additional cost. He must have forgotten that it existed. As soon as he found out, he had the insurance company remove my company from the policy.

During the period of writing this, I had dinner with my cousin, Harris. He kept pressing me as to how it is possible that my son and I do not speak. He had spent vacations with us and saw the relationship between my kids and me. He said he wanted to call him. I said do whatever you want.

His report to me of their conversation was that Adam said, "My father passed away three years ago."

After further discussion regarding the fact that Adam is the successor to the business I built, Harris said that Adam said, "My father had nothing to do with my success. I did it all myself."

Finally he let Harris know, "My sisters and I have agreed to eliminate him from our lives." When I told Amanda of the conversation, she discussed it with Adam, who said he never said those things and that Harris must have made them up.

Adam, Wendy, and Elyssa love Amanda and would not want to alienate her by letting her know that they are defiling her father.

The opportunities that were given to Adam make me wonder how my life would have turned out if, while building my business, I had just a few of the things that Adam had. Someone to teach me the ropes and teach me the mistakes that were made. Or to teach me about fax machines, cell phones, email, and Internet.

Or the opportunity to have relationship with my father's customers and suppliers and friends. If I had access to the tools and the union men that my father had. If my father put me in a business where he taught me from the time I was old enough to learn. If my father had me host his holiday parties and mingle with all the customers.

If my father showed me the best business model to emulate based on his experience. If my father took me to all the job meetings and let me watch the ways and means to get along. If my father pointed me in the direction to be a business major in college. If my father taught me that all the sophisticated and expensive computer software was a waste of time and money.

Success is never final. Failure is never fatal. What's in your wallet?

It is hard to believe how all three of these children have turned out so selfish, ambivalent, and dispassionate. I will always believe that it is Rich's influence along with not wanting to incur the wrath of Wendy that has corrupted them all. The only one I can say I am proud of is my son-in-law, Steve. There is hope for my grandchildren that there is a skipped generation in genes.

No longer wanting a relationship where I am an inconvenience, I notified them, through Amanda, that until such time that we seek a family counselor that I would rather not have a relationship.

If I am not entitled to feel pride in what I accomplished or respect for who I am, I no longer need to hang on to the past, but surge forward to today and tomorrow.

The result was no response.

On Chanukah, I sent money orders to my grandchildren; the parents returned them to me.

I understand who Wendy is; I understand who Adam is. I do not understand Elyssa. Is she so insecure that she threw me under the bus? Is she not intelligent enough to be able to handle a relationship with them and me separately?

Where is a parent, an ex-wife, an in-law, or Steve, to say, "All you had to do was meet with a counselor? For that you gave up your father?" How can Elyssa give me up so easily? How can they all deprive their children from their grandfather and their grandfather from their children?

It appears that the entitlement generation was designed without a sensitivity chip.

AMANDA

On a visit to New York, in 2002, Adam had lunch with Amanda, who was sixteen at the time. He complained to her that he was unhappy paying for some of my expenses. He complained loudly enough that Amanda repeated the conversation and his displeasure to her mother

That was catalyst number one in Denise's decision to seek greener pastures. From 2002 through 2008, while going through the divorce

I was paying for Amanda's car, car insurance, apartment at FSU, allowance, summer camp as C.I.T., health insurance, cell phone, sorority dues, books, and tuition in addition to alimony. The $15,000 I gave to her mother for part of these expenses was, of course, gone.

For Jordan, I was paying for summer camp, health insurance, and whatever else he needed or wanted. For myself, I was paying for a car, an apartment in Florida, miscellaneous expenses, and an apartment in New York. It was more economical to keep the apartment than to stay in hotels, as at the time I was going back and forth for business more frequently. During the period before and directly after the breakup of our marriage, Amanda had learned how to play each of us in order to get whatever she wanted. I naively believed that she would not lie to me until I realized she was smoking and denying it.

When I found out about the cigarettes, I was hurt and angry. Amanda's responses were defensive offense. This was all shortly before her departure from camp. It took four months before I received a letter of apology and acknowledgement of her being wrong that was not sprinkled with defense and offense.

In 2006, Mike was history, and Jake was his replacement. He was a much better alternative. I was in the height of the success of the generator business. The credit card processing company, in order to continue to process our customer's cards, required security deposits and personal guarantees of the officers. I had made Amanda president for two reasons. One: my credit was not good. Two: the business was heading into a success the likes of which I had never known. I felt the business, even without new sales, would provide a substantial annuity from the service contracts alone. Being 65 at the time, and since my father passed away at age 66, if I were to go suddenly, Amanda would own the stock.

With a manager and a couple of servicemen, it would be a six-figure absentee management income for Amanda and Jordan.

Jake had graduated from college and was working in New York. I let his brother and him use my apartment in New York for the cost of the utilities, which was about $300.00 per month.

When the generator business imploded, the cash flow stopped. I was not allowed to take new sales or deliver the million dollars' worth of paid-for generators that I had in inventory. Whatever money I could get my hands on went to pay back deposits of jobs we had sold.

People who paid their deposit with a credit card refused to accept the charge and did not pay the credit company. The processor was than out over $200,000, which they listed on Amanda's and my credit.

Meanwhile, all of Amanda's, Denise's, and Jordan's expenses were being paid. Late, but still paid. Other than no cash flow, I had corporate, personal, and criminal attorney's fees. Amongst the bills being paid late was the New York apartment where Jake and his brother were living. Apparently there were notices put under the door which I was never aware of. However, the rent was always paid prior to any legal action.

In 2008, I gave up my New York apartment. Jake shared an apartment with his friends in Manhattan. Amanda graduated, got a job with Macy's, and shared an apartment with her friends in Manhattan.

In 2009, they shared an apartment together.

Prior to getting an apartment, Amanda was diligent in trying to force me to get that credit scar off her name. Without paying, there was nothing I could do. I assured her that she would not have a problem with a lease,.

By attrition, the credit scar would come off her name. I am sure that the influence of others was a factor in her persistence.

The only thing I was still paying for was Amanda's cell phone, which ended as they were both working. I still paid for flights and miscellaneous when requested.

Over the next three years, I think that I stayed in their apartment twice when I went to New York. Not more than two nights, and as always, I paid for dinners.

In 2009, Amanda wanted to come to Florida for Thanksgiving. She asked if I could pay the airfare, which I did. Jake's family, who lives in Florida, were making Thanksgiving dinner. Amanda, Jake, Denise, David, and Jordan were invited. I, as usual, was spending another holiday without family. I was slighted and let Amanda know.

Her response, on October 13, 2009, was titled, "Sorry."

> *Hi,*
>
> *I have been thinking about what happened, and I now see that it was wrong of me to not invite you. Jake's parents left it in my hands, because they did not want to put me in an uncomfortable situation, and I thought about the consequence for me; my mother would be more upset than you would. I now see that it was wrong, and I should have invited you, as it is very important to me that we all spend time together since they will probably be a part of our lives for a long time. I did not mean to hurt your feelings, and I would love for you to come, but if you don't want to now I understand. Going forward I will look at the situation differently.*
>
> That was the most sincere acknowledgment I have ever received from Amanda

Entitlement

Cause and Effect

334

CHAPTER 36: SANDY

After two years of living together, it was now time to carry out my plea bargain sentence.

I was being confined to house arrest for seven of a sentenced nine months. During that period, I made breakfast, lunch, and dinner for both of us. In addition, I tried to regiment Sandy to take her enormous amount of anti-depression and anti-anxiety pills regularly. She never did.

The only people who visited were my friends. Still, with all the cracks in the armor starting to appear, I was appreciative of all she had done for me and committed to settle for this relationship for the rest of my life.

While living there, the signs of her depression and/or mental unbalance started to unfold. She would spend the entire day on the computer playing some moderate mind game or would sleep all day, and would make plans and cancel them on a regular basis.

Sandy was becoming increasingly insecure with my feelings for her. This was unwarranted but nevertheless was there. It started from the beginning and progressed as we went along. I am sure it was based on her prior relationships; none of them were meaningful. It started when I did not go to Paris, and especially when I went to New York for two days to see my kids.

The best part of our togetherness was every day we had happy hour with my sister and brother-in-law. That seemed to be the essence of Sandy's existence. I was very warm and affectionate, to the point that my brother-in-law would tease us continually.

There was no point in keeping my apartment in New York. Sandy was trying to sell her New Jersey town house.

Sandy went back to New York, got rid of the furniture, packed everything up, and that was the end of my apartment. Not being able to sell her place, she rented it to a tenant, and that worked out fine.

Sandy, aside from her need for medication, was fighting two battles:

1. As I was living with her in her house, her set of entitled children were very concerned that my financial situation and future needs would deplete their inheritance. They would continually press her buttons about how I had a lot of financial needs coming up, like Jordan's Bar Mitzvah, college, and car, as well as Amanda's wedding.

2. For whatever reason, her life experiences made her terribly insecure.

These battles created a tense and explosive atmosphere while confined to the house. Every weekend, Jordan came over. He slept over Friday and Saturday nights, and left Sunday.

Denise's boyfriend at the time did the delivery and pick up, sometimes with her, and sometimes not. This only occurred because Jordan wanted to be with me, and Denise wanted her weekend free. Jordan watched TV with me. We all played Scrabble, did a jigsaw puzzle, barbecued, and we all enjoyed each other's company. Jordan was twelve years old: mature, bright, undemanding, and fun to be with.

Denise, in her usual manner, was freaking out. She would say, "Why do I have to drive him and pick him up? You should pay me before restitution." Because of my cash flow constrictions, she still was getting her money, but not on the exact date it was due.

Denise wrote emails and phone messages calling Sandy "your f---n girlfriend." You can take the girl out of Brooklyn, not Brooklyn out of the girl. Denise had infuriated Sandy so much that Sandy thinks every time Denise says anything that she is being manipulative.

Therefore Sandy is always being defensive, and the one that suffers is Jordan. Sandy wants him picked up on Sunday. Early, not late, and he can sleep over one night, not two.

Denise hasn't the intelligence to be manipulative. She is just a self-centered combination of being histrionic and having Borderline Personality Disorder.

Sandy launched a campaign against my inability to say no to my kids. The result was that instead of every other weekend with Jordan, I was having him over every weekend. Nothing she was saying was true, but it was an argument I could not win.

Sandy was influenced by her kids' manipulation. She projected the costs of Jordan's college and my expenses over the next few years. She said I should get my own apartment and that we would meet for dinner on occasion.

The week prior, Sandy ambushed me into showing her all my accounts because she was convinced I was sneaking money to Amanda behind her back. Of course, it was not true. But the internal conflicts she had was taking over.

In my case, I did not mind the change, I just feared the expense.

Sandy, from all indications, she was not prepared to live alone, and on the surface she showed total love and devotion for me. So, again, the whole thing was confusing.

One of her other talking points was that a twelve year old was not in her plans. She referred to the two cruises we took with Jordan on Christmas. She said that she had a miserable time.

This was not true. I never saw her in any way not enjoy herself. Those trips were conceived, planned, and executed by her.

Sandy is now obsessing that Denise is manipulating me regarding Jordan coming over every weekend so that Denise can have free time. Denise, in her infinite wisdom, has offended Sandy to the point it has become a vendetta. The mere mention of Denise makes Sandy's blood boil.

Prior to the generator problems, Sandy and I were enjoying a social and romantic relationship. When she made me a surprise birthday party, her kids sent a bottle of champagne and a lovely card saying, "Thank you for making my mother happy." Happy, money, money, happy? I get confused. After the generator problems and the diminished cash flow, I was no longer being thanked by her kids.

During that period, Jordan spent a weekend with Sandy's daughter and family. They told Sandy that Jordan had told them that his dad lost all his money gambling. I spoke to Jordan; he had no idea what I was talking about. I figured they had misinterpreted something until now. Their father was left by Sandy because he had a gambling problem. They were planting seeds.

Not being able to understand, as Jordan is noninvasive and a pleasure to be with, I attributed it to the many "theys," who say, "He has a twelve year old; not for me."

Then I asked her, "What does this mean to our relationship?"

She never answered, and I never pushed it. For whatever reason I did not understand that she had succumbed to her offspring, and this was all about money. I guess they convinced her that I would not be able to pull my weight, and she would use up all her money, yadda, yadda, yadda.

I could not get a lease for an apartment or credit to buy a car, and Sandy put the leases on both in her name. We met for dinner three or four nights a week, and it was fine. Jordan came over and stayed with me. We had no one giving us things to do. I still did not understand where she was coming from. I was not interested in dating.

She created the new deal, and I liked it. We went along this way for several months. I drove her and picked her up from the airport; we met for dinner.

One night we met for dinner in Boynton Beach at the Ale House. They did not have what she wanted, so we walked over to Bonefish. On the way she said, "I would have thought things would have progressed further by now."

"In what way?" I asked.

"Well you should have at least met someone to have dinner with."

"You mean to tell me that if I went out with another woman it would not bother you?"

Her response was a chuckle. "Try me."

So for the first time I believed she was serious. I could not understand it because I know how tough it is to meet someone, and she had me. I really took care of her, aside from providing a social venue that was previously unavailable to her.

Being offended and confused, I had never thought that money could be the factor. Call me stupid.

I now believed her and said, "Okay, I will put myself out there again."

As coincidence would have it, within the next few days, I received an email from an old friend, Mardge. She had been married to my good friend, Richard. They had divorced years ago, and he subsequently died. The last I had seen her was fourteen years earlier.

In past single years, I tried to find her but could not. Several months prior, I was online searching a real estate website. There was a list of developers and John, the guy she was seeing, was listed. He knew me. We had them out to the Hamptons, and I solicited his firm for business back in the day.

I sent him an email. "How are you; how did things work out for you and Mardge?" That was in June or July. He never answered, and I forgot all about it. For some reason in their conversation in February my name came up, and he then informed Mardge of my email.

Hence the email, then a phone call. Mardge informed me that she was with John for four years, and then apart for ten, and they were recently back together, but she hated him. However, they just bought this house in Florida. He came down every other weekend, and for the moment decorating the house was giving her pleasure.

On February 13, 2009, we made a date for dinner. She had a girlfriend visiting, and I invited them both to join me. We had a lovely dinner. She looked great. Her girlfriend and her told me what a horrible guy John is, and on and on of how she cannot stand him.

On February 20, 2009, she wanted me to see her home. She invited me the following week to a dinner party she made for her gay cousin and her gay hairdresser so they could meet. Her friend was there as well, and it was a fun evening. When I left we walked outside, and in saying goodbye, I took her in my arms, and we passionately kissed and embraced as if our body parts were made for each other.

We then continued to see each other almost daily. We were very romantic and demonstrative in public.

On March 24th, Sandy took her granddaughter to Paris for spring break. I emailed Sandy in Europe, saying, "Hi, tried to call your cell. They said the number is not valid. How are you doing? Hope Izzy (her granddaughter) and you are enjoying."

On March 25th, she responded, "Your emails are so endearing. It's amazing how you express yourself."

Jubilantly I had told one male friend that I was in love and as thrilled as could be. He must have told his wife, who told Sandy, who called to say, "I hear you are in love. Why did I have to find out from someone else?"

Then the following email came on March 29, 2009:

> *Michael, I wrote this script. I knew you would meet someone. I needed you in a good place. You need someone to play with. I don't play with you. I am happy for you.*
>
> *I want to know about your life. I want to be able to have dinner and a drink, as friends do. I certainly do not want to be told by someone else that Michael is in love. Do you think me so shallow that I would not be able to handle this? I told you to do it. I am sure she is young and beautiful; don't I know you?*

She made like she was happy. She inquired as to all the facts, and I told her everything. At this point I was taking everything that Sandy said at face value, not realizing that it was all a smoke screen. I explained that Mardge was living with a guy part time who she hated, and who came to Florida every other weekend.

Sandy reaction was to anxiously suggest that Sandy and I go out as a couple together with Mardge and her friend so we could see how they interact with each other. I ignored the request.

The next evening I was at Mardge's at about 6:00 p.m. getting ready to meet another couple for dinner when Sandy called. She had been supposedly putting together financial records for a forensic accountant. She thought her deceased husband might have siphoned off money for his kids that should have gone to her. So as an excuse and as a test she informed me that she finished putting it all together and wanted to celebrate by meeting me for a drink.

I explained that I was already committed to other plans; however, she pushed and pushed even though I had plans with her for dinner the following evening. I said I would see what I could do and called back fortunately to get her voicemail. I left a message that I could not get out of my plans.

The following day she called about three times to confirm our dinner plans; we were to meet at Prime Catch. I arrived on time; she was at the bar amongst several patrons. I went over, ordered a drink, and got the following:

"I want the car back." Remember that the lease is in her name. "You couldn't go out of your way to meet me last night. Have your girlfriend lease it for you." She took out a pad and intimidated me to give her Mardge's last name, phone numbers, and addresses, and John's as well. I gave her some factual info along with some fiction, as I understood her intentions were not good.

All of this was being carried out in front of these other patrons in a very adversarial way on her part. After some other insulting remarks, she said something like she was going to come and take the car, but she is not a prick like me.

Again this all stems from me not meeting her the previous evening. With that, I put down my drink and walked out. I was leaving with Jordan the next day for Washington, D.C., and had agreed to return the car to her when I returned.

Three days before returning to Florida, she contacted me to say she wants the car "NOW." I said that we would be back in three days; her response was, "Too bad, leave now." After a few days of back and forth on that, she gave it up and agreed to wait. She had wanted me to drop it off at her house, so I needed someone to follow me there.

On Monday following the trip, I told her I would bring the car on Thursday. That evening while I was fast asleep, I was woken by Sandy standing over my bed. She assumed Mardge would be there and was very disappointed that Mardge was not there. She demanded the keys to the car. She came with a neighbor whom I knew well, and who was very embarrassed.

Following that, I was harassed by her with threats and innuendos by mail and by phone. In addition, Mardge's address was in the car when she took it, so she had all the info and tracked it all down. She called Mardge's house to speak to me, and by the emails attached you can get the gist of it all.

Sandy looked up the address online and got all the details of the house purchase, which she reported to me:

> Mardge's name is on the deed, but she has no more than 25% ownership. The way I see it, John can give her $10.00 and pay for her share. There is a $302,000 mortgage. He put down $75,000. In that same email you said you would do "anything in the world for me." That is a lie. I asked you to have a drink at 5:00, and you didn't come. Mardge's house is less than twelve miles from Boynton.

You should have told the other people involved, "Sandy is my friend. She kept me alive and free for three years. I must go." You should have been there for me anytime I needed you.

Sandy was now conjuring up in her mind that there was deceit all along that Mardge and I were together for a while. In an email in April, she requested a copy of my bank statements for the prior period, which I gladly gave. I was planning on moving to West Palm Beach so Mardge and I would be closer.

Sandy came over to see what furniture she wanted me to give her. The following day, I received this email:

Hope the vacation you selected to celebrate my birthday today is great. Have fun. It was the folded clothes that gave it away. I just miss you. I know you don't give a damn. Just ignore me. I am sorry.

My response was as follows:

Take your medicine regularly, and you will not be paranoid. The clothes were laundry returned and were on the bed to be put away. Happy birthday. This time, she said:

I think it was 2.5 glasses of wine, but you're right. I did forget to take my meds. But you must take clothes with you when you stay at Mardge's? Am I really paranoid? I hope that is my only ailment. Isn't this the last month before she goes back to New York? I honestly mean enjoy. It is not what you feel for Mardge, it is the lack of feeling towards me.

Whenever Sandy emails me she expects that I am sitting at the computer waiting and thinks I should respond within seconds. Ergo the following email:

There you go avoiding me again. Did you ever figure out what pissed me off that Friday night? When I asked you for their last names, I knew you were lying. Why you didn't give me their correct names? It hurts even as I write this.

When she took out that pad to write their names that Friday night, I did give her the wrong last names, fearing her intentions. My response was, "I do not know what you want from me."

Sandy then wrote:

I always told you how I wanted to be able to stay away. But I was always drawn back (like a magnet), because I love you! When I was going to New York, I told you I had a date with my daughter's friend's father. That was not true. I just wanted to see if you cared, and you showed you did not. I guess I just wanted to hurt you, because you were hurting me. But. It only hurts when you love someone. What a fool I was, am. Is Mardge with you? I hope I am not sending you mixed signals. The reason I wanted you to answer my email is that I had my eyes done with restylane, and I wanted you to stop by for your opinion.

I would try not to piss me off if I were you. Remember there are just so many straws before the last one. I guess you decided not to talk to me. You certainly aren't getting any wiser. Answer this within fifteen minutes. I have a date and must leave. I think this is it (John's email and phone number). But if not I will find it.

A long letter basically saying that because she helped me, she owned me. If she says "come," it means "come now." In the bank statements I gave her, she could not find any charges for me taking Mardge out; therefore I was hiding something.

I responded with the following facts:

> *I am not hiding anything. I gave you all I got; if it wasn't*
> *enough, not my fault. Never lied. I had vowed to myself to*
> *remain appreciative and not to enter into name calling and*
> *dwell on how you insulted me. You keep saying that you would*
> *never do the things to me that I did to you. The only thing I did*
> *to you was not jump when you said jump, ONCE. Apparently*
> *to live with the mistake of letting me go, you have to hate me.*

Prior to the next email, she apparently tried her key to get in my apartment. But as I always do when I go out, I lock the deadbolt section of the door. She said, "I could have had a locksmith come and break the door. I didn't because I had no intention of going in anyway. My daughter's best friend who lives in Florida is a locksmith. It wasn't the money."

Sandy had called Mardge's house, and whatever Mardge said, I do not know. This was the email I received:

> *I react sometimes quickly. Last night I did not think Mardge*
> *was going to answer. I should not have said what I said to her.*
> *But you have convinced her, and I think yourself, that I am just*
> *a jealous fool. Michael. You 'threw me away' by not being*
> *there for me, your friend. I was always there for you. I can*
> *never, ever express to you how you hurt me. Where are you*
> *moving to?"*

My response: *Cityplace.*

She wrote: *I want the address and apt number, please. And please do not tell me an untruth.*

My response: *Why is that important?*

She then responded: *Will you trust me??????????????*

My response: *Here it is.*

She than writes a lengthy email accusing that in my last overnight trip to New York I was with Mardge. We hadn't even reconnected at that point. In it, she said, "Ignore last message, it was to remind you who I am."

My response was: *You really need to see a good psychologist. The hotel was the Reserve in the Wall Street area. It was paid for via hotwire. I went alone, did what I had to do, and came back.*

Sandy said: *Straighten up fast, or I will bring you down slowly. You cannot ignore people or treat them the way you do me and expect to get away with it anymore.*

In conclusion, the only time I ever did anything other than what she requested and beyond, was not meet her when she wanted!

Once! I met her the next night, instead.

Entitlement

Cause and Effect

348

CHAPTER 37: ONE DOOR CLOSES AND ANOTHER ONE OPENS

There she was. Mardge had all of the characteristics I wanted: a long flowing blonde mane, a slender body with a great ass and medium-sized breasts, a manner of dressing to my taste. She wore the long sun dresses which just caressed her body and enhanced all of those magnificent features that I hold so dear.

From the very beginning we connected in that fairy tale way that I envisioned my life to be. The first time we slept together she laid in my arms, and I awoke every few minutes, and we kissed all night long as I ran my hands up and down her body as if it were the first time I ever felt a woman's body.

She revealed that never in her life did any one devour or satisfy her as I did, nor had she ever had anyone who was as much of an unselfish lover.

She would call her friends and tell them that for the first time in her life she was truly in love. She wrote letters of eternal love about how happy she was. We socialized with our respective friends and went out with my sister. She showered me with love, affection, nurturing, and mothering. She washed my clothes and made my drinks and meals. We walked our dogs and planned our future together.

The following is a series of writings between us which are the essence of which all men come into this world believing in, and we all leave knowing it does not exist.

This started when I left for New York.

> The house is clean. The dogs have been fed. The dogs have been walked. The bed is made (boo hoo). The sheets are clean (boo hoo). I don't smell you. Bye, I love you. So many kisses and hugs. I love your loving arms, hands, mouth, and fingers. And most of all I LOVE YOU SO VERY MUCH

And:

> *Hi darling. A girlfriend of mine, who lives in North Miami, just sent me an email asking if we could get together the 19th or the 20th. I don't want to answer her until I know when you are actually leaving for New York. I think you said you had to be there on April 20th (Monday). Does that mean you leave on 4/19 and return on 4/20?*

On April 13, 2009, she wrote:

> *I do not want to make any plans at all when you are free. I want to spend as much time with you as possible. Why, you ask? Need I say why? Yes, you say! Well, the answer is "I LOVE YOU."*

Another email on April 13:

> *My dearest, I didn't get a chance to call you, but I will before I go to sleep. I am watching Dancing. I just took a minute out to send you this email.*

On April 26, 2009, she said:

> *Michael darling! Being a true romantic, I had to send this to you. I believe it is what we have and pray that we can hold on to it with every fiber of our being.*

> *How to Dance in the Rain:*

> *It was a busy morning, about 8:30, when an elderly man in his 80s arrived to have stitches removed from his thumb. He said he was in a hurry as he had an appointment at 9:00 a.m. He said he needed to go to the nursing home to eat breakfast with his wife. I inquired as to her health.*

He told me she had been there for a while and that she was a victim of Alzheimer's disease. As we talked, I asked if she would be upset if he was a bit late. He replied she no longer knew who he was; she had not recognized him in five years. Now I was surprised and asked him, "You still go every morning, even though she doesn't know who you are?"

He smiled as he patted my hand and said, "She doesn't know me, but I still know who she is." That is the kind of love I want in my life.

True love is neither physical, nor romantic. True love is an acceptance of all that is, has been, will be, and will not be.

The happiest people do not necessarily have the best of everything.

They just make the best of everything they have.

Life isn't about how to survive the storm, but how to dance in the rain.

On May 5, 2009, she said:

Love, love, love. "Now and Forever Let It Be True, When I go to Sleep, I never Count Sheep, I count all the charms about me and you."

Michael, Michael, I can't get over Michael. "Love is in the Air." They asked me how I knew my true love was true.

My darling, tomorrow night I will be in your wonderful loving arms.

On June 7, 2009, she wrote:

I guess I have been (and seem to continue to be) totally enamored, without a thought to anything else but YOU. I never entered one online deposit since March! This is so much fun. Entering all these numbers into Quicken. Ah, love, you have worn me down, and I have forgotten about all else.

For more years than thou; I loved you from afar, and longed for you while being carried away when you could have found me on the fire escape on West 80th Street by calling any number of people. The names of which escaped you while I waited and waited. Oh my dear, darling, unequivocally, not quite. You were my knight who should have whisked me away from that evil man who you pretended was your friend! And me too, I miss you, you dummy. Yes I want you here next to me each and every night, morning, noon. Yes, I love you so, you boob.

On June 9, 2009, she said:

My Dearest,

Sometimes it is hard to put into words exactly how you feel about someone. This short path of ours has been the most loving, warmest, and most incredible path in my life. I finally, after so many years, found my soul mate. One never knows where this will bring us, as we are all in God's hands. Our timing has not been too wonderful, but that could also change. Then again, it might have been the best timing. That we will know in time. I want you to have love and happiness in your life as you so deserve. I will be here for you as much as I can, and perhaps one day, all the time.

But for now it is what it is, as you say. I act with my heart, say what is in my heart, and that is not always a good thing for me to do. It is, however, who I am. At times I am the nervous woman who gets scared. Sometimes I am the very brave and strong woman who can overcome anything. It changes depending what is happening at the time. I'll be going back to New York on July 4th, and more than likely, will be there until October. I might be able to steal a week or so, but that will depend upon the weather and other circumstances in my life as it currently is.

I don't want any promises, as I want you to leave yourself open to happiness if you should find someone that can give you what you need. It is not what I want to see happen, but it would be so unfair of me not to let you know that I would understand and will continue to want you, to love you, and to need you. What you have given me will always be with me, and I pray that you will too. Life is very uncertain, and one does not know what the next day will bring. I pray it brings you to me forever. I only ask that you be completely honest and open with me, as I will be with you. I love you with all my heart. You are my special man that I always wanted, and I pray to God every day that you are with me for as long as we are on this Earth.

The next two letters from Mardge are an introduction to my world, in search of love, passion, and the ever after. Okay, now reality comes in. Hold on!

On December 11, 2009, Mardge wrote:

> *I spent the night in jail and just got home a few hours ago. John is gone from my life forever. We had a very major discussion (ha ha) and because he walked into a glass vase that was broken due to his pushing me while I was holding the broken piece so as to throw it away so that my Muffin wouldn't get hurt, it stuck him in his knee, and he bled like a pig. I called the police as I was fearful of him. The police after seeing the blood trickling down his leg put me in handcuffs and off I went to spend the night in jail. It was the longest 22 hours of my life. No food, no nothing. Just back and forth to the court room to different station houses and Bellevue Hospital. I got a lawyer; went before the judge (John got a restraining order out on me) so that I wouldn't call, email, contact him at his office (he was afraid I would do something terrible and email his entire company to advise what a disgusting animal he is, he took out the restraining order. The Judge let me go, but I was told if I came near him I would be carted off to jail. Obviously, I will not go near him, call him, email or anything else. According to my lawyer, I can change my locks, which I will do tomorrow, but he put a chain and lock around the closet doors that houses his clothing. He is so sick. And I am very happy to be rid of him. I will deal with the house when this is over. Next court date is February 2nd. After that we will see what happens.*

> *As I would like to sue him for aggravated assault, misrepresentation, etc. It's been hell. I still plan on coming to Florida on 12/20, I think.*

It will depend on a lot of things, but I will let you know. I'm sure you are now in shock as I am. I cannot believe that I called the police, and he said I tried to stab him, which was a lie, and the police took him to the hospital and me to jail. It is not a fair system and I was treated like a criminal.

> *Okay, just got out of a very hot bath, drank a glass of wine and am going to bed. I am beyond exhausted and doubt that I can even sleep, but I give it the old college try.*
>
> *-Mardge*

My reaction, of course, is sad for what she went through, but it looks like I will finally have the full time love story I have so desperately yearned for.

Two weeks later, Mardge wrote:

> *There is so much to tell I don't know where to start. Right now we have a tentative court date to make this go away on January 12th. This could change. The original court date for my hearing was scheduled to be February 2nd. However, my lawyer got it pushed up with John's help in the letters he has been writing to the assistant district attorney pleading to get this done. Said he is so sorry and acted hastily and wants to come back home as he misses me, my grandchildren, Muffin, and of course his stepdaughter. I met with another lawyer yesterday who was recommended by my ex-boss and he was an incredible lawyer. Quite a gentlemen. He sat with me for one and a half hours and told me that he reached out to the ADA as he is acquainted with her parents. That might have helped my case a bit. Then he stated that I didn't have to change lawyers as it wasn't necessary. My lawyer was doing his job.*

However, he put me in touch with a counselor that John and I will have to go to, who deals with these problems and is familiar with the court and has testified on behalf of other people for this particular lawyer. He didn't charge for the time, which is $500/hour, and his retainer is $10,000. Fortunately, he was the most generous, warm, and kind human being.

Another email from Mardge:

I am beginning to feel hopeful about John and me. I realize that I did a lot that wasn't right, as he did. He realizes also the mistakes he made, as I do. It will take time and patience to sort this all out, but I am praying for the best and really want this relationship to work. I do love him and realized how much I missed him. If we can get through this we will be able to get through anything. I'm not sure when I will be back in Florida, as it will depend on the court date. But once it is over I plan to stay until June, but will have to come back for a week each month to see the counselor with John. Once the summer comes we will have to see him once a week until he says, "Enough." It will take one year for this to actually go away. It's considered a FACD (Family - something or other). I appreciate your concern, and I will be in touch and let you know what the date of the hearing is and when I will be back in Florida, We should have dinner and catch up on everything. I hope all is well with you and the family.

Love,
Mardge

Once she professed her feelings for him. I felt that any
communication could create an uncomfortable situation for her, so
again the fleeting, illusive, irresistible desire to be irresistibly desired
will have to wait.

Women, Women, Women

Why can't a woman be like a man?

Men are so gentle, so easy to love

Why can't a woman be

Like me?

Entitlement

Cause and Effect

358

CHAPTER 38: AMANDA AND JAKE

Amanda had some difficult experiences to get past, like receiving a trophy in camp for the most attendance to the infirmary, growing up amidst a tumultuous relationship between her mother and me. Her mother confiding in her as if she were a friend and not a daughter, and being pummeled with meritless vitriol towards me. The fact that she emerged as a responsible young lady is in itself a magnificent accomplishment, considering what she was put through, it is more like a miracle.

Her relationship with Jake appears to be healthy and mature. Her work ethic, ability, responsibility, and general demeanor is that of a very accomplished and responsible young lady

Over the next two years, Amanda was promoted, and her salary increased three times. Jake, according to his parents, was doing fabulously to the point that they were very pleasantly surprised.

In January of 2011, Amanda and Jake were engaged. Denise had her grandmother's diamond stone and gave it to Jake to have set and presented to Amanda. The engagement party was made at Denise's current boyfriend David's home. I went alone. I had no guests, and although I felt so disconnected, I put on a smile and made no complaints.

The pictures from the engagement party were posted on Amanda's Facebook page. There wasn't even an attempt to make believe I had some significance.

As the wedding plans were being formulated, I was hardly consulted except for an obligatory gesture here and there. But it was apparent that Denise and David, Bernie and Beth, and Amanda were making the rehearsal dinner, wedding, and brunch.

Feeling very disconnected from the planning of all the festivities, the engagement party, rehearsal dinner, and brunch were at David's house. There were wedding plans, social meetings of everyone but me, and pictures in Amanda's apartment of everyone but me. But this is the penalty of being the participant with the least money. I accepted it and kept it in.

As the wedding plans progressed, the budget was to be divided between Denise, her boyfriend, myself, and Jake's parents. I was asked to commit to $8,000. I did so because at the time, I had a good profitable job, and as an eternal optimist, I thought the economy was gaining momentum. And no matter what, I never said no to hardly anyone, and never to my kids.

It was not clear as to whether Denise and David were going to remain together, as she was as happy with him as everyone else that was in her life. I was willing to pay my share, but I wanted it to be credited toward my obligations to Denise. Jordan was going on 16; my obligation to Denise was until he was 18. There is no way that I would not get him a new car for his birthday, as all my other kids did.

If David and her were not together, the same addiction for money would start all over again and would result in another attempt to put me in jail. The judge would say to get rid of the car and pay her. I wanted to take this opportunity to avoid that potential.

This is all in addition to the continual slanderous deadbeat dad and other vial defiling statements that she makes. With my newly-found knowledge of the legal system, and the ability to sue pro se, I sent the following letter to Denise:

From 9/15/2008 until this 5/5/2011, I have paid in, on behalf of Jordan, as child support $69,100.00, which includes $32,000 you received from my Social Security. As of 9/15/2008, an executed agreement required me to pay $51,040.

Therefore, I have paid more than required. Going forward, I am willing to pay fifty percent of all Jordan's expenses, over and above the Social Security check of $1,000 per month you receive on my behalf for Jordan. Those expenses will be excluding car expenses. I am willing to pay fifty percent of the cost of a car and fifty percent of the insurance, gas, repair, etc.

The above will be adhered to only by executed agreement registered with the court. Any discussion with Jordan as to my obligations not being met are grounds for contempt and an action of such will be commenced.

Any discussion outside of Jordan as to my obligations not being met, will be responded to by an action of libel and defamation. The two voicemails alone left on my phone on 4/27/2011 are grounds for contempt.

If this agreement meets with your approval, I will adhere to the committed $8,000 for the wedding.

Denise objected, telling Amanda how bad I am, and wrote to Amanda that I was not paying my share of the wedding. Amanda complained that she was being put in the middle, and the argument was not her problem. I explained that no matter what I would pay my share, and everything would work out fine, but Amanda would not stop the pursuit of being assured that she is getting what she wanted.

The agreement I wrote to Denise disappeared. I was asked to pay the florist deposit of $1500, which I did. Amanda continually complained of the stress that her mother was putting on her.

The future in-laws socialized with and continually invited Denise and David to their home. Amanda continued to complain of how difficult it was for them to save money. They were continually going to destination weddings.

One of my customers is a sophisticated florist who specializes in weddings. I told Amanda that they would do the flowers, and my work would pay for it. That would have paid my obligation. She refused.

When I was requested to give more money, I did not have it. I suggested to leave the balance of my commitment to the end, and hopefully I would have it then.

Meanwhile, the few times I was in Jakes parents' company, they were ecstatic as to how well he was doing to the point that they never would have expected him to do so well. Amanda was also continually getting raises. She continued to complain and never said anything about Jake's success.

In December of 2011, I sent the following email:

Because at times it is necessary, I come to New York. My cost of living for Jordan's and my modest existence requires an income of $80,000 per year. Normally, this would not be a problem, but, due to the economy, it is a problem.

When I committed to paying my share of the wedding, I was in the middle of a very profitable contract. Being an optimist, I assumed that my regular business on top of that job would allow me the ability to meet my wedding commitment. As things do not always work out as well as you would like or plan, business got worse instead of better.

As I have done for all my other children, on the birthday that legalizes driving, I bought Jordan a car. Jordan contributed to the down payment as a loan.

My lease was up on my car. I bought a used Chevrolet with a modest down payment. These necessary expenditures prevented me from having the money for the wedding.

Both Amanda and Jake earn enough to have a reserve and would also be receiving a substantial amount of cash as wedding gifts. I assumed that by paying them $500 per month for the balance committed would not be a hardship for anyone other than myself. I advised them several weeks before the wedding that this was the way I had to handle it.

The wedding was beautiful. I had two couples as guests. Amanda looked exquisite. Even though I was the oldest parent there, the honor of saying the Motzie (the prayer over the bread before eating) was given to Jake's father and was never even discussed with me. I never complained.

That is where it all sat, and I was satisfied that I would be able to meet that obligation and that we can all go about being happy. But, as in the godfather, "Just as I think I am out, they drag me right back in." Happiness can be elusive as demonstrated by the following: In the beginning of May, I was working on two jobs that were on progress payments. One was in Manhattan at $2500 per month, and another in Queens at $1000 per week. Both clients were complaining that I had not been to the job. I arranged that on Monday, May 21, I would personally pick up $2500 from one and $2000 from the other.

My cash flow as usual was a disaster, especially now in hard times. I had to come to New York. I purchased airline tickets, used a credit I had at a hotel in West Hampton, reserved a car with Avis, who I had recently used before. Each time, they accepted my debit card without even reserving an additional amount.

They either changed their policy, or else the addition of a car loan on my name reduced my credit score. First they check your credit, and then they accept the debit card. I did not pass their credit criteria; they would not even process the card.

The only money I had access to was for the car, the room was no charge. On Monday I was picking up money. I had to get from Saturday, May 19 to Monday, May 21. I was stuck at the airport without a car; the Hamptons would not work. I had lunch and figured that the only thing to do was to stay at my daughter's place and use public transportation. I called from the airport to see if it was even possible to stay at Amanda's. She was home and watching TV. They were staying in Saturday night. Invited me to stay, I headed over.

Between lunch and transportation to the city, I used up the money I had reserved for the car. I arrived and watched TV. Jake was at a friend's.

For dinner, Amanda ordered in. I had a sandwich. I didn't offer to pay, as I was broke.

Sunday we went to my cousin's for dinner. The cab to Grand Central Amanda paid for; it cost $10.00. Amanda paid the $45.00 for the three of us on the train, and noted with a smile that she would add it to the wedding money I owed her.

The next day I was collecting $2,500 and $2,000, so I asked Jake to cash a check for three hundred dollars, which he could deposit on Wednesday. I saw he was laboring over it. I said, "If you can't, no problem." He said he couldn't. We went on to have a good evening, went back to their apartment, and went to sleep.

I was traveling with a carry-on with all my things, neatly tucked away, out of everyone's way. I stayed in bed until after they left for work, as to not to be in their way.

On Monday morning, my customers paid me by credit card, which is processed through PayPal. I told PayPal to invoice them. They gave PayPal the credit card info. When it is approved, PayPal notifies me and transfers the money to my business account. This process usually takes less than 48 hours. On Wednesday morning the funds would be in my account.

On Monday evening, when Amanda and Jake came home, Amanda cooked dinner. Jake watched TV and all was fine. We sat down for dinner.

Jake said, "How do you like your daughter's cooking?"

"Delicious," I said.

Jake asked, "Why don't you tell her so?"

"Amanda, you're a great cook. This is delicious."

Amanda then asked, "How long will you be staying with us?"

"Probably leaving in the morning," I said.

"It would have been nice if we had some notice you were coming," Amanda said.

Jake chimed in with, "Anyone who stays here gives us notice when they are coming, and we just got back from our honeymoon." They had gotten back from their honeymoon four days prior.

The decibel level of his tone increased with each sentence, as well as a notch of contentiousness. I reminded them of the fact that I could not get a car and was planning on staying in the Hampton.

Jake said with even more contentious than before, "That makes no sense to me. They probably didn't take your card because there was no money." He then went on in a seething tone.

"You let Amanda pay for the cabs and the train to Larchmont." (Altogether those charges totaled $86.00, which I sent as soon as I returned to Florida.) He continued. "You did not even ask her. You never apologized for ruining her credit. You asked me to 'spot' you three hundred dollars when I probably will never see the money from the wedding. I believe your situation with your other children is also about money."

I just listened, not commenting, as I knew any comment I would make would be as contentious.

Jake than pushed further. "Why don't you respond? You're nodding your head. What do you have to say? Don't just sit there, say something."

Mulling over in my brain something to say to what I perceived as a declaration of war without acknowledging its existence. Finally I answered, "I am not answering you because I am searching for the words to use other than go fuck yourself."

"That's it," he said. "You have to leave."

"No," I said. "I do not have to leave, I want to leave." I walked to my carry-on to close it up and folded the bedding.

At that point he rushed toward me to get in my face, as if he was going to start a fight, and said, "You have never done anything for me."

"I thought I let you rent my apartment for the cost of utilities!" I said.

He replied with the most selfish, unappreciative, rude, inexplicable remarks that I have ever heard. "That was six years ago, and I kept getting collection notices under the door." The fact that he felt entitled and not appreciative of letting him use my place. Showed me who he really is.

I thanked him for saving me the wedding money and left. I had no money, nowhere to go, and it was pouring rain. I called a friend who had a one-bedroom apartment. He graciously offered me his living room chair, where I cried myself to sleep.

When I returned to Florida, I made up my mind that I was not going to let this go any further. On the outside I am going to make believe it never happened.

On Wednesday, May 23, Amanda sent me five IMs saying that it was wrong of me to speak to Jake that way and presenting an offense in her defense.

I said I would just like to forget the whole thing and asked if we can all move on.

She continued wanting to be absolved from any wrong doing after five times of me stating to move on. She would not stop. She then told me I should at least apologize to Jake.

Entitlement

Cause and Effect

368

CHAPTER 39: SHAME ON YOU

It is commonality to find the cause of a plan gone wrong within someone other than yourself. I would hope that I am at least smart enough not to do that, but after soul searching for many years regarding how my relationships with my children have shattered—Amanda now makes this four out of five—common sense dictates that by being the common denominator, I must be the cause.

Failing to have us all see a professional to rectify the situation. I have written what I believe to be all the facts that caused the problems in hope of getting some feedback as to whether my role has been different than what I believe and portray.

Without any rebuttal or professional evaluation, I am convinced that my children were poisoned.

A typical example would be at the wedding brunch where all five of my children were sitting at a table with spouses and grandchildren. My ex-wife, Denise, walked over to the table and commented on Wendy's jewelry by saying, "Nice jewelry, Wendy. Just like I used to have when I was married to your father."

Rich's immediate retort was, "But hers is paid for."

This is the same Rich who accepted all my hospitality, dinners, vacations, parties, and more without ever even feigning an attempt to put his hand in his pocket. This is the same Rich who, without any reservations, would denigrate and defile me in front of Amanda, Jordan, and my grandchildren. This is the same Rich, who from the first time I met him, whined, monopolized, disrespected, and displayed his selfishness and unappealing personality. But my daughter picked him, and I accepted him as part of the family, not realizing that he was as contagious as he was. Instead of anything from our family rubbing off on him, the opposite took place.

This is one cause of the poisonous disease that negated my proven record as a parent, as a loving father, as a loving husband, as a loving friend, as a charitable member of society, as a provider of comfort, education, and safe guidance through times that led many others of their generation down unrecoverable paths. I built my business from an existing base. I added businesses and built those from no base. I survived the storms, the mistakes, and the circumstances beyond my control.

In order to survive, I inadvertently caused a few minor blemishes on those who wallowed in my generosity. I apologize for that; I certainly would never have intentionally caused any discomfort for my loved ones.

Refusing to fail, my tenacity stemmed from my need to continue to provide a comfortable lifestyle for our family. If by doing so caused me to lose your respect, than I deserve it. As a parent and mentor, it was my failure not to have instilled respect.

If it were necessary for me to financially survive, to provide for my family, and faced with the same alternatives, I wouldn't change a stroke. It would be a small price to pay for what was accomplished.

To my Children:

If a blemish or a poison can cause your loss of respect for me:
SHAME ON YOU.

If a person stands in judgment of others without the credentials to do so, and you allow it:
SHAME ON YOU.

If you haven't learned to live, teach, and walk in respect, and not fall prey to envy and disrespect, then I failed:
SHAME ON ME.

Respect is the catalyst of true love; words of love are meaningless if not seeded by respect.

I married a woman who had no respect; I thought I could teach her respect. I thought I could mend the disrespect she had for her mother and father. Unfortunately, her poison grew the same way. But I did not say, "You don't like your father? Me too! You don't like my kids? Me too! You don't like my friends? Me too!"

No, I said, "Why?" I said, "There is no reason." I said, "Honor thy father." I said, "Love my children." I said everything I could to counteract a family divided. I failed there too.

The acquisition of some materialistic rewards is not a presumption of success, nor an empowerment of intelligence or judgment.

As you naturally mature and meander through the trials and tribulations of life, remember:

you took from me, your father, all the amenities a patriarch has earned as he gets closer to his demise.

when you see a parent shown love, compassion, and concern from an adult child.

when you see grandchildren laughing with their grandfather.

when you look at the pictures of how it was and how it is.

All of the above from a life of earned dividends, you have denied your father without cause, without reason, without respect and without compassion.

SHAME ON YOU.

Entitlement

Cause and Effect

372

CHAPTER 40: PRE-CONCLUSION

Today is November 2, 2013. Denise has been dating David from 2008 on. He is ten years her senior, and about the same time they started dating, he seems to have achieved a comfortable financial level.

David's divorced from his first wife, who bore a son, who hardly speaks to or sees him. His second wife passed away about the same time he started dating Denise, from an eating disorder, possibly anorexia. That marriage bore a daughter, Allyson, now twenty.

During the period that Denise and David were dating, he paid her rent for her. She, of course told the kids, "Don't tell your father," and continued to try to extort as much money as she could from me, knowing that I didn't have it but with the attitude and statement "not my problem."

Their relationship is a relationship of convenience. He has the capacity to support her. She has the need to be supported, which is fine. They decided to live together, in a new community of Parkland, which is a fabulous opportunity for both Denise and Jordan. Jordan will live near his friends in a country club community in a decent house, with his own room.

The day Denise moved in to this beautiful new home with David, one would think, after all the misery she has endured over the past seven years, that she would be entering into this new endeavor with happy thoughts. Unfortunately, Denise could ruin a wet dream. She is still miserable, crying, and burdening Jordan with all her personal and histrionic thoughts as if he was her confidant, not her fifteen-year-old son.

Jordan handles it all very well. He loves his mother, as he should. He is thrilled with the new house and his new room. However, as they prepared to decorate and order furniture, Jordan was treated like the male version of Cinderella by David, without any rebuttal by Denise. Thereby tension followed. However he is not taking any of the petty stuff that David wants to put on him; he is quite a kid.

After they moved in, David would continually tell Denise that Jordan did or did not do some silly thing. She would yell at Jordan, who had no idea of what he was being accused of. In addition, David had some concerns about Jordan and wanted him to abide by his rules. He had Denise arrange for the three of them and myself to have dinner and go over it, as he realized, he would need my cooperation.

David's concerns were:

1. Jordan cannot have any visitors at the house
2. He was not going to pay for his college
3. He was not going to pay for a car
4. He should not be social or go to parties as a pretty girl or peer pressure would corrupt him
5. He has to be more diligent in planning his social life
6. He cannot keep a car on the premises, as he (David) would be liable
7. And, finally, Jordan orders food at dinner that is too costly

In response to his concerns, I agreed that whatever is fair Jordan and I certainly would agree to.

Not allowing him to have friends at the house is a decision David has a right to, although Jordan is a very responsible young man, and would be respectful of all his concerns.

There is no possible way that either Jordan or I would expect, want, or need David to pay for his college education.

There is no possible way that either Jordan or I would expect, want, or need David to pay for his transportation requirements.

Jordan gets all A's, and he is a smart, happy, social kid. He has been brought up well and is very aware of drugs and alcohol, and as of the moment, his father is very aware of everything he does and knows that he has no interest in any of those things.

A pre-driving teenager is a pain in the ass. They make plans at the last minute, and then they need a ride. As a parent, you have your own plans and the driving or picking up is an inconvenience. But it comes with the territory. It is annoying, and it is a pain in the ass, but that's the way it is.

David finds that too difficult for him, and he wants Jordan either to plan properly or stay home. That age, to my experience, cannot plan properly, as everything changes, and a social life is a factor of enjoying one's existence on this planet. So, David complains, Denise complains, Ally complains, and Jordan overhears them.

With regard to him living there and David being liable, I researched and presented him with the facts of liability and insurance.

David's complaint was when they are out to dinner, even though Ally, Denise, and him order steak, Jordan should order a hamburger, because he is a kid.

I think as far as ordering dinner that he should ask David if it is alright before he orders. (He later told Jordan he should not even ask.)

I wrote to Denise:

> David and Ally as well as yourself will get great pleasure out
> of Jordan's accomplishments and relationships. Jordan is very
> fair, he should be treated accordingly. If Jordan is given chores

to do around the house, it would be his pleasure, and he understands that he too, has responsibilities.

If he is to be reprimanded, let it be for something he knows he did wrong, thereby maintaining his respect.

He should be treated with trust until that trust is broken.

David needs continual acknowledgment that he is rich, benevolent, and intelligent, none of which he has displayed so far. He taunts Jordan with disrespect and accusations of improprieties, none of which have any basis. When he makes these accusations, he fuels Denise with a need for her to berate Jordan, thus making Jordan distance himself from all of them.

David acts the way he does out of a need to control, by making Jordan do things his way, because he is paying the bill. That type of behavior is hypocritical, stems from a deep-seated insecurity of his own, feeding his need to feel superior. He cannot come to terms with the fact that a fifteen-year-old is smarter than him; I can, he is smarter than me.

Recently, in November, 2011, Denise, her mother, Bob, Steven, her brother, Amanda, Jake, and Jordan had dinner in a restaurant in New Jersey. After dinner, several hours later, at the table the owner asked if they would not mind just moving to the next table, as he needed to set this one for a party coming in.

After mother and daughter were finished breaking dishes and teaching the owner a new vocabulary, six squad cars were sent to the restaurant to escort them out. Amanda, Jake, and Jordan were devastated.

Jordan is now seventeen. He has a car, a cell phone, insurance, spending money, gas money, a college advisor, and anything else he may need, all from and with the pleasure and the love of his father.

That does not stop the phone messages, emails, or public defiling of me. With the most outrageous accusations, lies and venom.

HEDONIC ADAPTATION

Denise (like many others) is a product of hedonic adaption; she is never happy with today, only to aspire for fleeting materialistic thrills. That is not only a road less traveled, but a road to nowhere: a person of intellect would understand that we humans have the remarkable ability to get used to things, and quickly the thrill dies.

Those that are not understanding think that there is something wrong. Perfectly good families, relationships, and/or employment are abandoned for reasons that will only reoccur.

The lasting satisfaction is that of loving and being loved, by being a friend and having a friend, helping others or giving back to the community.

"Ask not what could be done for you, but what you could do for others."

Entitlement

Cause and Effect

378

CHAPTER 41: JORDAN ROBERT SCHEFFLER

There is a picture in Dan's papers from Yom Kippur in 1996, where all the participants of the West Hampton Synagogue, not yet built, congregated for the traditional casting of their sins into the ocean.

That group picture taken from behind us, has Jordan in my arms, sleeping on my shoulder, with as loving a vision between father and son that one would ever hope for.

When we vacationed at our Florida house, the music on the stereo was an old CD of mine and a new CD of mine.

The song was from Harry Belafonte:

When I was a lad, just three foot three
Certain questions occurred to me
So, I asked my father quite seriously
To tell me the story about the bird and the bee
He stammered and he stuttered pathetically
And this is what he said to me

Son, from the beginning of time and creativity
There existed the force of relativity
Pi R square and minus ten
Is rooted only when

The woman piaba and the man piaba
And the dan dan coal back lemon grass
The lily root, gully root, belly root, huh
And the famous granny scratch scratch

And the Mambo #5:

A little bit of Monica in my life
A little bit of Erica by my side
A little bit of Rita is all I need
A little bit of Tina is what I see
A little bit of Sandra in the sun
A little bit of Mary all night long
A little bit of Jessica here I am
A little bit of you makes me your man

In 1999, at three years old, we would get in the car to go somewhere. Jordan would be in the back in his car seat. We would do a duet of those two songs and he knew every word and every tune.

You could tell from the very beginning that there was something very special about this boy.

Now going on eighteen, he's living through tumultuous situations because of a histrionic mother. He is a mensch. He is smart, charming, polite, respectful, and charitable. He could hold his own in any Adult situation. I believe that he will achieve great things in his life, in spite of or because of his experiences.

I never favored one child over the other, but as circumstances developed in the relationships with my three older children, they are no longer in the mix.

Amanda, who I love equally with Jordan, married in New York. She works, plays, and has myriads of friends, little time for me. As it should be. But, I still hold out hope that her sensitivity gene will appear

Jordan is different. Jordan really grew up with the worst of circumstances. He loves his mother and me. He was being told continually that I was a liar, despicable, not a father, and more.

Entitlement

Cause and Effect

When his mother and I went into divorce mode at seven years old, he became her son, confidant, friend, father, etc. The fact that he is who he is is an absolutely amazing feat.

Based on my experiences, the genes one is born with are a mixture of the blood lines. Similar to thoroughbreds, if the gene mixture of the stud and the mare is the proper formula, you have a champion. If the formula varies, you have all the different grades below.

Jordan got the right mixture. In addition to the genes, his daytime supervision was left to our housekeeper, Gail. That supervision took away the overbearing pampering that Amanda had as a baby, thereby giving him a foundation of respect, manners, and obedience.

As he gets older it will probably change, but he calls me every day. He checks on my health and when requested, has mature, common-sense opinions. I do not say that with tongue in cheek. His ability to reason and understand situations is way beyond his years, and he has intelligence that surpasses most adults.

He completely understands who his mother is. He loves her, he deals with her intelligently, and when she frustrates him, he comes to me, just as Amanda did. And I remind him to just say, "Yes, Mother."

He also knows who I am and deals with me accordingly, but has much fewer eggshells to walk over with me. Jordan will not take anything said to him as the facts; he must confirm them before he will believe them. As I do, and as he was taught.

He is currently set up as a DJ on his own. He is seventeen years old as of February 19th, 2013. He also assists a more experienced DJ. He is designing a line of T-shirts, and whenever an opportunity to make money occurs, he takes advantage of it.

He deals with an excessive amount of drama and takes it all in stride. With all of that he, so far, is maintaining a straight-A average. This is a very special young man; I hope I am able to live long enough to watch his accomplishments.

I am equally as proud of Amanda and her accomplishments.

I came across an interesting analogy, which is another factor of learning to live a fruitful life. I was able to make Jordan understand it, and he seems to have adopted it. As follows:

TWO WOLVES

One evening an old Cherokee told his grandson about a
Battle that goes on inside people
He said, "My son, the battle is between two wolves
Inside us all.

One is Evil. It is anger, envy, jealousy, sorrow, regret, greed
Arrogance, self pity, guilt, resentment, inferiority,
Lies, false pride, aging, superiority, and ego.

The other is good. It is joy, peace, love, hope, serenity,
Humility, kindness, benevolence, empathy, generosity,
Truth, compassion, and faith."

The grandson thought about it for a minute and then
Asked his grandfather:
"Which wolf wins?"

The old Cherokee simply replied:

"The one you feed."

CHAPTER 42: IN CONCLUSION

At seventy-two, after spending the past five years attempting to summarize my experiences, I conclude as follows:

I have tasted the delicious and joyous sweetness of life, love, family, and success. I have also tasted the bitter sting of loss, betrayal, and defeat. Now, as a short timer, with an unknown portion of my life left to live, it is time to reflect on it all.

As I traveled through life's path, I learned that my truest happiness was my children. This was a safe place for me. I could count on their emotion, words, and actions to be sincere. Nothing gave me more pleasure then being with them and giving and doing for them.

Almost every vacation was a family vacation. Friends, acquaintances, and strangers would tell me what a good father I am. I would continually respond, "It is not so much that I am a good father as much as I am being a hedonist, as it gives me more pleasure than them." Everyone was in awe of my love, devotion, dedication to education, vacations, family values, and relationship with my kids.

As the three children born of my first marriage grew to be adult members of society, I realized that our parent/child bond would change as they concentrated on their own mates and their children. It was expected that the adulation of child for parent would morph into a more sophisticated adult relationship. Still, I expected to enjoy a portion of the respect and love which I had given to them and which I had received from them as they grew. The fracturing of our familial union was unimaginable to me.

The day came when my calls to my two oldest daughters went to answering machines or my daughters were too rushed to spend time chatting with their father. My calls never occurred at a convenient time for them.

Wendy, my oldest daughter, became disrespectful to me, causing me great distress. Her condition for any reconciliation was my agreement to refrain from any discussion regarding the cause and effect of her disrespect.

Elyssa reacted in much the same manner as Wendy with our discussions limited to her approved subjects.

An obligatory Father's Day message left for me was the last communication with my second daughter. Realizing that my daughters had no interest in a continuing relationship with me, I stopped calling. Perhaps I could have maintained a polite, superficial relationship with my elder children, but my heart yearned for a closer and more honest, more loving, and more intellectual link with my children. In an effort to regain our former closeness, I informed them that in the interest of gaining and maintaining a relationship between Wendy, Elyssa, Adam, and me, we would need to work with a professional arbitrator or family counselor.

Their reaction was to sever our ties, thus rejecting what I consider the one and only way to regain the love and respect which we had previously enjoyed. In their rejection of my proposal, they deny me access to my grandchildren. This brings me great sadness.

As I review the record to convey accuracy, Elyssa and Adam seem to feel that I do not say please or thank you. I accept that constructive criticism, but as I read their emails, neither do they.

While waiting on line for a table at a restaurant to have lunch, a table became available for two. The woman behind me was alone; I asked her to join me rather than wait for a table for one. She was a neighborhood married woman with children about the same age as my older daughters. We had lunch and enjoyed such a lovely conversation. I left scratching my head. I never had that with my daughters.

My life, as I age, is missing the relationships I worked so diligently to attain. I miss a friendship with my children, the opportunity to enjoy and mentor my grandchildren, the social satisfaction resulting from family adventures, learning from each other during the sharing and the playing together. The special relationship which, typically, exists between grandchildren and grandfathers is sorely missed. Laughter of grandchildren lightens the burden of old age.

The irony is how I created the entitlement mentality and then became victimized by it is the perfect metaphor for modern America. Even the employee thefts were from a mindset of entitlement that dominates today's society.

A parent's responsibility is to enable the child to be self-sufficient. Being able to earn one's own living gives a person self-respect and dignity. I have done that as well as all the tools required to prepare for and execute a responsible and successful life. But, there are elements that we think we are doing right that may not be. As Jerry Weintraub writes:

> *I ask myself have I been a good father?*

> *I sometimes feel that the root of the problem is the life we have given our children, the money, the cars, vacations, have possibly spoiled the everyday world for them. Can a child of affluence have the same ambition as the child of a lesser experience?*

If there is a parent out there who is suffering from the same mindset, my heart goes out to you as a parent. I hope that I have enlightened you in time to have your children read my story.

Denise abandoned me for fear of diminished lifestyle, somehow thinking that she would benefit financially through the court rather than through the marriage. What she and others before and after do not realize is that the only true asset that you have is your children. And no matter what the circumstances, a divorce decreases the value of that asset. No matter how amicable or obvious a divorce is, the relationship with the children of the family as a unit is never the same.

Her shortsighted selfishness has stolen my final years on this Earth. She took away the pleasure of a mutual parenting of our children, the pleasure of sharing all occasions as a family, and the Sundays I loved so much to be with Amanda and Jordan.

She took away a cadre of social relationships, which are so important as the years pass. She stole this with no gain to herself and to the loss of the children as well. As I compensated during our marriage for her inability to love, so do I now. I compartmentalize my life, then and now, as I refuse to embrace the bad and instead find the good and enjoy each day.

With all the heart-wrenching misery Denise has put me through, I knew then as I know now, we both would have been better off staying together. Now, ten years later, I venture to say that her journey from there to here was much more difficult than mine.

At my current age, which is so hard to believe, I still feel like a kid and really do not know how these years have passed so quickly. I like me; I like the life I lived; I like the things I accomplished. I am proud of how I brought up my children, and how I prevented them from falling prey to the drug era and peer pressure and established a good sense of values in them.

I am not afraid of death. I do fear, as I age, contracting a debilitating illness where I can no longer take care of myself. I have no idea of what the outcome of that would be.

I cannot think of a thing I would want to do other than what I am doing, with the exception, of course, of a true love affair, or Jordan living with me. As I keep looking back, there is very little that I would have done differently. All in all I had a great trip. I am comfortable staying home, dining alone, enjoying my son, and enjoying my friends.

My days are always occupied with business that I now conduct in a very relaxed atmosphere without any pressure, and I usually have fun. It was not my plan to be here at this juncture of my life. However, based on family history, I never thought I would live this long.

Whenever I go to a restaurant for dinner, invariably I meet people who I have done business with, befriended, served on boards with, was former members of the same clubs, high school, summers. It is always a warm, friendly, well-received greeting.

I appreciate these are bonus years. I am probably happier then I have ever been. Currently living alone, except for Lola, in the most beautiful, fun-filled complex Mizner Park, in Boca Raton, Florida.

I wake up each morning with my most unconditional love "Lola", my rescue MaltiPoo, walk down by the water and say, "Good morning, world," and, "Thank you, God."

"Things turn out best for people who make the best out of the way things turn out."

Entitlement

Cause and Effect

388

Entitlement

Cause and Effect

My dearest, most loyal friends Penny and Dale write:

When Mike attained success, he enjoyed living large. In doing so, he took a lot of people along with him and he happily paid the tab. Doing things his way included loving, giving, and sharing. Those were the things he enjoyed most. In the writing of his memoirs, Mike is still giving, giving all he has left to give. Write your story. Keep it honest and tell it all.

Your children enjoyed all the affluence and advantages you gave them and, by golly, they have no right to look down their noses at what it took for you to provide them with all that splendor. I know you, warts and all, and I love you. We both do! My only complaint is that you don't communicate with us often enough!

-Penny

Entitlement

Cause and Effect

390

AUTHOR'S NOTE:

Writing this book has been a labor of compulsive, obsessive behavior, having to continually add, delete, and edit, never being satisfied that what I am trying to present is properly captured.

In this year, I have been able to find some partial closure to issues.

I have located and spoken to Theresa.

I have been contacted by and reunited with Mardge.

I have successfully marketed, sold, and installed whole-house emergency standby generators in the northeast because of Hurricane Sandy. With the same ability and criteria as Florida, the only difference being that the townships involved are sympathetic to the devastating human suffering that living without electricity has caused and made the permit process realistic.

This has put me back in a place where I can enjoy an income to support my lifestyle and my son's needs.

I think about those relationships I have lost because of money. And I keep replaying the scene from *Pretty Woman*, when Julia Roberts's character walks back into a shop on Rodeo Drive in Beverly Hills, dressed expensively immaculate, carrying boxes of clothing from all the neighboring stores, flashing a black American express card.

"You work on commission, right? Remember me? When I came in yesterday and you would not acknowledge me? Big mistake, big mistake."

In the early 1960s, songwriters Jerry Lieber and Mike Stoller created lyrics from an adaption of a short story called "Disillusionment." While the story was more depressing than emotionally stimulating, the songwriters somewhat captured where I believe it belongs today.

Entitlement

Cause and Effect

The song was recorded by many artists of the time in various forms, the one that succeeded was Peggy Lee's version of "Is That All There Is."

The lyrics, combined with a book called *The Myths of Happiness*, by psychology professor Sonja Lyubomirsky, pretty much symbolizes the formula that I believe, if understood, would make for a much more stable and happier existence in the short time we have.

If one would be truthful with themselves and realize that we have a remarkable ability to get used to things, the thrill then fades, the new car, the bigger house, the larger ring, the mid-life crisis; it does not mean you should not aspire for or obtain whatever material goals you have, just realize that the biggest thrill is in the quest and initial possession, and then it becomes second nature.

Money makes you happy only when it prevents you from being miserable.

Many valuable relationships and careers have been jettisoned for the thrill of the new. When the new fades you will wonder:

Is that all there is, is that all there is?
If that's all there is my friends, then let's keep dancing
Let's break out the booze and have a ball.

I had the feeling that something was missing.
I don't know what, but when it was over,
I said to myself, "Is that all there is?"

The real thrills that do not fade: friendships, learning, challenging, contributing, helping others. These are not bragging rights, but they are lasting, not fading things like romance, which will dim, but if there is a substantial investment then those that invested have to put an all-out effort into rekindling those flames.

AND THAT IS ALL THERE IS.